AFRICAN AMERICAN BIOGRAPHY

AFRICAN AMERICAN BIOGRAPHY

VOLUME 4
S–Z

WITHDRAWN

An Imprint of Gale Research Inc.

Jefferson-Madison
Regional Library
Charlottesville, Virginia

AFRICAN AMERICAN BIOGRAPHY

STAFF

Carol DeKane Nagel, *U•X•L Developmental Editor*
Thomas L. Romig, *U•X•L Publisher*

Amy Marcaccio, *Acquisitions Editor*

Barbara A. Wallace, *Permissions Assistant (Pictures)*
Shanna P. Heilveil, *Production Assistant*
Evi Seoud, *Assistant Production Manager*
Mary Beth Trimper, *Production Director*

Cynthia Baldwin, *Art Director*

Weigl Educational Publishers Limited, *Page and Cover Design and Typesetting*

Library of Congress Cataloging-in-Publication Data

African American biography.
      p. cm. -- (African American reference library)
    Includes index.
    Contents: v. 1. A-D -- v. 2. E-J -- v. 3 K-R -- v. 4 S-Z
    ISBN 0-8103-9234-8 (Set : alk. paper); 0-8103-9235-6 (v. 1); 0-8103-9236-4 (v. 2); 0-8103-9237-2
      (v. 3); 0-8103-9238-0 (v. 4)
    1. Afro-Americans--Biography. I. U•X•L. II. Series.
E185.96.A44 1993
920'.009296073--dc20
[B]
                                         93-45651
                                             CIP

This publication is a creative work fully protected by all applicable copyright laws, as well as by misappropriation, trade secret, unfair competition, and other applicable laws. The author and editor of this work have added value to the underlying factual material herein through one or more of the following: unique and original selection, coordination, expression, arrangement, and classification of the information. All rights to this publication will be vigorously defended.

Copyright © 1994
U•X•L
An Imprint of Gale Research

All rights reserved, including the right of reproduction in whole or in part in any form.

∞™ This book is printed on acid-free paper that meets the minimum requirements of American National Standard for Information Sciences--Permanence Paper for Printed Library Materials, ANSI Z39.48-1984.

Printed in the United States of America

10 9 8 7 6 5 4 3 2

AFRICAN AMERICAN REFERENCE LIBRARY

ADVISORY BOARD

Alton Hornsby, Jr.
Professor of History
Morehouse College

Jean Blackwell Hutson
Former Curator and Director
Schomburg Center for Research in Black Culture

William C. Matney, Jr.
Public Affairs Coordinator
U.S. Bureau of the Census

Carole McCullough
Professor of Library Science
Wayne State University

Brenda Mitchell-Powell
Editor
Multicultural Review

Jessie Carney Smith
University Librarian
Fisk University

AFRICAN AMERICAN REFERENCE LIBRARY

The **African American Reference Library** fills the need for a comprehensive, curriculum-related reference covering all aspects of African American life and culture. Aimed primarily at middle school and junior high school students, this nine-volume set combines appropriate reading level and fascinating subject matter with quality biographies, statistics, essays, chronologies, document and speech excerpts, and more.

The **African American Reference Library** consists of three separate components:

African American Biography (four volumes) profiles three hundred African Americans, both living and deceased, prominent in their fields, from civil rights to athletics, politics to literature, entertainment to science, religion to the military. A black-and-white portrait accompanies each entry, and a cumulative subject index lists all individuals by field of endeavor.

African American Almanac (three volumes) provides a comprehensive range of historical and current information on African American life and culture. Organized by subject, the volumes contain 270 black-and-white illustrations, a selected bibliography, and a cumulative subject index.

African American Chronology (two volumes) explores significant social, political, economic, cultural, and educational milestones in black history. Arranged by year and then by month and day, the volumes span from 1492 until June 30, 1993, and contain 106 illustrations and maps, extensive cross references, and a cumulative subject index.

Comments and suggestions

We welcome your comments on *African American Biography* as well as your suggestions for topics to be featured in future **African American Reference Library** series. Please write:

Editors, **African American Reference Library,** U•X•L, 835 Penobscot Bldg., Detroit, Michigan 48226-4094; call toll-free: 1-800-877-4253; or fax: 313-961-6348.

CONTENTS

AFRICAN AMERICAN BIOGRAPHY

Elizabeth Cotten
Ellen Craft
Countee Cullen
Angela Davis
Benjamin O. Davis, Sr.
Miles Davis
Ossie Davis
Sammy Davis, Jr.
Juliette Derricotte
Irene Diggs
David Dinkins
Sharon Pratt Dixon
See Sharon Pratt Kelly
Thomas A. Dorsey
Frederick Douglass
Charles Richard Drew
William Edward Burghardt (W.E.B.) DuBois
Paul Laurence Dunbar
Katherine Dunham

Volume 2: E-J

Marian Wright Edelman
Elleanor Eldridge
Duke Ellington
Effie O'Neal Ellis
Ralph Ellison
Medgar Evers
James Farmer
Louis Farrakhan
Ella Fitzgerald
Aretha Franklin
John Hope Franklin
Mary Hatwood Futrell
Ernest J. Gaines
Marcus Garvey
Arthur Gaston
Henry Louis Gates, Jr.
Zelma Watson George

Althea Gibson
Dizzy Gillespie
Nikki Giovanni
Robin Givens
Danny Glover
Whoopi Goldberg
W. Wilson Goode
Charles Gordone
Berry Gordy, Jr.
Dick Gregory
Angelina Weld Grimké
Bryant Gumbel
Lucille C. Gunning
Clara Hale
Alex Haley
Arsenio Hall
Fannie Lou Hamer
Virginia Hamilton
Hammer
Lionel Hampton
Lorraine Hansberry
The Harlem Globetrotters
Barbara Harris
Marcelite Harris
Patricia Harris
Robert Hayden, Jr.
Dorothy Height
Jimi Hendrix
Matthew Henson
Aileen Hernandez
Anita Hill
Chester Himes
Gregory Hines
Billie Holiday
Benjamin L. Hooks
Lena Horne
Whitney Houston
Langston Hughes

Pauli Murray
Gloria Naylor
Huey Newton
Jessye Norman
Hazel O'Leary
Shaquille O'Neal
Jesse Owens
Satchel Paige
Gordon Parks
Rosa Parks
Sidney Poitier
Adam Clayton Powell, Jr.
Colin Powell
Leontyne Price
Charley Pride
Barbara Gardner Proctor
Richard Pryor
Public Enemy
Lloyd Albert Quarterman
Queen Latifah
Dudley Randall
A. Philip Randolph
William Raspberry
Ishmael Reed
Eslanda Goode Robeson
Paul Robeson
Jackie Robinson
Charlemae Hill Rollins
Diana Ross
Carl T. Rowan
Wilma Rudolph
Bill Russell
Bayard Rustin

Volume 4: S-Z

Edith Sampson
Sonia Sanchez
Dred Scott

Gloria Scott
Bobby Seale
Attalah Shabazz
Ntozake Shange
Al Sharpton
Althea T.L. Simmons
Carole Simpson
Naomi Sims
John Singleton
Bessie Smith
Wesley Snipes
George Stallings, Jr.
Shelby Steele
William Grant Still
Juanita Kidd Stout
Niara Sudarkasa
Henry Ossawa Tanner
Mildred Taylor
Susan Taylor
Susie Baker King Taylor
Mary Church Terrell
Clarence Thomas
Jean Toomer
Jackie Torrence
Toussaint-Louverture
Robert Townsend
William Monroe Trotter
Sojourner Truth
Harriet Tubman
Nat Turner
Mario Van Peebles
Sarah Vaughan
Denmark Vesey
Charleszetta Waddles
Alice Walker
Madame C.J. Walker
Maggie L. Walker
Sippie Wallace

Edith Sampson

Lawyer, judge
Born October 13, 1901, Pittsburgh,
Pennsylvania
Died 1979

"Color never bothered me very much. I know what I am, and a blonde I am not."

Edith Sampson

In every profession there is someone who has to lead the way. When it comes to law, that person was Edith Sampson. She was the first black woman to receive a master of laws degree from Loyola University, one of the first black women to practice before the Supreme Court, the first black woman elected judge in the United States, and the first black person appointed as delegate to the United Nations. She was a frequent speaker on the situation of blacks in the U.S. and was a strong believer that America was the land of opportunity for people of all races.

Leaves school to find work

Sampson was the daughter of Louis and Elizabeth Spurlock. Her father managed a cleaning and drying business, while her mother made buckram hat frames and false hairpieces. The family was very poor, and Sampson had to leave school on several occasions to find work. She eventually graduated from Peabody High School in Pittsburgh and her Sunday school teacher helped her gain admission to the New York School of Social Work.

After graduating, Sampson worked as a social worker at the Illinois Children's Home and Aid Society. While there she ran into one of her former teachers, George Kirchwey of the Columbia University School of Law, who was giving a lecture. The two chatted, and he convinced her to seek a law career. She enrolled in the John Marshall Law School at night and became the highest ranking student among ninety-five in the course on jurisprudence. She also received a special commendation from Dean Edward T. Lee.

Sampson applied for the bar but was unsuccessful. She said she was overconfident entering the exam, but it was still one of the best things that could have happened to her. She enrolled in a master of laws program at the graduate law school of Loyola University. In 1927, she was the first woman to receive the LL.M. degree from the university. Later that year she was admitted to the Illinois bar.

While attending law school, Sampson became a probation officer and eventually a referee for the Juvenile Court of Cook County,

Illinois. She also began a law practice in 1924 that specialized in criminal law and domestic relations. Ten years later she joined a handful of black women who practiced before the United States Supreme Court. That same year she married attorney Joseph E. Clayton, who joined her Chicago practice. She later married Rufus Sampson, a field agent for Tuskegee Institute in Alabama. Although she later divorced him, she kept his last name.

Sampson's law office became a drop-in center for thousands of poor people who had difficulty receiving legal advice. She wound down her practice in 1942 and five years later was appointed assistant state attorney of Cook County.

"America's Town Meeting of the Air"

During the late 1940s the National Council of Negro Women (NACW) selected Sampson to represent the association at "America's Town Meeting of the Air" radio program. This was a seventy-two day around-the-world trip, which featured representatives of different American interest groups discussing their problems in twelve countries. Sampson spoke on the misinformation that was being spread about the status of blacks living in America. Most outsiders thought blacks still lived in virtual slavery. They were often amazed to hear that Sampson had a law degree, attended a white church, and had never been to a segregated school.

When the trip finished, the delegates organized the World Town Hall Seminar and elected Sampson president of the group. In *Negro Digest* she said, "My decision to make the Town Hall trip proved to be the turning point of my life. After visiting and talking with the peoples of other countries, I knew that I could never make my law practice the primary business of my life; I would have to devote myself to the course of world brotherhood and world peace."

In 1950 President Harry Truman appointed Sampson to serve as an alternate United States delegate to the fifth regular session of the United Nations General Assembly. When her appointment was announced, she was canning peaches in the kitchen of her Chicago home. She received reporters, but went on with her canning. She had a strong personality and impressed many with her force of will. "She works like a dynamo; talks like a pneumatic drill; and her warmth penetrates any room she enters," was the way the *Chicago Defender* described her.

As a United Nations delegate, Sampson served on the social, humanitarian, and cultural committees. She also served on Committee Three, which was responsible for several areas including land reform, reparation of prisoners, the repatriation of Greek children, a general resolution on the work of the Commission on Human Rights, and radio jamming. She was reappointed alternate delegate in 1952 and was a member-at-large of the U.S. Commission for UNESCO early in the Eisenhower administration.

As a member of the United Nations, Sampson spent a great deal of time traveling overseas to discuss America's race situation. She told *Ebony* that "there were times when I had to bow my head in shame when talking about how some Negroes have been treated in the United States.... But I could truthfully point out that these cases, bad as they are, are the exceptions—the Negro got justice for every one where justice was denied. I could tell them that Negroes have a greater opportunity in America to work out their salvation than anywhere else in the world."

Sampson's descriptions of the situation were sometimes criticized by those in the black community. William Worthy, a writer for *Crisis,* criticized comments about the status of blacks she made in a speech in Copenhagen in 1952. Marguerite Cartwright, an educator at Phelps Stokes Institute in New York City, also discussed the controversial question of Sampson's characterization of the status of blacks in her overseas lectures.

Ebony supports her

The criticism never seemed to affect Sampson and she continued to voice her support of the status of blacks. She was also a strong opponent of communism. Many blacks looked to her for encouragement and *Ebony* once published an editorial supporting her. "The very career of Mrs. Sampson in itself is a symbol of the greatness of American democracy with its story of a girl born in the slums, and unable to finish grade school working her way through law school and becoming a member of the U.S. delegation to the world tribunal. *Ebony* insists that is precisely because America is great that Negroes will continue to uphold, protect and fight for their native land as unceasingly as they battle to correct the flaws in the democracy they cherish."

The vice-president appointed Sampson to serve on the United States Citizens Commission on the North Atlantic Treaty Organization in 1961 and 1962. She was also a member of the Advisory Committee on Private Enterprise in Foreign Aid in 1964 and 1965.

Sampson became the first black woman elected associate judge in the United States in 1962. Her law career continued to rise and by the late 1960s she was judge of a branch of the Circuit Court of Cook County, handling landlord cases. Her election to the court was in part due to her close relations with Mayor Richard Daley. He considered her a friend and supported her as a candidate for the court when William Dawson, a leader of Chicago's predominantly black South Side, opposed her.

Sampson was awarded an honorary degree of doctor of laws from the John Marshall Law School. Although she had no children, she was very involved in the lives of her nieces and nephews. She had a powerful impact on her entire family, and two of her nephews followed her into the legal profession and eventually became judges. They are Oliver Spurlock in Chicago and Charles T. Spurlock in Boston. Sampson died in 1979.

Sonia Sanchez

Poet
Born September 9, 1934, Birmingham,
   Alabama

"Sanchez has been an inspiration to a generation of young poets."—Marilyn K. Basel

 s well as being a distinguished poet, playwright, and professor, Sonia

Sanchez has long been a committed activist. In the 1960s she joined the Congress of Racial Equality, and for three years during the 1970s she was a member of the Nation of Islam, the Black Muslim organization. It has been said that Sanchez "lives the life she sings about in her songs." She has matched her militant poetry by taking action on behalf of the black community wherever she sees the need, whether by supporting nationalist organizations or by getting courses on African American literature established in colleges and universities.

Even Sanchez's poetry recitations are a form of action. She regards the readings as a way of bringing African Americans together and instilling a sense of pride so that people have the strength and confidence to tackle political problems. Poetry, for Sanchez, is very much a spoken art—something to be declaimed and shared, not just read in private.

Sanchez is the author of more than half dozen books of poetry, including *homegirls and handgrenades* (1984), which won the American Book Award. She has also recorded an album, *A Sun Lady for All Seasons Reads Her Poetry* (1971). As well, she has written plays, short stories, and three books for children: *It's a New Day: Poems for Young Brothas and Sistuhs* (1971), *The Adventures of Fat Head, Small Head, and Square Head* (1973), and *A Sound Investment and Other Stories* (1979).

Lead black studies movement

Listening to Sonia Sanchez eloquently declaim her poems today, it is hard to believe that she was shy and stuttering as a child. Born Wilsonia Driver, she had an unsettled childhood. Her mother, Lena (Jones) Driver, died when Sanchez was one year old, and Sanchez and her sister Pat spent their early years being shuffled from relative to relative. When Sanchez was nine she had yet another disruption when her father, Wilson Driver, moved the family to Harlem, New York.

After graduating from high school in Harlem, Sanchez enrolled at Hunter College, where she earned her B.A. in political science in 1955. She then took a postgraduate course in poetry at New York University. She first had her work published in the early 1960s when her poems appeared in such magazines as the *Liberator* and the *Journal of Black Poetry*.

Intense political activity occupied Sanchez during the 1960s as she enthusiastically threw herself into the civil rights movement. As well as agitating for political and social change, she joined with playwright Amiri Baraka and others in calling for reforms in the educational system. Teaching at San Francisco State College during the late 1960s, she was one of the leaders of the Black Studies Movement who worked to establish African American studies programs in colleges and universities. Sanchez taught at several universities during the 1960s and 1970s, eventually settling at Temple University, Philadelphia, in 1977.

Not disturbed by her critics

From the very beginning Sanchez used her writing as a form of activism. Her early poetry, in particular, was influenced by the philosophy of the black nationalist Malcolm X, and her first book bristles with scorn for "white America." Titled *Homecoming* (1969), this

Sonia Sanchez

collection of outspoken verses represents Sanchez's return to the black urban viewpoint, after having seen things through the viewpoint of the white culture in which she was educated.

As a champion of African American culture, Sanchez has made a point of writing in "black" language, often spelling words the way they are spoken. This is particularly true of her second book of poetry, *We a BaddDDD People* (1970), which makes frequent use of words such as "mothas," "blk men," and "witeness," as well as the long-drawn-out "baddDDD." By incorporating these phonetic spellings in her poems and using black speech patterns, Sanchez has turned everyday black speech into literature.

Sanchez has always paid particular attention to how her poems sound when read aloud. "When I write," she says, "I always read my poems aloud, even as I construct the poem and also at the end of the poem. I've always

told people that on some levels every poem is threefold. One is the private self when you read a poem silently. The other is when you hear a poet read her or his poem, which brings another self. And then of course there's the point of you reading it aloud yourself."

To hear Sanchez reading her own poems is a thrilling experience. Sometimes her voice rises to a scream—and then drops to a moan or sob. At other times the words roll along in a sonorous chant, or swing in a jazz-like rhythm. Sanchez's aim is to capture the truly black rhythms, the rhythms of West African languages. As well, she wants to show that poetry is not only for intellectuals. It can be shared and enjoyed by everyone. Because Sanchez believes so strongly in public readings, she has given her dramatic performances of poetry on campuses throughout the United States as well as in Cuba, the West Indies, Europe, China, and many other parts of the world.

Many of Sanchez's poems are about her personal experiences, either as an activist or as a woman. Some of her love poems reflect her unhappy marriage and divorce, as does her well known story, "After Saturday Night Comes Sunday," which appeared in *homegirls and handgrenades* (1984). Some of her poems are written with her three children in mind, and others are written specifically for them. Sanchez has three children—a daughter, Anita, and twin sons, Mungu and Morani.

Sanchez's other works include a range of prose pieces and several plays. Her best known play is *Sister Son/ji* (1972), which exposes the contradictions of a black freedom movement that is dominated by men and does not offer women liberation. This has been a recurring theme in Sanchez's poetry as well as in such prose works as *A Blues Book for Blue Black Magical Women* (1973).

Sanchez's outspokenness about the downtrodden position of black women has often aroused controversy—she is accused of betraying her race by criticizing black men. But Sanchez can shoulder such criticism. She has never been one to avoid difficult issues. Although now a respected university professor, she is still a committed activist, supporting such groups as MOMS in Alabama as well as worldwide organizations like the antinuclear Project Plowshares. Meanwhile, her poems and plays continue to be an essential part of her activism. "I recognize that my writing must serve a dual purpose," she has said. "It must be a clarion call to the value of change while it also speaks to the beauty of a nonexploitative age."

Dred Scott

Slave
Born 1795, Southampton County, Virginia
Died September 17, 1858, St. Louis,
    Missouri

One of the most important legal battles in United States history took place between Dred Scott, a slave, and his master, John Sanford. Scott's previous owner, John Emerson, had taken him to live in states that were considered "free," so when he became Sanford's property, Scott argued all the way to the Supreme Court that his time spent on free soil had entitled him to his freedom. The Court ruled against him on the basis that he was a slave and a Negro. The decision had reverberations across the country, causing Southerners to rejoice and angering free blacks and abolitionists.

Sold for $500 to an army doctor

Scott was born a slave in Southampton County, Virginia, in 1795. He worked in a variety of positions including farmhand, laborer, craftsman, and general handyman. In 1819, his original owner moved to Huntsville, Alabama, and later to St. Louis, Missouri. After his owner died in 1832, Scott was sold for $500 to U.S. Army doctor John Emerson, who took him to the free state of Illinois in 1834, then to the free territory of Minnesota, and later to Missouri.

When Emerson died, Scott became the property of John Sanford. During these years he married and had two daughters. He unsuccessfully tried to escape from slavery and later to buy his freedom. In 1846, he filed suit in the Missouri state courts for his freedom on the grounds that residence in a free territory had liberated him.

After nine years, his case was heard by the U.S. Supreme Court, where five of the nine justices were Southerners. The Court considered three questions: Was Scott a citizen of Missouri, and hence within the jurisdiction of the federal court there? Did residence in a free area of the United States automatically entitle Scott to his freedom? Was the Missouri Compromise constitutional?

The court case attracted national attention. There existed a widespread feeling at this time that the slavery question, which Con-

Dred Scott

gress seemed unable to resolve, should be dealt with in the courts. President Buchanan stated in his inaugural address on March 4, 1857, that he hoped the Court would bring down a decision in the *Scott* case that all people could live with.

Two days later, a verdict was handed down in *Dred Scott v. John Sanford*. After much debate, the Court ruled against Scott, seven to two. Each of the judges handed down a separate opinion, although that of Chief Justice Roger B. Taney, a Southerner, is usually cited for the majority. According to Taney, Scott could not sue Sanford because he was not a U.S. citizen, because he was both a Negro and a slave.

In making his ruling, Taney stated: "If the Constitution recognizes the right of property of the master in a slave, and makes no distinction between that description of property and other property owned by a citizen, no tribunal, acting under the authority of the United States, whether it be legislative, executive, or judicial, has a right to draw such a distinction, or deny to it the benefit of the provisions and guarantees which have been provided for the protection of private property against the encroachments of the government....

"Upon the whole, therefore, it is the judgement of this court, that it appears by the record before us that the plaintiff in error is not a citizen of Missouri, in the sense in which that word is used in the Constitution; and that the Circuit Court of the United States, for that reason, had no jurisdiction in the case, and could give no judgment in it."

Ramifications across the country

The decision electrified the country. The Court had ruled that black people were not citizens of the United States and that an act of Congress (the Missouri Compromise of 1820) was unconstitutional. It also redefined the relationship between the states and the federal government, making it possible for slavery to expand into the territories. The decision was a clear-cut victory for the South; the North viewed it with alarm. With the highest court in the land supporting slavery, many abolitionists felt there was little hope that anything short of a dramatic political or social revolution would bring an end to slavery. All abolitionists were not as optimistic as Frederick Douglass, but they shared his hope that "the Supreme Court ... [was] not the only power in this world. We, the abolitionists and colored people, should meet this decision, unlooked for and monstrous as it appears, in a cheerful spirit. This very attempt to blot out forever the hopes of an enslaved people may be one necessary link in the chain of events preparatory to the complete overthrow of the whole slave system."

The response by free blacks to the decision was swift and angry. They objected to the ruling that black slaves and the freed descendants of slaves could not claim citizenship or bring suit in court. Robert Purvis made several protest resolutions at a Negro meeting at Israel Church in Philadelphia, Pennsylvania, on April 3, 1857, which were typical of the reaction of blacks. He resolved that "this atrocious decision furnishes final confirmation of the already well-known fact that, under the Constitution and government of the United States, the colored people are nothing but an alien, disfranchised, and degraded class. Resolved, that to attempt, as some do, to prove that there is no support given to slavery in the Constitution and essential structure of the American government is to argue against reason and common sense, to ignore history, and shut our eyes against palpable facts; and that while it may suit white men, who do not feel the iron heel, to please themselves with such theories, it ill becomes the man of color, whose daily experiences refutes the absurdity, to indulge in any such idle fantasies."

His concerns were echoed by others at the meeting including Charles Remond, who resolved that "though many of our fathers and some of us have, in time past, exercised the right of American citizenship, this was when a better spirit pervaded the land, and when the patriotic services of colored men in the defense of the country were fresh in the minds of the people; but that the power to oppress us lurked all the time in the Constitution, only waiting to be developed; and that now, when it suits the slave oligarchy to assert that power, we are made to feel its grinding weight."

Despite the furor over the case, Scott's owner freed him, a few months after the decision, on May 26, 1857. Scott continued to live in St. Louis until his death on September 17, 1858. Although black men would not become American citizens until the ratification of the fourteenth Amendment in 1868, Scott's bid for freedom remained the most momentous judicial event of the century.

Gloria Scott

Educator
Born April 14, 1938, Houston, Texas

"Giving something back, influencing what happens to Black people has always been important.... I suppose I'm one of the vestiges of what you call 'race women'—people who really believe in African Americans."

A noted educator and a member of numerous associations and organizations, Gloria Dean Randle Scott has frequently been selected Woman of the Year and Woman of Achievement and was one of the Seventy-five Black Women Who Changed America in the exhibit I Dream a World.

Since 1987 Scott has been president of Bennett College in Greensboro, North Carolina, the second woman to be president of this black women's liberal arts college. She has also played a leading role in the Girl Scouts movement, serving as vice-president (1972–75) and then national president (1975–78). Scott was the first African American to be president of the Girl Scouts, USA.

In all her work, Scott has been a strong advocate of racial equality and women's rights. "Giving something back, influencing what happens to Black people has always been important," she says. "I suppose I'm one of the vestiges of what you call 'race women'—people who really believe in African Americans."

Grew up in a working-class family

Gloria Dean Randle Scott was the middle child in a family of five, the daughter of Freeman and Juanita (Bell) Randle. She came from a working-class family where her father was a cook and her mother a domestic and where she had plenty of love and encouragement both at home and at school. Her first grade teacher was a particularly strong influence. "She made learning interesting," recalls Scott, "and let us know that, because we were black, we had to be doubly achievement-oriented."

Scott took this message to heart so well that she graduated from Jack Yates High School in 1955 as salutatorian. She then enrolled at Indiana University, where she earned her B.A. in zoology and botany (1959), M.A. in zoology and botany (1960), and Ph.D. in higher education, zoology, and botany (1965).

During the years she was preparing for her Ph.D., Scott taught at Marian College, Indianapolis, Indiana. After receiving the doctorate in 1965, she moved to Knoxville College, Knoxville, Tennessee, where she served as dean of students and deputy director of the Upward Bound program until 1967. In the

next few years she was involved in university planning at several colleges, including North Carolina Agricultural and Technical State University, where she developed a ten-year plan for the university. This was followed by nine years as a university teacher and as vice-president of Clark College in Atlanta, Georgia, 1978–87.

Modernized Girl Scout programs

While Scott pursued her university career she was also involved in numerous volunteer organizations, including the Girl Scouts. She had gained a love of scouting as a teenager when she was taken on her first nature trip, and as an adult she remained closely involved in the scouting movement. Before her appointment as vice-president in 1972, Scott spent three years chairing the Girl Scout Program Committee, and she was also a member of the Minority Task Force.

Gloria Scott

As Girl Scout president, 1975–78, Scott introduced a range of innovative programs. They included leadership training for black and Puerto Rican teenagers; programs for mentally handicapped girls; a campaign to get more African Americans to join the Girl Scouts; and conferences on women's issues, land use, and justice for juveniles. Classes on venereal disease were also introduced during Scott's term as president. Her aim was to update the organization, making it relevant to the needs of today's young people. She particularly wanted to attract girls from poor homes, so that they could benefit from the instruction and camaraderie offered by the Girl Scout movement.

Being president of the Girls Scouts, USA, brought international commitments, too. Scott was regularly in touch with Girl Scout leaders of other nations, especially those in the Americas. At the World Association of Girl Guides and Girl Scouts in Rio de Janeiro in 1977, she conducted training sessions for delegates from Central America, South America, and the Caribbean.

Named president of Bennett College

When Scott was appointed president of Bennett College in 1987, she approached this challenge with the same energy and imagination she had shown as Girl Scout president. From the first, she aimed to give Bennett's 600 black women students an all-round education that would truly fit them for the modern world. This has meant going beyond the usual subjects. "I hope to educate Bennett women in the area of applied technology," says Scott. "This started to change our lives and will change it in the future. Women must harness that learning. They must take on the role of being informed citizens and influence social and economic policy. They must be educated to become parents. Attention needs to be given to being a new kind of parent."

Whenever asked whether her students would get a better preparation for life at a coeducational college, Scott points out the advantages of colleges such as Bennett: "If you attend a women's college, you have the opportunity to be everything.… You don't have to deal with the competitive personal development issue of whether you challenge the males, or, if you're a good student, the question of whether you tailor that so you won't appear to be too smart."

Scott would like to see many more black women taking leadership roles. "Part of my leadership style is to help … younger women, especially, to develop leadership qualities," she says. She has written a number of papers on women's education, including "Educational Needs of Black Women" (1977). She has also been involved in educational committees and commissions, including the 1975 Task Force on Equal Education Opportunity for Women. From 1976 to 1978 Scott served on the National Commission on International Women's Year, to which she was appointed by both President Gerald Ford and President Jimmy Carter. Then, in 1978, President Carter appointed her to the National Commission on the International Year of the Child.

Since 1959 Scott has been married to Dr. Will Braxton Scott, currently professor of sociology and social work at Bennett College.

Although the couple have no children, they have guided the affairs of many young people over the years, including more than 3 million Girl Scouts and hundreds of former students.

Bobby Seale

Political activist, author
Born October 22, 1936, in Dallas, Texas

"We began to understand the unwritten law of force. They, the police, have guns, and what the law actually says ain't worth a damn. We started to think of a program that defines and offsets this physical fact of the ghetto."

Disillusioned from poverty and poor job prospects, Bobby Seale joined Huey Newton to begin one of the most controversial groups in U.S. history—the Black Panther Party. Seale hoped the party would teach the less fortunate to gain control of the institutions that controlled their lives. Seale's tenure as chairman of the party often brought him into conflict with the law, and he served several years in prison. In the early 1970s he softened his stance and moved the party toward developing community action programs. Eventually he left the Panthers, but he is still involved with organizations committed to political and social change.

Formed the Black Panther Party with Huey Newton

Seale was born on October 22, 1936, in Dallas, Texas, to George and Thelma Seale. He had poor grades in school and eventually dropped out to join the U.S. Air Force. He trained to become an aircraft sheet-metal mechanic, but after three years, he was dishonorably discharged for disobeying a colonel. He returned home, finished high school at night, and found occasional work as a sheet-metal mechanic at various aircraft plants in the late 1950s.

In 1959 Seale studied engineering draftsmanship at Merritt College, a two-year institution located on the fringe of West Oakland's ghetto. He joined the Afro-American Association (AAA) on campus and became involved in the civil rights struggle. He also met Huey Newton, and the two often sat in coffeehouses discussing literary classics of black nationalism and revolution. They soon became disenchanted with the AAA, because they thought it did little to alleviate the economic and political oppression felt by blacks. They formed the Black Panthers for Self Defense Party a year later. Their objective was to create a grass roots political organization that would attract the less fortunate and teach them to use the electoral process as one way of gaining control of the institutions affecting their lives.

The Black Panthers walked the streets of Oakland's ghettos with firearms with the intention of protecting residents from police brutality. Tensions increased between the police and the black community, with the police trying to stem the Panther's appeal and effectiveness.

Disrupted the California State Assembly

In an effort to limit the Panther's power, state legislators planned to repeal the California law

657

Bobby Seale

allowing firearms to be carried in public. To protest, Seale led a group of thirty armed Panthers into the California State Assembly on May 2, 1967. After talking with the press the Panthers walked out and were arrested on a variety of charges. Seale pleaded guilty to disrupting the state legislature, so that the majority of Panthers could be released. He spent five months in prison, but the incident received national media coverage and helped the Panthers increase their membership.

After his release from prison Seale established contacts with other radical groups, both in the black protest movement and the mostly white peace movement. "You don't fight racism with racism," Seale said in *Time* magazine. "The best way to fight racism is with solidarity." In 1968 Seale acted on this belief by forming the Peace and Freedom Party with several white radical groups.

Later that year Seale participated with antiwar leaders in demonstrations at the Demo-

cratic National Convention in Chicago. He and seven others were indicted under the new antiriot provision of the 1968 Civil Rights Act, which made it illegal to cross state lines to incite a riot or instruct in the use of riot weapons. This group, nicknamed the "Chicago Eight," went on trial on September 24, 1969.

Seale's attorney, Charles Garry, was recovering from surgery, and when he could not be present, Seale asked the presiding judge, U.S. district judge Julius Hoffman, for a delay until his lawyer could recover. Judge Hoffman refused, so Seale retained William Kunstler, who was representing the other seven defendants. But Garry recommended that Seale fire Kunstler and represent himself. Judge Hoffman refused this request as well, saying that Kunstler and his colleagues were sufficient representation for Seale.

Tried as part of the group called the "Chicago Eight"

Believing Judge Hoffman's decision infringed on his constitutional rights, Seale began disrupting courtroom procedure with repeated outbursts against Judge Hoffman. In his autobiography, *A Lonely Rage,* Seale recounted one of his many tirades against Hoffman for the judge's continual denial of his requests for representation. "If you suppress my constitutional right to speak out in behalf of my constitutional rights, then I can only see you as a bigot, a racist, and a fascist." Seale also called the judge a pig during the trial.

His behavior brought him notoriety nationwide as a symbol of black anger and protest. A month into the trial Judge Hoffman ordered Seale bound and gagged, but he still managed to disrupt the proceedings. Judge Hoffman eventually ruled a mistrial for Seale and found him guilty on sixteen counts of contempt of court, each count having a sentence of three months in prison. Seale faced a retrial on the riot charges, but in 1972, after he served two years, the federal government rescinded all charges against him.

During his prison term, in March 1971, Seale stood trial in New Haven, Connecticut, for charges of conspiracy to kidnap and murder in the death of Alex Rackley, a New York-based Black Panther suspected by the party of being a police informant. The Federal Bureau of Investigation believed Seale gave the order for Rackley's murder. On May 24, 1971, the jury deadlocked on a verdict, and a mistrial was declared. The judge dismissed the charges, saying there had been too much publicity for a new trial to be fair.

At the beginning of the 1970s Seale moved the Black Panther Party towards community action programs, and he purged the party of any individuals with criminal intentions. These actions put a better face on the party, and coincided with a book Seale published in 1970 called *Seize the Time,* in which he attempted to debunk the perception that the Panthers had once been racists or cop killers.

In 1973 Seale exchanged the Panther's traditional black leather jacket for a suit and tie. He ran a Democratic campaign for mayor of Oakland and finished second in a field of nine candidates, with 43,710 votes. Since Seale's beliefs began to deviate further from the Black Panthers, he left the party in 1974. He formed the Advocates Scene, an organiza-tion aimed at helping the underprivileged form political coalitions. He also began writing *A Lonely Rage,* an autobiography exploring his psychological state during his childhood and activist years.

Seale became an outspoken proponent of handgun control in the 1980s, and he continued developing and helping organizations committed to social change. He served as a community liaison for Temple University's African American Studies Department and has lectured on his past activism and the continued need for civil rights involvement.

Attalah Shabazz

Activist
Born November 16, 1958, New York, New York

"All I understood life was changing, and there were places we couldn't go or be. People who once were around weren't. I didn't question this. I felt no fear. I was a child."

Attalah Shabazz has continued the fight for African American civil rights where her father, Malcolm X, left off. Working closely with Yolanda King, the daughter of slain activist Martin Luther King Jr., she formed Nucleus Inc., a drama troupe that performs in about fifty cities a year. Nucleus Inc.'s chief play is *Stepping into Tomorrow,* which warns against dropping out of school, doing drugs, and teenage pregnancy. Shabazz and King also co-authored *Of One Mind,* which looks at what might have happened if their fathers had not been assassinated. Shabazz has toured the country giving lectures on civil rights and on her father's dreams and visions.

An awareness of her heritage

Shabazz is the daughter of slain civil rights activist Malcolm X and Betty Shabazz. Although her father was a determined and aggressive campaigner for civil rights, and faced violence because of his activities, Shabazz has described him as being playful, understanding, and tolerant. As a child, she was made aware of her African, Arabic, Caribbean, and Native American heritage. Shabazz was raised as a Muslim, but was sent to a Roman Catholic school to learn other religious beliefs. Her diverse, complex upbringing was a testament to the type of individual her father was. In an interview, she said that most people have the wrong impression of her father. "People only see pieces, the fiery speaker, the street hustler of Boston and New York. But it seems that every five years he went through a radical change. In the end, he was so much more than anyone knew. I can tell you, no picture on a T-shirt captures him."

Shabazz's first grade teacher was uncomfortable with who her father was. One day her father came to pick her up at a public school in Queens. Malcolm X appeared to be a regular father in a Lacoste shirt coming to get his little girl, and the teacher overcame his mystic idea of the man. The teacher eventually became a good friend of Shabazz.

Her parents did not hide the events of the civil rights movement from her. She would watch the news when a church was being bombed, during President John Kennedy's funeral, and for other momentous events.

Shabazz told *Rolling Stone* that she did not fully comprehend the events that were happening around her when Malcolm X left the Nation of Islam. "All I understood was life was changing, and there were places we couldn't go or be. People who once were around weren't. I didn't question this. I felt no fear. I was a child. We just consolidated our family—which was always very strong, very tightly knit—and turned further inward."

When Malcolm X broke away from the Nation of Islam, the family was worried that he might be assassinated. If he heard a noise, he would calmly call his family together and keep them under cover until it was safe. On February 14, 1965, the Shabazz home was bombed by a Molotov cocktail. Malcom X

Attalah Shabazz

led them out the door and to a friend's house where they were safe.

Shabazz's father is killed

A week later Malcom X was assassinated at the Audubon Ballroom in Harlem. Shabazz recalled the incident in *Rolling Stone*. "Bullets are shot. Pandemonium. She's [her mother] telling me, 'Get down!' reaching her arms out to hold us all down on the ground. Simultaneously she's yelling, 'That's my husband they're killing!' And a kid wants to look and see. Her husband means it's my father So I keep looking, I see the men. I see it. They start to beat one of the perpetrators. People are up on stage, saying, 'Is he breathing?'"

After the incident, the family moved to their old home in Westchester. Shabazz continued her education and was especially interested in the arts. She enjoyed sculpting, writing, and acting. By the time she finished high school, she had decided to pursue an acting career. While studying at New York University, a friend introduced Shabazz to Yolanda King. The two discovered they had a lot in common—age, career goals, outlook in life, as well as the previously untapped tragic emotions about their respective fathers' deaths.

Shabazz and King decided to collaborate on a play that would combine their artistic and social concerns. They created *Stepping into Tomorrow,* a seventy-five minute play that combines comedy, drama, and music. The play is about a ten-year reunion of six high school friends. It aims to motivate youths to overcome certain dangers when growing up. "All of the things that we fall prey to—peer pres-

sure, drugs, gang violence—the reason is because of low self-esteem, not liking yourself, and having a small will or none at all," Shabazz said in an interview.

They also collaborated on *Of One Mind,* a play that discusses the possible shared dreams and goals of their fathers had both men not been assassinated. They believed King and Malcolm X were moving closer in their analysis of the civil rights movement. The two men were beginning to see racism, sexism, and ethnic division as symptoms of a deeper conflict between the rich and poor.

In 1980 Shabazz and King formed Nucleus Inc., a performing arts troupe. The company travels to about fifty cities each year and performs *Stepping into Tomorrow* in schools, churches, community centers, and local theaters. In 1988 the Los Angeles County Board of Supervisors honored King and Shabazz for their motivational play, which the board deemed "entertaining and enlightening." In 1990 the play celebrated its tenth anniversary with a gala presentation to actress Marla Gibbs's new Crossroads Arts Academy in Los Angeles. King's mother, Coretta Scott King, and Shabazz's mother attended the anniversary show.

Shabazz continues to perform and to co-direct Nucleus with King. She has branched out in the acting community, taking on credits as producer of theatrical and other productions. In the early 1990s, Shabazz was an associate producer of gospel music's Stellar Awards and the National Association for the Advancement of Colored People Image Awards.

Ntozake Shange

Playwright, poet
Born October 18, 1948, Trenton, New Jersey

"Bein alive & bein a woman & bein colored is a metaphysical dilemma I haven't yet conquered."

A gifted writer and performer, Ntozake Shange is best known for her play *For Colored Girls Who Have Considered Suicide/ When the Rainbow Is Enuf,* which took New York by storm in 1975. A blend of poetry, music, dance, and drama, it ran for two years on Broadway before going on a highly successful tour, and it is still being produced around the country.

Shange's other works include poetry and novels, as well as plays and theatrical productions. Like *For Colored Girls,* they focus on the difficulty of being black and female in America. Shange was one of the first to express the fury of African American women over their disadvantaged position in a country dominated by white males. As part of her personal protest, she adopted her African name. In Zulu, Ntozake Shange means "she who comes with her own things" and "one who walks like a lion."

A cultured upbringing

Until Shange changed her name in 1971, she was called Paulette Williams. She was named after her father, air force surgeon Paul Williams. Her mother, Eloise Williams, was a psychiatric social worker and educator. Shange was the oldest of four children, and she grew up in a cultured middle-class home. At the Williams's house there was usually somebody playing music or reciting poetry or simply curled up in a corner reading a book. There were trips to the theater and the ballet, and travel to Europe, Mexico, and the Caribbean.

On Sunday afternoons, the family often staged variety shows, as Shange later described in *Ms.* magazine: "My mama wd read from dunbar, shakespeare, countee cullen, t. s. eliot. my dad wd play congas & do magic tricks. my two sisters & my brother & i wd do a soft-shoe & then pick up the instruments for a quartet of some sort: a violin, a cello, flute & saxophone."

When Shange was eight, her family moved to St. Louis, Missouri, where they came to know many of the local musicians and writers. Jazzmen Dizzy Gillespie, Charlie Parker, and Miles Davis were all friends of the family, as was the civil rights leader and author W. E. B. Du Bois. During the five years Shange lived in St. Louis, she thoroughly enjoyed the artistic atmosphere, but she hated the blatant racism she so often encountered.

At the time, St. Louis was a segregated city, though the schools had recently been desegregated as a result of the 1954 Supreme Court ruling. Shange was bused to a German-American school, where she experience first-hand many of the cruelties of racism. It was this experience that gave birth to the anger that glows like a burning thread through so much of her work. Later, while at high school, she became aware of the other injustice that features so largely in her work—the way women are treated.

Ntozake Shange

Shange attended high school in New Jersey, for her family returned there when she was thirteen. By the time she was eighteen, she was a married woman studying for a bachelor's degree at Barnard College in New York. But the marriage did not last. By her second year at college, Shange was separated from her husband, and she felt so bitter and depressed that she tried to commit suicide. As a young black woman, she felt that everything was stacked against her. Fortunately, none of Shange's suicide attempts succeeded and after graduating with honors in 1970, she went on to the University of Southern California, Los Angeles, where she earned her M.A. in 1973.

For the next two years, Shange taught women's studies and Afro-American studies at Sonoma State College and Mills College in California. She was also deeply involved in dance and poetry groups—writing poetry and giving readings, as well as performing with such groups as the Third World Collective and West Coast Dance Works. Meanwhile, she formed her own company, which she called For Colored Girls Who Have Considered Suicide.

For Colored Girls Who Have Considered Suicide

In 1975, Shange moved to New York City, where she put on her show, *For Colored Girls Who Have Considered Suicide/When the Rainbow Is Enuf.* This "choreopoem," as she called it, consisted of twenty poems that Shange had written during the previous few years. The poems were acted out by seven black actresses, to the accompaniment of dance and music. Symbolically, the actresses were dressed in the colors of Shange's personal rainbow: brown, yellow, orange, red, purple, blue, and green.

The main theme of *For Colored Girls* is the survival of black women despite all that is ranged against them. Through dance and poetry, the seven female characters dramatize the abuse they have suffered from the men in their lives, telling how they have endured pain, rape, loneliness, and disappointment. Instead of despairing, they draw strength from one another and find hope for the future in their joint rainbow.

Some reviewers criticized *For Colored Girls* because of its negative picture of African American men; nearly all the men depicted are thoroughly vicious. Yet the show was so powerful that it quickly became the talk of New York. When it first opened in 1975, it was just a small, informal show put on in a Soho jazz loft called Studio Rivbea. There it was seen by the director Oz Scott, who developed it for production in the bars on the Lower East Side. This led to its off-Broadway production at the New Federal Theater, from where it was transferred to the Public Theater. By the end of 1976, it was playing on Broadway at the Booth Theater. The successes continued as the choreopoem toured the United States and then went overseas.

In 1977 *For Colored Girls* won Shange an Obie award, the Outer Critics Circle Award, an Audelco Award, and the *Mademoiselle* Award. It was also nominated for a Tony, a Grammy, and an Emmy. Since then, it has been performed in many parts of the world, and in 1982 it was adapted for the "American Playhouse" series on public television.

Other works

The success of *For Colored Girls* has tended to overshadow Shange's other works, yet she has had a successful career as a writer, performer, and director, as well as holding university appointments. She currently teaches drama at the University of Houston and has given lectures at Yale University, Howard University, the Detroit Institute of Arts, New York University, and many other institutions.

Shange's volumes of poetry include *Nappy Edges* (1978), *A Daughter's Geography* (1983), *From Okra to Greens* (1984), and *The Love Space Demands* (1991). Of the plays she has written in recent years, the most acclaimed are *Three Pieces* (1981), which won the *Los Angeles Times* Book Prize for Poetry, and *Mother Courage and Her Children* (1980), which won Shange a second Obie award. Her fiction includes *Sassafras, Cypress & Indigo* (1976), a novella that centers on the lives of two sisters, and *Betsey Brown* (1985), an autobiographical novel.

In 1977, Shange married the musician David Murray, from whom she has since been divorced. She has one daughter, who has been a great source of inspiration to her, for Shange's writings are suffused with a protective love for young black American girls. She sees it as her mission to provide them with the information she feels they need. "When I die," she says, "I will not be guilty of having left a generation of girls behind thinking that anyone can tend to their emotional health other than themselves."

Al Sharpton

Civil rights activist
Born 1955, New York, New York

"What I'm sayin' needs to be said, I ain't makin' no apologies. I ain't puttin' on no Brooks Brothers suit. This is how we are. But we can still deal."

He's been called Al Charlatan, the Reverend Soundbite, and the Minister of Hate, but the name-calling has never bothered him. Reverend Al Sharpton is a firm believer in black civil rights and has the battle scars to prove it. He has been stabbed, served time in jail, and led demonstrations that shut down the New York subway and the Brooklyn Bridge. Despite his run-ins with the law, Sharpton has remained a popular figure in New York's poor black community. In 1992, he ran for the Democratic party nomination to the U.S. Senate. Although he was unsuccessful, Sharpton impressed many with his campaign to end racial injustice in the city.

First sermon at age four

Sharpton was born in Crown Heights, a New York City suburb, in 1955, and even before he learned to read and write he gave sermons. His first sermon, "Let not your heart be troubled," was presented when he was four years old at the Washington Temple Church of God in Christ in Brooklyn. By the time Sharpton was seven, he was called the Wonderboy Preacher of the New York gospel circuit.

Sharpton was raised in a ten-family building in Queens. His father owned the building, along with thirty houses in Brooklyn. When Sharpton was ten, his father took all their money and left. Sharpton's mother moved her family to Flatbush and became a maid for a rabbi. It was a difficult period for Sharpton, and the experience shaped his future endeavors.

"I knew the world was better than this," he told the *New York Times Magazine*. "In the [housing] project I thought: 'No, I don't have to accept this. I know there's good schools. I know that the garbage man picks up garbage in some neighborhoods because I lived in them.' So that really gave me indignation."

When Sharpton was eleven, he met Congressman Adam Clayton Powell and was so impressed that he stopped preaching to become a civil rights worker. In 1969, at the age of fourteen, he was named youth director of the New York chapter of Operation Breadbasket, the economic program of Martin Luther King, Jr.'s Southern Christian Leadership Conference. Sharpton coordinated the activities of about four hundred children. They campaigned for jobs and other rights from white businesses in the ghetto. Two years later Sharpton started his own group, the National Youth Movement. The NYM targeted companies at first, then turned to politics. By 1972, several presidential candidates sought Sharpton's support.

When not attending to his political duties, Sharpton attended an all-white school in Flatbush. He was vice-president of the student council and associate editor of the school newspaper. Sometimes he would gather his supporters together before school began and declare a boycott against cafeteria food, dress codes, or anything else that struck his fancy.

Turns to street preaching

At nineteen, Sharpton met James Brown, the legendary "Godfather of Soul." Sharpton toured with him, booked his shows, and hired his bands. When he was not living the high life, Sharpton could be found in New York, registering voters, marching against crack cocaine, and even uncovering a police drug-and-fencing operation. He became a popular street preacher and worked hard to attract support from the area's residents. His wife worked as an army reservist.

During this time Sharpton also bid on a garbage contract with the local Con Ed public utility, but he was disqualified when it was discovered his financial backer was an organized crime figure called Matty the Horse. He also had a stint as an FBI informant and had run-ins with the law for nonpayment of rent and for disorderly conduct.

In the mid-1980s, a series of racial incidents occurred in various New York neighborhoods that disturbed Sharpton: four black youths were shot in a subway, a young black man was killed in Howard Beach after he was chased on the highway by some whites, and a young black man named Yusuf Hawkins was shot in Bensonhurst. These events caused Sharpton to bring his demonstrations out of the ghetto and into white areas. He staged protests at Howard Beach and Bensonhurst, and on December 21, 1987, shut down the subway and the Brooklyn Bridge. In February 1990, Sharpton was convicted for his role in organizing the Brooklyn protest. Despite several appeals, he began a forty-five-day jail term on March 5, 1993. He worked out an agreement with the Corrections Department that allowed him to work from his office, attend meetings, and make speeches, returning to jail each night.

In 1987 Sharpton alienated many civil rights moderates with his unwavering support of Tawana Brawley. He sided with this fifteen-year-old black girl who claimed to have been raped, smeared with dog feces, and abandoned by a group of white men. He took on the state attorney general's office and staged a series of stunts and confrontations that many felt were done for self-promotion. He came across as obsessed with racism, aiming to heighten racial tensions. When a special grand jury called the case a hoax, he did not budge. Sharpton still maintains that Brawley was raped and then abused by a judicial system that would not listen to her.

In 1989 Sharpton ran afoul of the law again when he was charged with sixty-seven

Al Sharpton

counts. Among the charges—that he stole $250,000 from charitable donors and cheated on his income taxes. He was ultimately acquitted on all charges. Of three other tax charges that lingered, two were later dropped, after he pleaded guilty to failing to file a tax return in 1986 and was fined $5,000.

Stabbed near his heart

Sharpton's tough stance on black civil rights ran him into trouble on several occasions, but the most serious occurred on January 12, 1991. A drunk man named Michael Riccardi stabbed him two inches away from his heart with a five-inch steak knife. "I remember something brush past," he said in an *Esquire* interview. "But when I looked down, there was a knife sticking out of my chest. Instinctively, I grabbed the knife out and that's when the air hit and I went down." Sharpton was rushed to Coney Island Hospital. While convalescing, he met with civil rights leader Jesse Jackson, who advised him to calm his speaking style down and to make room for other points of view.

In 1992, a rejuvenated Sharpton ran for the U.S. Senate. He talked passionately about injustice, but he seemed softer, more focused, and intellectually polished. He told the *New York Times Magazine,* "it was time to bring down the volume and bring up the program." His campaign appealed to the poor and neglected citizens—those who had traditionally turned away from politics. He held his own during television debates and held his temper during the campaign trail. Edolphus Towns, a Brooklyn Democrat and former chairman of the Congressional Black Caucus told the *New York Times Magazine* that, "no question about it, he's matured. He's been out there so long that sometimes people think he is older than he is. But when he started he was literally a kid." When the election ended, 166,665 people had voted for Sharpton, giving him about 15 percent of the vote in the Democratic primary and landing him third in a field of four.

Since the election, Sharpton has met with Edward J. Perkins, the United States representative to the United Nations to talk about the Somalian civil war. He devotes himself daily to meetings with prominent blacks and appearances at some of the most high-profile political events.

Many Americans still see him as a dangerous media manipulator. One white columnist called him "a racial ambulance chaser" and another dubbed him a "race racketeer." A *New York Daily News* poll stated that 90 percent of whites and 73 percent of blacks believe he is harming race relations.

Opinions on Sharpton's activities vary. Major Owens, a black Democrat from New York, says Sharpton's history "shows he has no principles. He's not to be trusted." Andrew Cooper, publisher of the *City Sun*, a black newspaper in New York, says, "Most middle-class blacks are embarrassed by him." His supporters, like Rev. Timothy Mitchell, pastor of Ebenezer Baptist Church in Queens, says, "He's some sort of a hero to young people. They admire his courage." Rev. Williams Augustus Jones, pastor of Bethany Baptist Church, the oldest congregation in Brooklyn, says, "We recognize his gift. We applaud his spirit. We thank God for the fact that he has been consistently on the firing line on behalf of our people and our cause."

For his part, Sharpton defends all his actions. He told *Esquire*, "I wanted to build a grass-roots movement with a little pizzazz. That's what [Martin Luther] King did. He brought theater into the movement. King said, 'We will close down the bus company.' It was TV. That's how King changed America."

Althea T.L. Simmons

Lawyer, NAACP Washington Bureau director
Born April 17, 1924, Shreveport, Louisiana
Died September 13, 1990, Washington, D.C.

"The job must go on. There is little time for rest."

Althea T.L. Simmons was born with a fierce desire to end racial injustice and prejudice. She rose through the ranks of the

Althea T.L. Simmons

National Association for the Advancement of Colored People (NAACP) from fieldworker to Washington Bureau director and the organization's chief lobbyist. She fought hard for voting rights extensions, a strengthened Fair Housing Law, and a bill to establish a Martin Luther King holiday. Confined to a hospital room during her final months, Simmons maintained a bedside office to continue her relentless struggle for civil rights.

Studying to meet career goals

Simmons was born on April 17, 1924, in Shreveport, Louisiana, to M.M. Simmons, a high school principal, and Lillian Simmons, a high school teacher. As far back as kindergarten, Simmons used the initials "T.L." When asked once what the initials meant, she replied, "That's one secret I will keep."

In 1945 Simmons received a bachelor of science degree with honors from Southern University, a black, state-supported institution in New Orleans, Louisiana. She received a master's degree from the University of Illinois in Urbana in 1951, and a law degree from Howard University in Washington, D.C., in 1956. She also took courses at the University of California at Los Angeles and did additional work at the American Society for Training Development, the American Management Association, the New School for Social Work in New York City, and the National Training Laboratory. All this training was necessary. After graduating from law school, Simmons set high career goals and was particularly interested in the civil rights movement.

From 1956 to 1961, Simmons was associated with the W.J. Durham law office. She became an NAACP volunteer as executive secretary of the Texas State Conference of NAACP branches and chairperson of the executive committee of the Dallas branch. In 1961 she became a field secretary, working out of the subregional office in Los Angeles. When activist Medgar Evers was killed by a white supremacist, the NAACP sent Simmons to assist his widow, Myrlie, and the Evers family and to relocate them to Los Angeles. Civil rights leader Benjamin L. Hooks said, "Her quiet courage and demeanor was a source of strength to Myrlie and the children."

In 1964 a management consultant firm recommended to the NAACP board of directors that an office of secretary for training be established. Roy L. Wilkins, executive secretary, appointed Simmons to the position, and she remained there for ten years. As well that year, Simmons was named director of the NAACP's National Voter Registration Drive. Appointed the NAACP national education director from 1974 to 1977, Simmons developed textbooks, pamphlets, programs, and other materials to inspire black youths. As associate director of branch and field services, Simmons supervised the NAACP's nationwide network of branches, field staff, and the membership and youth and college division from 1977 to 1979.

Simmons was appointed director of the Washington Bureau and chief lobbyist in 1979. She had established a solid reputation in her past positions, and she said her years of field service "taught her the value of grassroots mobilization." While in Washington, Simmons's work gained her national respect, but the shadow of her predecessor hung over her head. Her leadership was often compared to that of the legendary Clarence Mitchell. Some people felt she was an unworthy successor to Mitchell because she was black and a woman—a double liability.

Lobbying for civil rights legislation

Simmons did not let her detractors interfere with her work. She began her usual routine of working late into the evening and on the weekend to get the job completed. She never viewed her role as one of self-promotion. She was a civil rights expert and had a comprehensive understanding of the civil rights agenda. Simmons would often corner representatives and senators and, according to *Crisis*, "cajoled them...into supporting Civil Rights legislation." Her hardnosed lobbying helped bring about extensions of voting rights, passage of the Fair Housing Act, and a bill to establish a national holiday in honor of Martin Luther King, Jr. She played a pivotal role in causing

Congress to deny Robert Bork's appointment to the United States Supreme Court and facilitated the work of the Resolutions Committee at NAACP conventions by planning summits, conferences, marches, and various protests and demonstrations. Senator Orrin G. Hatch, a Republican from Utah, called her "one of the most effective, intelligent lobbyists on the Hill."

Simmons was noted for her forcefulness and resolve. These qualities made her an awesome opponent and a fearless leader. She was straightforward and never let herself be distracted in an argument. She had a brisk walk, always appearing to be in a hurry.

Besides her work with the NAACP, Simmons was a member of the National Manpower Advisory Committee for the United States Department of Labor, vice-president of the American Society for Training and Development, a vice-president of NOW's Legal Defense and Education Fund, a member of the United States Census Advisory Committee on Black Populations, a member of the board of directors of the National Council on the Aging, and a member of the executive board of Delta Sigma Theta Sorority.

She received several awards for her professional and community service, including Washburn University's President's Award in 1975; a 1987 Distinguished Alumni Award; and a 1988 Leadership Award from the National Association for Equal Opportunity in Education. Simmons also received the National Bar Association's Gertrude E. Rush Award in 1990.

Toward the end of her life, Simmons fell ill for several months, but still set up an office at her hospital room in Howard University. She wanted to continue her work rather than rest. "The job must go on. There is little time to rest," she said. After a long illness, she died in her hospital room on September 13, 1990.

Carole Simpson

Broadcast journalist
Born December 7, 1940, Chicago, Illinois

"I want to cover black stories because I feel I bring them sensitivity and a perspective that white reporters don't have. I wouldn't want to cover just black news though, because you often lose your credibility that way."

W hen Americans turn on their televisions Saturday night to watch the news, more often than not, they're tuning in to watch Carole Simpson. As host of ABC's "World News Saturday," Simpson has provided her audience with a sensitive perspective when covering news and features about black America. She has covered a wide array of topics including Capitol Hill, health care, housing, education, the environment, and the release of Nelson Mandela. With her articulate style and a rhythmic flow in her news delivery, Simpson has made an outstanding contribution not only to broadcast journalism, but also to society in general.

A stringer for Voice of America

Simpson was born on December 7, 1940, in Chicago, Illinois. She received a bachelor of arts degree in journalism at the University of Michigan in 1962. She later did graduate study in journalism at the University of Iowa. Early in her career she worked as a stringer correspondent for the Voice of America radio network and spent two years as a journalism instructor and director of the Information Bureau at Tuskegee Institute in Alabama.

In 1965 she joined the staff of WCFL-Radio in Chicago as a news reporter and anchor, and also reviewed books and movies. Three years later she served as a special correspondent and weekend anchor at WBBM-Radio in Chicago. She was also a commentator on "Our People," a minority affairs program on WTTW-TV, a public television station in Chicago. From there she became the first black woman television reporter in Chicago.

Simpson's reputation as a top-notch journalist continued to grow. She became a television news correspondent for WMAQ-TV and worked at that station from 1970 to 1974. She also worked as a journalism instructor for Northwestern University's Medill School of Journalism from 1971 to 1974. It was during her time at WMAQ that she began specializing in feature stories that gave her more creativity. She also wanted to cover stories about African Americans because she felt she could be more sensitive and objective than a white reporter. "I want to cover black stories because I feel I bring them sensitivity and a perspective that white reporters don't have. I wouldn't want to cover just black news though, because you often lose your credibility that way," she told *Ebony*.

In time, Simpson moved to Washington to host a women's public affairs program called "HerRah," which aired on WRC-TV,

Carole Simpson

an NBC affiliate. She also became a substitute anchor for "NBC Nightly News" and anchored NBC's "Newsbreak" on the weekends. Her news delivery, style, camera presence, and on-air finesse made her a popular television personality, and she was selected to cover Capitol Hill as a news correspondent. Simpson held that position from 1978 until 1981, when she was chosen to serve as a perimeter reporter during the Republican and Democratic party conventions in 1980. She received national recognition and earned the respect of her colleagues. In 1982 she joined ABC in Washington as a general assignment correspondent.

News anchor

Her primary assignment during the 1980s was to cover George Bush. She accompanied him on domestic and foreign trips. In 1984 she covered his vice-presidential reelection campaign, and his 1988 bid for the presidency. She also served as a perimeter reporter during the 1988 Republican convention in New Orleans.

Simpson's journalistic skills, combined with years of experience, made her the ideal choice for the anchor of ABC's "World News Saturday" in 1988. She also contributes reports about family issues for the "American Agenda" segment on "World News Tonight" with Peter Jennings. Some of her segments have dealt with controversial subjects, such as children under stress, battered women, and teen pregnancy. In 1988 she received an Emmy nomination for a story on children with AIDS. Simpson is also seen on "Nightline" and "20/20."

Besides anchoring half-hour news shows and providing segments, Simpson has also anchored three hour-long ABC news specials: "The Changing American Family," "Public Schools in Conflict," and "Sex and Violence in the Media." One of the most important stories she covered was the release of Nelson Mandela, who was imprisoned in South Africa for twenty-seven years. While covering a church service the day before Mandela was released, Simpson was assaulted by a South Africa police officer at a disturbance in Johannesburg. During her stay, she also did a special report on South African women.

Simpson has received many honors and awards. She is listed in *Who's Who in America* and *Who's Who Among Black Americans*. From 1982 to 1983, she was president of the Radio and Television Correspondents Association. Simpson was named to the University of Iowa's School of Communications Hall of Fame, and in 1986 she was elected chairperson of the ABC News Women's Advisory

Board. She is also a member of the board of directors for the Washington chapter of the Society of Professional Journalists of the Fund for Investigative Journalism and of the Distinguished Journalists Advisory Committee of the American University. In 1988 she was the recipient of the Milestone Award in Broadcast Journalism from the National Commission on Working Women and received the Silver Bell Award from the Ad Council in 1989.

When Simpson turned 50 in 1990, she told *Ebony* it was a chance to sit back and evaluate her life. "It was very sobering because it became apparent to me that two-thirds of my life was over," she said. "It was a time to really take stock of what I wanted to do with the rest of my life."

Simpson is married to James Marshall. They have two children, a daughter named Mallika and a son named Adam.

Naomi Sims

Model, business executive
Born March 30, 1949, Oxford, Mississippi

"Once you've got success, it's empty. The fun is in reaching for it."

In the late 1960s Naomi Sims blazed the trail for thousands of young black women by proving to the fashion world that "black is beautiful." She was the first African American to appear on the cover of major publications such as the *New York Times* fashion supplement, and she was also widely seen in television commercials. Never before had such a dark-skinned model been used to portray beauty in North American media.

Having achieved celebrity as a top fashion model, Sims launched a second successful career as a business executive with her own brand of beauty products. She has also written the books *All about Health and Beauty for the Black Woman* (1975), *How to be a Top Model* (1979), *All about Hair Care for the Black Woman* (1982), and *All about Success for the Black Woman* (1983).

Felt "tall, dark, and different"

Naomi Sims's parents divorced when she was a baby, and she has only faint memories of her father. She was brought up by her mother until the age of eight, when her mother had a nervous breakdown. Sims was then put in a home for girls until a place was found for her in a foster home. This was a miserable, lonely time for her, for she was separated from her two sisters as well as her mother.

Sims recalls that she used to cry every night: "The social worker promised me that I would return to my mother, who she said was very sick. But when I was ten I realized I would never be placed with my natural mother again." Her childhood was spent in a series of foster homes.

Sims was educated at integrated schools, where she felt "tall and dark and different." Slender and already 5 ft. 10 in. when she was thirteen, she dressed well, to the admiration of her friends. Sims was so fashion conscious that when she was at Westinghouse High School in Pittsburgh, she often went without lunch so she could spend her lunch money on a pair of earrings or some other accessory.

On graduation from Westinghouse High in 1966, Sims went to New York and enrolled at the Fashion Institute of Technology to study fashion. When she ran short of money, she found part-time work posing for a fashion illustrator for $6 an hour. This was still too little to live on, so Sims decided to act as her own agent—since she could not possibly afford to hire one—and telephoned the prominent fashion photographer Gosta Peterson. It was unheard of for a would-be model to take such a step, but Peterson agreed to see Sims and then agreed to try her as a model. As a result, Sims was soon earning $60 an hour.

Broke onto the covers of "white" fashion mags

Sims could now afford to sign up with a modeling agency, but a black model was still such a rarity that she sometimes went for weeks without work. But in 1967 the *New York Times* featured her on the cover of its fall fashion section, *Fashion of the Times,* a breakthrough not only for Sims but for the fashion world in general.

Sims regards the 1967 AT&T television commercial as her big break. She had been out of work for eight weeks when she was offered the commercial, which featured her and two other strikingly beautiful women— one Asian and one white. "After it was aired, people wanted to find out about me and use me, " she said. Her career suddenly took off, with her picture appearing in such traditionally white magazines as *Vogue, Ladies Home Journal,* and *Cosmopolitan.* She was the first black model to appear in most of these journals, and in many of them her photograph appeared on the cover.

In 1969 Sims won the Model of the Year Award, the first of many modeling and beauty awards to come her way. Her success in the wake of the civil rights movement was an overdue tribute to all black women. In 1971 Sims was honored with the key to the city of Cleveland, Ohio, and two years later the governor of Illinois proclaimed September 23, 1973, to be Naomi Sims Day.

Pursued successful business career

By the time Sims was twenty-four she was so securely at the top of her field that she was finding life rather dull. "Once you've got success, it's empty," she said. "The fun is in reaching for it." She soon found something new to reach for by going into business. Her first enterprise was designing wigs for African Americans—really attractive wigs made out

Naomi Sims

of synthetic fiber which she had invented and patented. When stores doubted whether the wigs would sell, Sims put together a slide show, which convinced even the most dubious to market them.

Naomi Sims Beauty Products Ltd. was Sims's next enterprise, a business she founded in 1985 with her former brother-in-law, Alex Erwiah, who owned a cosmetics import-export business in New York. As there were existing cosmetic companies supplying the needs of African American women, Sims focused on skin treatment rather than makeup. She pointed out that stress, fast foods, and pollution were each doing their bit to harm the black complexion, and she offered three products to counter their effects: a cleansing milk, a chamomile cream soap, and a primrose rinsing lotion. If black women used these products for only three minutes each day, she said, they could have skin as healthy as their mothers'.

During summer 1987 Sims advertised extensively in the media. As part of the advertising campaign, she invited black women to visit her and other consultants at a store in Brooklyn, where she promised to give personal advice on skin care. The response was overwhelming. Women lined up for hours awaiting their turn. The enterprise was such a success that by the following year Naomi Sims Beauty Products Ltd. was offering some 60 different products, which were carried in 125 department stores. The sales from these products grossed $5 million.

As wife of art dealer Michael Findlay and mother of their son John Phillip, Sims has a full private life in addition to her business career. Yet she also finds time to involve herself in charitable work, supporting such causes as research into sickle-cell anemia and drug rehabilitation programs. Remembering her disadvantaged childhood, she is especially concerned with the well-being of children and is on the board of directors of the Northside Center Child Development in Harlem.

John Singleton

Screenwriter, director
Born 1968, Los Angeles, California

"I always wanted to do a real film about what it's like growing up black. There are always stories about how whites grow up, films like American Graffiti or Rebel Without a Cause."

In the late 1980s and early 1990s, a new class of films were being produced in Hollywood. Black filmmakers were producing movies for black audiences about black issues. While black movies in the 1970s usually stereotyped blacks and were produced by whites, these new films were produced, directed, and written by blacks. Film critic Susan Stark of the *Detroit News* wrote that these filmmakers "are an extraordinary group of artists. They are energizing American movies on a scale not seen since World War II, when Hitler forced many of Europe's greats to seek refuge in Hollywood."

One of the best examples of this new type of filmmaker is John Singleton. While still in college, Singleton signed a three-year contract with Columbia Pictures to develop and direct films. The result was the critically acclaimed *Boyz N the Hood,* released in 1991. "He's the most impressive of this year's debuting young black filmmakers because he puts his anger into words, not just camera angles—into detailed screenwriting that makes audiences feel what he has felt." Although Singleton directed the movie, he feels his bigger accomplishment was in writing the screenplay. "In this business you get hired for your vision, and your vision begins with your script," he told the *New York Times Magazine.* "I'm a writer first and I direct in order to protect my vision. *Boyz* is a good story, a *real* story, and they wanted it. Simple as that."

Gorged himself on movies

Singleton was born in 1968 in Los Angeles, California, to Danny Singleton, a mortgage broker, and Sheila Ward, a pharmaceutical company sales executive. He spent his early years shuttling back and forth between his unmarried parents. Since his parents did not have a lot of money, Singleton would steal candy and toys. He never stole anything more serious because his parents devoted a lot of attention to him. His father, for example, used to take him to the movies, and by the time he was nine he began to think about making films. "He gorged on films by Orson Welles, Francois Truffaut, Steven Spielberg, Akira Kurosawa, John Cassavetes, Martin Scorsese, and Francis Ford Coppola," Karen Grigsby Bates wrote in the *New York Times Magazine.* Singleton learned a lot from their pictures, and he developed the idea of producing his own film about growing up black.

While in high school, Singleton heard that the film business was controlled by screen-plays, and so he set about learning how to write. He graduated from high school in 1986 and was accepted to the University of Southern California School of Cinema-Television's prestigious Filmic Writing Program. He won three writing awards in his four-year stay.

During his sophmore year, Singleton's agent sent his screenplay, *Boyz N the Hood,* to Columbia Pictures. The response was immediate. "I thought John's script had a distinctive voice and great insight," Columbia chairman Frank Price told the *New York Times.* "He's not just a good writer, but he has enormous self-confidence and assurance. In fact, the last time I'd met someone that young with so much self-assurance was Steven Spielberg." Columbia wanted to produce the movie but did not want Singleton to direct it. Singleton refused to let anyone else direct it, and eventually Columbia agreed to his demands.

Columbia gave Singleton $7 million to produce a movie that would provide a realistic portrayal of what it is like to be young, black, and American in the 1990s. The film followed the lives of three people at two different stages of their lives. First at the age of ten, then at the age of seventeen. The film begins with Tre Styles, the protagonist, being sent by his mother, Reva, to live with his father, Furious. She hopes the father will discipline the young man to become a respectable adult. In his new neighborhood, Tre meets two half-brothers who live across the street: Rickey and Doughboy. These three grow up in an inner city, which *New York* magazine described as "all day, jets heading for LAX come in low over the small tract houses; at night, police headquarters join in the din, training down their lights. The sun shines regularly, but the little boys play football with a corpse lying nearby, and a teenage girl tries to read through the rattling of gunfire."

Unlike the others, Tre has a concerned and caring father. Furious tells him to treat people with respect, work hard, and stay away from crime. His advice convinces Tre to stay away from life on the streets and to become responsible. Since his two friends do not have a strong father figure, their lives are not as fortunate. Rickey is a gifted athlete and his mother's favorite, but he must pass his SATs to win a scholarship. Doughboy, who is disliked by his mother, is a complex character who makes his living selling drugs.

The opening line of *Boyz N the Hood* is "One out of every twenty-one black males will be murdered. Most will be shot by another black male." This statement holds true

John Singleton

at the end of the movie. Only Tre survives, guided by his father's advice, and enrolls in a college. The *New York Times* had strong praise for the ending. "In the end, *Boyz N the Hood* asks the all-important question of whether there is such a thing as changing one's fate. If there is—and Mr. Singleton holds out a powerful glimmer of hope in the story's closing moments—then for this film's young characters it hinges on the attitudes of their fathers."

Reaction to the movie mostly positive

Reaction to the movie was mostly positive. Critics raved about Singleton's ability to recreate an inner city neighborhood on screen. One of the best reviews came from the *New York Times Magazine,* which described it as a "challenging film, a disconcertingly gritty peek into a facet of life to which virtually no white audiences have been privy—and that a fair number of black middle-class viewers will find alien as well." *New York* lauded his ability to depict the "insane combustibility in ordinary encounters—the jostling among teenagers that ends with guns blazing. He gets the heat and sass of young women, the despair of the older ones. He presents a coherent picture of a tragic way of life." The film, very popular among moviegoers, made more than $57 million.

But there were some who were critical of portions of the movie. *Time* said the women in the movie were "shown as doped-up, career-obsessed, or irrelevant to the man's work of raising a son in an American war zone." *People* went as far as stating that none of the characters was realistically outlined, and that only the actors kept Singleton's "too-symbolic characters from turning into cardboard."

In addition to this negative press, the movie suffered bad publicity when it opened on July 12, 1991. Shootings and knifings left two dead and more than thirty injured in incidents at about twenty theaters from Los Angeles to Chicago to Detroit. Twenty-one theaters immediately dropped the film. Singleton responded to this decision by stating he did not create the conditions under which people shoot each other. He added that shootings happen because there's a whole generation of blacks who feel disenfranchised. In *Newsweek* he said: "It was the fact that a whole generation (of black men) doesn't respect themselves, which makes it easier for them to shoot each other. This is a generation of kids who don't have father figures. They're looking for their manhood, and they get a gun. The more of those people that get together, the higher the potential for violence."

A strong explanation has yet to be made regarding the relationship between the film and the violence during its opening. Singleton hoped the film would help end violence in inner cities rather than spur on new violence. "If you make a film," Singleton told *Time,* "you have a responsibility to say something socially relevant. This is a film that makes a plea for conscientious parenting. This is a film that shows self-respect and hard work as the only hope for children. This is a film that concludes with a challenge, written in bold titles across the screen: 'Increase the peace.'"

Bessie Smith

Blues singer
Born April 15, 1894, Chattanooga, Tennessee
Died September 26, 1937, Clarksdale, Mississippi

"More than any other singer, she set the blues tradition in terms of style and quality."
—Gunther Schuller

B essie Smith, the biggest-selling recording artist of her day, was widely known as the Empress of the Blues. More than any other artist, she popularized blues singing, attracting literally thousands of fans to her concerts. Often there were near riots as those waiting outside tried to get in and those inside refused to leave. With her majestic stage presence and wicked sense of humor, Smith knew instinctively how to communicate with her audience.

"She was one of those rare beings, a completely integrated artist capable of projecting her whole personality into music," said critic and promoter John Hammond. "She was blessed not only with great emotion but with a tremendous voice that could penetrate the inner recesses of the listener." Smith's voice was a rich contralto, and its moody tones set the style for a whole generation of jazz singers. Billie Holiday, Mahalia Jackson, and many other performers were strongly influenced by Smith's style of singing.

Traveling road shows

So many stories have grown up around Bessie Smith that it can be hard to sift the fact from the fiction. Contrary to popular belief, she was not related to three other early blues singers, Clara, Mamie, and Trixie Smith. She was the daughter of William Smith, who died soon after her birth, and of Laura Smith, who died when Bessie was nine years old. There were six children in the family, the oldest being Viola, who took care of her younger brothers and sisters when their mother died. She supported them by taking in laundry, just as her mother had done, and occasionally the children themselves earned a few cents by singing in the streets.

When Smith was about fourteen she joined a traveling show as a dancer in the chorus. These road shows were a common feature at the time. Small troupes of entertainers would tour the towns and cities, setting up their tents at each stop and putting on a vaudeville act or minstrel show. During her teens, Smith toured with several groups. As she polished her skills, she moved up the ladder from chorus girl to solo performer, doing an act that combined singing, dancing, and comedy.

Around 1912, Smith first worked in a show with Ma Rainey, "the Mother of the Blues." As the two toured together and became friends, Smith picked up various musical ideas from the older woman. However, Smith's style was very much her own, as was her delivery. Her earthy voice was so strong that it could easily fill a hall—an essential quality in those pre-microphone days. The audiences were mesmerized. As guitarist Danny Barker described it, "Bessie Smith was

a fabulous deal to watch. She was a large, pretty woman and she dominated the stage. You didn't turn your head when she went on."

By 1920, Smith was producing her own shows for the 81 Theater in Atlanta and then taking them on the road. She did so well that two years later she was able to buy a house in Philadelphia. Yet she was still only in the early stages of her career. Her big successes came when she started making records.

Record sales

The first record of blues singing was made in 1920 by Mamie Smith. It proved so popular—especially in the South, where it attracted white as well as black buyers—that record companies moved quickly to bring out more records of black performers.

Bessie Smith made her first recording in 1923 with the songs "Down-Hearted Blues" and "Gulf Coast Blues," which were accompanied on the piano by Clarence Williams. The record was an immediate hit, selling 780,000 copies in the first six months. This was the first of 160 records that Smith made for Columbia Records—and in the process she helped restore the fortunes of the ailing company. In 1923 Columbia was on the brink of failure, but thanks largely to Smith's popularity, it survived to become a highly prosperous business.

Smith's recordings for Columbia were made with some of the most famous names in jazz. These included trumpeter Louis Armstrong, with whom she recorded the classic "St. Louis Blues," as well as such numbers as "Cold in Hand Blues," "Careless Love Blues," "Nashville Woman's Blues," and "I

Bessie Smith

Ain't Gonna Play No Second Fiddle." Other partnerships included those with trombonist Charlie Green and cornetist Joe Smith, with whom she recorded such songs as "The Yellow Dog Blues," "Empty Bed Blues," "Trombone Cholly," and "Young Woman's Blues." Then there was the brilliant pianist James P. Johnson, who teamed up with Smith to record "Preachin' the Blues" and "Back Water Blues" in 1927, and "He's Got Me Goin'," "Worn Out Papa Blues," and "You Don't Understand" in 1929.

Smith's success as a recording artist made her much sought after as a concert performer, and throughout the 1920s she was constantly on the move, mobbed by adoring crowds in every city where she performed. Despite her star status, she usually had difficulty finding somewhere to stay because so many hotels and restaurants would not admit African Americans. To avoid frustrating humiliations for herself and her troupe, Smith bought an eighty-foot Pullman railroad car in 1925 and fitted it up luxuriously so that they could all live and travel in comfort. She also saw to the comforts of her family by supporting her many relatives, and she bought her sister, Viola, a house near her own in Philadelphia and set her up in the restaurant business.

The depression years

When the Great Depression hit in 1929, Smith was still making good money. Although she was doing less recording than earlier in the decade, she had a busy schedule of concert appearances and was the star of the film *St. Louis Blues,* which ran for the next two years. But gradually she too felt the effects of the Depression. The record industry had to cut back in order to stay in business, and theaters had to reduce the price of tickets to attract the public. Meanwhile, the beginning of the radio age meant that many people preferred to stay home and listen to the radio rather than go out to a show. As a result of all this, even the most popular performers experienced a sharp drop in income. Although Smith continued to get concert appearances, she could no longer afford to keep up her railroad car. Touring once again became a thoroughly unpleasant business.

Smith's personal life, too, was at a low ebb. After the death of her first husband, whom she had wed in her early twenties, she married a night watchman named Jack Gee, who became her part-time manager. Three years later, in 1926, they adopted a son, Jack Gee, Jr., but the child proved to be a cause of further strife in what was already a stormy relationship. When the couple separated in 1929, Gee took the boy and kept him from Smith by hiding him in various boarding homes.

In the 1930s Smith formed a happier relationship with Richard Morgan, the uncle of jazz musician Lionel Hampton. As well, her career began to turn a corner. By the mid-1930s, although the country was still in the grip of the Depression, prospects were looking brighter for performers because of a new and gutsy type of music that was sweeping the dance halls, called "swing." Smith quickly adapted her style, proving that she could swing with the best of them, and in 1936 she gave a memorable performance at New York's prestigious Famous Door on Fifty-second Street. So superb was her performance that Mildred Bailey, who was booked to follow her, decided to bow out. She knew that however well she sang, it would be an anticlimax after Smith's magnificent act.

Clearly, Smith's star was once more on the rise. As a result of her Famous Door appearance, Benny Goodman, "the King of Swing," was eager to record with her, as was bandleader Count Basie. Another film was planned, and the future seemed rosy. But there was to be no future. In the early hours of a September morning in 1937, when Smith and Morgan were driving from a show in Memphis, Smith was fatally wounded in a car accident. She died at a black hospital in Clarksdale, Mississippi, a few hours later.

Soon afterwards, someone started a rumor that Smith had bled to death in a white hospital, which had refused to treat her because she was black. Although there was no truth in the story, it spread rapidly and was repeated by John Hammond in his *Downbeat* magazine article a month later. It was repeated again in Edward Albee's 1960 play *The Death of Bessie Smith*. As a result, it has become part of the Smith legend along with other titillating myths, such as the story that, as a teenager, Smith had been kidnapped by Ma Rainey and forced to perform with her troupe.

While such inventions add drama to Smith's life, the truth is dramatic enough on its own. The child who sang for pennies on street corners in Chattanooga, Tennessee, became famed throughout the world as the Empress of the Blues—and today, more than half a century after her death, she is still remembered as one of the all-time greats in the history of jazz.

Wesley Snipes

Actor
Born July 31, 1962, Orlando, Florida

"You will never hear me say I don't see myself as a black actor but just an actor who happens to be black. Every chance I get I'm going to tell you I'm an African American man who is acting."

F ew young actors have been as successful as Wesley Snipes, who became so well known in his twenties that he was featured on the cover of *Newsweek* and *Jet* magazines. The *New Yorker* magazine called him one of the most impressive members of the new generation of American actors.

Snipes gives a totally riveting performance whatever role he takes on, and he has played such diverse characters as boxer, architect, and paralyzed patient in a rehabilitation center. One of his strengths is his versatility. During his meteoric career he has performed in films, videos, stage plays, and on television, and in 1987 he won cable television's ACE Award for best actor for his performance in *Vietnam Story.*

"Felt like mold on white bread"

The youngest in a family of seven children, Wesley Snipes was brought up by his mother, Marian, who worked as a teacher's aide. He saw little of his father during his childhood, since his parents divorced when he was barely a year old, and his mother took him and two of his siblings to live in the South Bronx, New York.

Snipes began his acting career early, for an aunt frequently entered him in talent shows. At the age of twelve he landed a small role in the Off-Broadway play *The Me Nobody Knows.* After elementary school, he enrolled at the High School of the Performing Arts, where he excelled in basketball as well as acting and dancing. Life in New York was fun, and Snipes was not pleased when his mother decided to move back to Orlando, Florida. The predominantly black Jones High School that Snipes attended there seemed very slow-paced compared with his New York schools. However, he settled in happily once he became involved in the school production of *Damn Yankees.*

As well as acting in school plays, Snipes joined a city-sponsored drama troupe called Struttin' Street Stuff, which performed puppet show in parks and schools—and charged up

Wesley Snipes

to $70 a week for doing so. Thus he had already taken his first steps as a professional when he won a scholarship to attend the theater arts program of the State University of New York at Purchase. Snipes was one of only four black students in the theater arts program: "I felt like mold on white bread," he later told *Ebony* magazine. "What saved me was being exposed to Malcolm X."

As a young black man surrounded by whites, Snipes gained both confidence and racial pride from the writings of the militant Black Muslim, Malcolm X, and during his second semester he became a Muslim like his hero. But he gave up the faith a few years later. Meantime, he was making a strong impression at the college. One of his teachers remembers that Snipes was exceptionally versatile even then: "He was extremely funny, he could do straight drama, he could sing and he would stop shows with the dance numbers he had choreographed."

681

Snipes graduated with a B.A. in 1984, but there was no acting part waiting for him, so he took a job installing telephones in New York. However, the following year saw the beginning of his film career. It also saw the beginning of his five-year marriage, which brought him a son, Jelani.

Won an ACE for *Vietnam Story*

Snipes's first film role was in *Wildcats,* which was released in 1985. Then came several stage appearances. He had a lead role in *The Boys of Winter,* the grueling play about the effects of the Vietnam war on American soldiers. Next came two very different stage roles, one of which was drag queen Sister Boom-Boom in the Broadway play *Execution of Justice.* In 1986 he was back in films, playing a boxer in *Streets of Gold.* But then came the type of lull that every actor fears.

The year 1987 began very badly for Snipes—he was reduced to taking a job parking cars, just to bring in some money. Yet this year also proved to be a turning point in his career. He landed his first television role, in HBO's *Vietnam Story,* a role that won him cable television's ACE Award for best actor. Even more significant, he had a small part as a gang leader in Michael Jackson's *Bad* video, which he played so convincingly that he attracted the attention of director Spike Lee. This caused him to be noticed by other filmmakers so that Snipes was suddenly a very sought-after actor. He had so much work coming in that he turned down a minor role in one of Lee's films in order to take a better part in the baseball comedy *Major League* (1989). Next came a small role in *King of New York*

(1990) and then the part of the saxophone player Shadow Henderson in Lee's *Mo' Better Blues* (1990).

Gained fame as a real box-office draw

One of Snipes's most powerful performances was his portrayal of Nino Brown, a Harlem gangster and drug king, in Mario Van Peebles's *New Jack City* (1991). Some critics maintained that Snipes played the part too powerfully—*New Jack City* was intended to be an antidrug and anti-gangster film, but it seemed to have the opposite effect, for there were outbreaks of shootings and other forms of violence at several of the theaters where the movie was shown.

The real problem, according to Snipes, was that the film was too popular (it was an instant smash hit) and there were too many frustrated people who could not get to see it. "They oversold the showings by 1500 tickets," he explained, "and the theater owners didn't give their money back. The same thing would happen with a Menudo concert, or the Rolling Stones." Nevertheless the film brought in an incredible $22.3 million during its first three weeks.

Snipes's next movie, *Jungle Fever* (1991), also was controversial, though in a different way. Directed by Spike Lee, the film was about color consciousness and cultural differences between whites and blacks, with Snipes playing a married architect who has an affair with his white secretary. Snipes confessed that he had no personal experience of interracial love affairs: "It's more important for me to try and develop a good … relationship between a black man and a black woman. That's the agenda … and that's totally where my head is—to redefine the image of black male/female relationships and how important they are."

By this time Snipes had a wide choice of roles. Producers knew that his presence in a movie could make all the difference to its success. In 1992 *White Men Can't Jump* and *Passenger 57* were both top money-makers because Snipes was starring in them, and *The Waterdance,* in which he played a paraplegic, won several awards at the Sundance Film Festival.

Snipes kept up the pressure in 1993 by beginning the year with another winner, the top-grossing film *Boiling Point.* Two years earlier, in an interview with *People* magazine, he had stated, "I want to do everything, and I'm blessed to be in the right place at the right time."

George Stallings

Religious leader
Born March 17, 1948, New Bern,
   North Carolina

"This is a church for all people; it's just run by us black folk, that's all."

If you enter the Imani Temple African American Catholic Congregation in Washington, D.C., you'll find a church service that's a bit different from what you may be used to. You'll discover intense lighting, drums, bells, rattles, clapping and swaying, and readings by black writers rather than texts

George Stallings

from the New Testament. This is the church that George Stallings built.

Originally a Roman Catholic priest, Stallings became disenchanted with the Church's ability to meet the needs of its black congregations. He initially broke away to operate an independent church still under the auspices of the Pope. Faced with stiff opposition from the Catholic hierarchy, Stallings finally severed all ties with the Catholic Church, which eventually excommunicated him. Although his motives and methods have been called into question, Stallings has forced the Church to reconsider its treatment of African Americans and to look at new ways of including them in its rites.

Gains notoriety in the Church

Stalling was born on March 17, 1948, in New Bern, North Carolina. He received a B.A. in philosophy at St. Pius X Seminary in 1970 and his M.A. in pastoral theology in 1974 from the University of St. Thomas Aquinas. He began his career in the ministry as an associate pastor at Our Lady Queen of Peace in Washington, D.C. In 1976 he became the pastor of St. Teresa of Avila in Washington.

During his tenure as pastor, Stallings gained notoriety among the Church's hierarchy for his refusal to live in a rectory and for questions about whether his expensively decorated private residence had been partly funded by church offerings. He also came under attack for having sexual relations with a sixteen-year-old altar boy in 1977, but these allegations were never proven.

Despite these criticisms, Stallings became highly regarded in the Church for his evangelical flair. Bishop Emerson Moore, Auxiliary Bishop of New York and Vicar for Social Development and Black Community Development, said in an *America* interview, "Years ago, shortly after [Stallings] was ordained, a group of us invited him to a revival, up in Harlem, and he came and was very, very good. I mention that, because that is one aspect of his ministry he has excelled in—preaching and teaching the word of God. As a preacher and a revivalist, George has built up a national reputation."

Despite his national reputation, Stallings was relatively unknown outside religious circles. That all changed in June 1989, when he defied the Catholic Church's orders and established the Imani Temple African American Catholic Congregation (imani means *faith* in Swahili). He said he formed the AACC because the establishment Church no longer adequately met the needs of the black community. He also complained that the Church did not recognize and nurture talent. In an interview with *Black Enterprise,* Stallings said, "The reality is that a split exists in the American church just as it exists in American society, and its cause is racism. There are not enough black priests (only 300 of 54,000), not enough black church members, and some of the relatively few black churches that exist are being closed or consolidated. The black experience and black needs are addressed minimally in church services and church life." Stallings's move stirred widespread opposition within the Church's upper echelon, and he became front page news across the country. Despite his departure, Stallings stated he wanted to remain a part of the Church.

Avoids excommunication

Stallings's departure put Church officials in a difficult position. Since the Church has tradianally been much weaker among black than white Americans, many did not want to risk a confrontation with him since he had not totally divorced himself from the Church. Officials responded by prohibiting him from performing the sacraments, but they stopped short at threatening excommunication. The Church seemed anxious to avoid a showdown that could trigger an even bigger rebellion among black Catholics. Reverend William Lori, a spokesman for Cardinal James A. Hickey, Archbishop of Washington, D.C., told *Black Enterprise,* "for now the Church will watch, [and] will pray. It will not rush into the next step. It will do its best to call Father Stallings home."

Black bishops were not as kind. Many called his move "ill-advised" and "selfish."

They also rejected his claims that the Church has ignored the importance of African American traditions during services. Stallings countered by stressing his crusade was a grass roots movement comprised of people who were fed up with racism at all levels of society.

In charge of his own congregation in a rented high-school auditorium in a Maryland suburb, Stallings began refocussing Christian teachings away from a European bias toward recognizing the role Africa and black people have played in Christianity. His services featured strong colors, intense lighting, drums, bells, rattles, electronically amplified instruments, jiggling and skipping, clapping and swaying. He also read prominent black writers rather than New Testament readings and dispensed with the act of kneeling. A champion fund-raiser, Stallings began raising money furiously to build a $1 million temple with a convention center, an academy, a hotel, and various community buildings.

In July 1989, black bishops made a noteworthy concession to Stallings. They announced that they would consider "very preliminary" studies aimed at including a possible African American rite within the Catholic Church. They also produced a report speaking critically of the lack of "cultural relevance" to black people in the current American church.

Stallings's new church attracted ex-Catholics and ex-Protestants. He gave eight to ten speeches a month across the United States, and many local blacks wanted to set up their own churches. Stallings established satellite congregations in Norfolk, Virginia; Baltimore, Maryland; and Philadelphia, Pennsylvania. But some reports, most notably by the *Washington Post,* claimed that church membership had actually declined since Stallings opened the AACC. Stallings was quoted in the *National Catholic Reporter* as denying these reports. "Some of these journalists don't know the basic principles of mathematics. Let me set the record straight: The numbers are going up."

AACC goes solo

Stallings announced on the *Phil Donahue Show* taped January 30, 1990, that, "as of today, the African American Catholic Congregation is going independent and will no longer be under Rome." On February 4, 1990, Stallings told nine hundred followers in his church that the AACC would allow women to be ordained and priests to marry. Divorced people would be allowed to remarry, and the use of artificial contraception would be allowed. He also stated, according to the *National Catholic Reporter,* that abortion is "the responsibility of that particular woman who is in that particular predicament." Individual confession would not be offered, all baptized Christians would be eligible to receive communion, and homosexuals would be welcome in the church. These actions caused the Catholic Church to excommunicate him.

In a prepared statement, William Kane, Vicar of the Archdiocese of Washington, stated that Stallings was excommunicated because he no longer followed the Church's teachings. The statement also warned that "any Catholic who would knowingly and willingly recant his or her faith to become a full and active member of Father Stallings' congregation would also incur excommunication." The threat of excommunication drove many of his congregants back into the Catholic Church.

A few months later Archbishop Richard Bridges of the Independent Old Catholic Church in Highland, California, a like-minded prelate, consecrated Stallings as a bishop. This allowed him to ordain his own priests.

Although many Catholic priests have disagreed with Stallings's actions, many also understand the frustrations he has felt in trying to bring black concerns to the Church's attention. Bishop Moore said in *America* that Stallings has "raised certain issues and has put black Catholics on the map in such a way that we can't use the fact that he's excommunicated now, that there are sexual allegations against him, as smokescreens for denying the real issues, like institutional racism and the need for more cultural experimentation in the church. It's wrong to dismiss George. We've got to take a look at some of these things he has surfaced and deal with them as a Christian community, in love and in charity."

Shelby Steele

Social critic, author and educator
Born 1946, Chicago, Illinois

"The reason I write is because I believe in black people. I believe they can do anything. I believe they can overcome any obstacle. I write out of love."

As racial issues emerged into the nation's consciousness in the late 1980s, a little-known Californian professor added his voice to America's on-going racial debates. Shelby Steele told blacks that they must define themselves in other than racial ways if they wanted to be free from racism. He believes that blacks who say that white society is inherently racist and that black grievances must be redressed through social programs are wrong. These programs transform whites into patrons, creating black dependency on whites. Steele's ideas have been both applauded and condemned, but many reviewers consider him to be among the best black essayists in the country.

His parents were founding members of CORE

Steele and his twin brother, Claude, a social psychologist, were born in 1946 to mixed-race parents who were deeply committed to the civil rights movement. His mother, a social worker, and his father, a truck driver, were founding members of the Congress of Racial Equality (CORE). They raised their family in Phoenix, a working-class area of Chicago, Illinois. His parents emphasized reading and writing, even though his father was a high school dropout. Steele attended a segregated school, and one of the elementary teachers consistently belittled his efforts. With the negative comments demoralizing Steele, his parents organized a parents committee against the teacher.

Steele traces his racial self-awareness back to an incident when he was fourteen. The white mother of a friend criticized his speech and grammar, and he responded that she must be racist to make such a comment. She told him that she wanted to make him aware of

Shelby Steele

good speech so he would one day find better employment. In his book, *The Context of Our Character: A New Vision of Race in America,* Steele realized he made a mistake calling her a racist. "I was shocked to realize that my comment had genuinely hurt her and that her motive in correcting my English had been no more than simple human kindness. If she had been black, I might have seen this more easily. But she was white and this fact alone set off a very specific response pattern to which vulnerability to racial shame was the trigger, denial and recomposition the reaction, and a distorted view of the situation the result."

After attending Coe College, a small school in Iowa where he was one of eighteen blacks, Steele set out to teach high school in the slums of East St. Louis. "It's the best teaching experience I've had, in the worst ghetto I've ever been in," he told the *Washington Post*. Through night courses he was able to obtain his master's degree in sociology.

Wishing to continue with his education, Steele enrolled at the University of Utah, where he earned a doctoral degree in literature. It was here that he met his future wife, Rita, a psychology graduate student.

After graduating he received a position with the English department at San Jose State. Since 1969 he has taught a course entitled "Literature and Personality," which studies the works of Primo Levi, Toni Morrison, Ernest Hemingway, and Fedor Dostoevski. He also teaches a course in creative writing called "Creative Nonfiction." Steele's favorite essayists are often studied in this course, including William Gass, Annie Dillard, Phillip Lopate, and James Baldwin.

During the 1980s Shelby emerged as a clear voice on the racial debate. He began to call into question the view, which many blacks believe, that white society is inherently racist, that blacks are victims of this racism, and that it is up to white society to redress these grievances through programs such as affirmative action and minority contact set-asides. Shelby feels this thinking is outdated. He wrote, "Such policies have the effect of transforming whites from victimizers into patrons and keeping blacks where they have always been—dependent on the largesse of whites."

Skewered for essays he wrote "out of love"

In time his essays began appearing in national publications such as the *New York Times Magazine* and *Harper's*. In summer 1990 these essays were collected and published by St. Martin's Press as *The Content of Our Character: A New Vision of Race in America*. Reaction was mixed. He found a supportive audience among conservative and neoconservative thinkers who were pleased to find a black man who stated he did not need special privileges to become successful. Many blacks and civil rights leaders were outraged at his opinions. They criticized his mixed-race background and questioned his credentials to generalize about black life. Martin Wilson, Harvard's first tenured black professor, said his arguments were "slick sophistry." Benjamin Hooks, an executive with the National Association for the Advancement of Colored People, said Steele's ideas were "nothing but a conservative viewpoint in black skin." Roger Wilkins, a Justice Department civil rights lawyer in the 1960s, told the *Washington Post* that Steele lacked "intellectual candle power" and merely provided "comfortable" ideas to white conservatives.

The *New York Times* said Steele's experiences were not complimented by outside corroboration and he offered insufficient evidence for his theories. In one episode in the book, Steele describes a well-dressed black woman in a mainly white-patronized supermarket who regularly passes by him without comment. Steele feels this means that just because they are black, that is not enough reason for her to speak to him. The *New York Times* said that there may be another reason why she does not talk him: "It never occurs to him that maybe she just doesn't like him."

Walter Williams, a professor of economics at George Mason University in Virginia, was one of Steele's defenders. He said Steele's critics would lose their credibility if his opinions became generally accepted. He told

Newsday, "At least (he is) saying some of the things that have needed to be said for a long time."

Steele has responded to his critics with a viewpoint that is articulate and graceful. Some reviewers have placed him in the same class as other noteworthy black essayists such as James Baldwin, Martin Luther King, Jr., and Frederick Douglass. His introduction to *The Content of Our Character* sums up his defense: "To retrieve our individuality and find opportunity, blacks today must—consciously or unconsciously—disregard the prevailing victim-focused black identity. Though it espouses black pride, it is actually a repressive identity that generates a victimized self-image, curbs individualism and initiative, diminishes our sense of possibility, and contributes to our demoralization and inertia. It is a skin that needs shedding."

As his ideas gained prominence, Steele was invited to speak on several talk shows, including ABC's "Good Morning America" and CBS's "This Morning." He was also invited to write and narrate a PBS documentary on the murder of a young black man in Brooklyn called *Seven Days in Besonhurst.*

In spite of his eloquent defense, Steele is still criticized that he is isolated from the black mainstream. His is the only black family in his neighborhood and his wife is white. "For me to be among large numbers of blacks requires conscientiousness and a long car ride, and in truth I have not been very conscientious lately," he wrote in *The Content of Our Character.* "I only occasionally feel nostalgia (for an all-black environment). Trips to the barbershop now and then usually satisfy this need, though recently, in the interest of convenience, I've taken to letting my wife cut my hair."

Steele lives with his wife and their two children in what he describes as a bicultural home. They teach their children about their Jewish heritage and about their black heritage. He intends to continue expressing his ideas about black social issues. "The reason I write is because I believe in black people," he told the *Washington Post*. "I believe they can do anything. I believe they can overcome any obstacle. I write out of love."

William Grant Still

Composer
Born May 11, 1895, Woodville, Mississippi
Died December 3, 1978, Los Angeles,
   California

"My favorite diversion is the study of life with a view to learning that which will enable me to make my life more serviceable to mankind."

W illiam Grant Still was the first African American to conduct a major orchestra, the first to have a symphony performed by a major orchestra, the first to have an opera performed by a major company, and one of the first to write for film, radio, and television.

Still's best-known work is the *Afro-American Symphony* (1930), which incorporates themes from jazz and folk music. As well as symphonies, operas, and film music, Still wrote a wide range of works, including songs for Broadway shows and several ballets. An

William Grant Still

avant-garde experimenter as a young man, he later turned to more conventional harmonies and rhythms. Many of his pieces are noted for their freshness and graceful melodies.

Decided to make music his career

Still was named after his father, who was the town bandmaster in Woodville, Mississippi, but who died when Still was a small boy. The family then moved to Little Rock, Arkansas, where Still's mother, Carrie (Fambro) Still, found a job teaching literature in the high school.

Still was given a thorough education, which included being taught the violin. His first choice of career was medicine rather than music, and with this in mind he enrolled at Wilberforce College. There he came across the music of the celebrated Afro-English composer, Samuel Coleridge-Taylor, which so impressed him that he decided to make music his career. Leaving Wilberforce without graduating, Still worked with various music ensembles and then enrolled at Oberlin Conservatory of Music.

At Oberlin, Still's teachers encouraged him to compose and he won a scholarship in composition. But in 1917, World War I interrupted his studies. Returning to Oberlin after serving in the navy, Still completed a year's work in less than three months. He then went to New York in search of work, accompanied by his wife, Grace (Bundy) Still, whom he had married a few years earlier.

His compositions earned him international fame

In New York, Still was taken on by music publisher W. C. Handy. He also had occasional engagements playing the oboe in theater orchestras. Meanwhile, he studied under the French American composer Edgard Varèse, who proved to be a strong influence. Varèse was an innovator who experimented with electronic music; dissonant sounds became his hallmark. Intrigued by the possibilities of such an approach, Still began to experiment in his own compositions. The 1920s marked his avant-garde period.

During Still's early years he also arranged popular music for jazz orchestras, and he kept many of the jazz idioms when he wrote his classical works. Encouraged to write specifically American music, he incorporated jazz and traditional folk tunes into his compositions. These themes are evident in his symphonic poems *Darker America* (1924), *Dismal Swamp* (1933), and *Old California* (1941), and in such suites as *From the Black Belt* (1926).

Still first attracted wide notice in 1926 when the International Guild of Composers featured four of his songs at a concert in New York. The following year saw the debut of *Darker America,* which was played by the Rochester Philharmonic Orchestra at its annual festival. It was performed again later in the year at the International Music Festival in Frankfurt, Germany.

In 1930 Still completed the first of his five symphonies, the *Afro-American Symphony.* Given its premier performance the following year by the Rochester Philharmonic Orchestra, this was the first symphony by a black American to be played by a leading orchestra. The symphony attracted considerable attention and was given repeat performances by prestigious orchestras, including the New York Philharmonic and the Philadelphia Symphony Orchestra. It also drew praise in Europe and was performed in several cities in Germany.

Another symphony that was extremely popular was *New Symphony in G Minor.* First performed by the Philadelphia Symphony Orchestra in 1937, it was based on jazz, blues, and other traditional idioms, following the Afro-American pattern of so much of Still's music.

The previous year Still had again drawn attention—and made history—by conducting a selection of his works in a concert given by the Hollywood Bowl Orchestra. This was the first time a major American orchestra had been conducted by a black musician. Still made history again when his operas were performed. His best-known opera is *Troubled Island* (1941), which is based on Langston Hughes's play *Drums of Haiti*. The opera was composed in conjunction with Hughes, who wrote the libretto. Still's other well-known operas include *Costaso* (1950) and *Minette Fontaine* (1958).

Some of Still's most delightful works are his ballets *La Guiablesse* (1927), *Sahdji* (1930), *Lenox Avenue* (1937), and *Miss Sally's Party* (1940). His most moving work may well be *And They Lynched Him to a Tree*. This ballad poem, with words by Katherine Garrison Chapin, was first performed in 1940 during the summer season at the Lewisohn Stadium in New York City. An extremely powerful piece, it is performed by a contralto solo accompanied by a double chorus and orchestra.

Still received many honors during his lifetime, including the Harmon Award (1927). He received prizes from the League of Composers and leading American orchestras and was given honorary doctorate degrees by Howard University, Oberlin College, Bates College, and the University of Arkansas. One of Still's most satisfying awards was the prize he won at the New York World's Fair in 1939. Of all the composers whose works were considered, the jury selected two pieces by William Grant Still. As a result, it was his tone poem that accompanied each six-minute showing of "Democracity"—the city of the future—that was seen by the millions of people who visited the fair.

Juanita Kidd Stout

Judge
Born March 7, 1919, Wewoka, Oklahoma

In the court of law, few have made more firsts than Juanita Kidd Stout. She was the first black woman to serve on the highest appellate court of any state. In 1959 she became the first black woman to be elected to a court of record. Stout later served on the Court of Common Pleas, the court of general trial jurisdiction, and the supreme court of Pennsylvania. When she turned seventy, Stout retired from the supreme court and returned to the Court of Common Pleas as a senior judge in the homicide division.

Finished school at the top of her class

Stout was born on March 7, 1919, in Wewoka, Oklahoma, to Henry and Mary Kidd. Her parents were schoolteachers who taught her to be obedient and studious. Since they taught her to read by the time she was three, she started school at grade three. Stout finished at the top of her class in elementary and high school, and at sixteen she began to study music at Lincoln University in Jefferson City, Missouri. In 1937 she transferred to the University of Iowa in Iowa City and two years later received a bachelor of arts degree in music. For two summers she did graduate work in piano at the University of Colorado in Boulder and at the University of Minnesota in Minneapolis.

After graduating from university, Stout taught grade school and high school music for two years at Booker T. Washington High School. She also taught for a year at Sand Springs, near Tulsa, Oklahoma, and it was here that she met her future husband, Charles Otis Stout. He taught history and Spanish and spent time as boys' counselor. Some of Scout's

Juanita Kidd Stout

students were older than she, and a few were bigger (she weighed only eighty-eight pounds). She felt discipline was the key to a successful classroom, but her principal was often found lacking in that area. Since Stout's future husband had a strong physical stature, she began to send the older troublemakers to him.

The two teachers became very close, spending much of their spare time together playing the piano, singing, and playing bridge. During World War II, he went to the army, while she and another Sand Spring teacher, Eula Mae Smith, went to Washington, D.C., where she found work as a secretary with the National Housing Authority. She later passed the examination for a job as junior professional assistant. Since passing the test was the only qualification for the job, she wondered why she was turned down, when others with similar credentials received the job. After an angry exchange with the personnel manager,

Stout quit rather than stay in a job that only paid $1,800 a year.

Later that night, Smith told her that Houston, Houston & Hastie, a prestigious law office, needed an extra secretary. Since Scout was excellent at typing and shorthand and also because she loved the law, she was hired. She worked directly for Charles Hamilton Houston, who later described her as "the best lawyer I have ever met."

Before his first military leave, Stout's future husband managed to get her address through their former high school principal. He went to Washington to find her. "He never asked me to marry him. He just walked in and said, 'We're getting married.' He never gave me a chance to say 'No'." They were married on June 23, 1942.

Award-winning jurist achieved many firsts

With encouragement from Charles Houston, Stout decided to begin legal training at Howard University. She later transferred to Indiana University in Bloomington, where her husband was completing his doctoral studies. In 1948 she received a doctor of jurisprudence, and six years later she obtained her master of law degree, specializing in legislation.

Stout passed the Pennsylvania Bar examination in 1954 and entered a private practice with Mabel G. Turner, who would go on to become assistant U.S. attorney. In April 1956 Stout joined the Philadelphia district attorney's office. Three-and-one-half years later she was promoted to chief of the Appeals, Pardons, and Parole Division. She still maintained a private practice, but she was limited to civil cases.

In September 1959 Governor David L. Lawrence appointed Stout as judge of the municipal court. She was the first black woman judge in Philadelphia. Two months later she ran in a citywide election and won a ten-year term (beating her opponent by a two-to-one margin) and became the country's first elected black woman to sit on the bench.

Stout began to attract national attention in the mid-1960s for handling a series of cases regarding young gangs. Some of these gangs were turning neighborhoods into war zones. *Life* profiled her in an article entitled "Her Honor Bops the Hoodlums," which paid a special tribute to her for being fair but tough. *Time* quoted the American Civil Liberties Union as saying she did not pay enough attention to the "constitutional niceties" in administering her "swift justice." Stout claimed that she did not understand what the criticism meant. *Ebony* stated many of her colleagues feel that "she knows when to take the long-term view."

Her peers are impressed with the clarity of her legal writing and opinions. She has published several articles and has been active in many professional and civic organizations, including the American Judicature Society, American Bar Association, National Association of Women Lawyers, and the American Judges Association. Her board memberships are with Rockford College, Saint Augustine's College, the National Conference of Christians and Jews, and the Women's Medical College of Pennsylvania.

Eleven universities have presented Stout with honorary degrees, and she has received more than 200 awards from professional and civic organizations. In 1988 she was named the justice of the year by the National Association of Women Judges, and the next year she was awarded the Gimbel Award for Humanitarian Services by the Medical College of Pennsyl-vania. She was also named a distinguished daughter of Pennsylvania by Governor Robert P. Casey. Presidents John F. Kennedy and Lyndon B. Johnson each named her to missions in Africa. She was inducted into the Oklahoma Women's Hall of Fame on November 18, 1983.

Stout credits many of her accomplishments to her parents, who taught her a strong work ethic, and the unswerving support of her husband, Charles Otis Stout, who died on August 15, 1988. Stout continues to form new law theories and applies the law in a manner "that will serve people, make for the overall good, and be useful to American society."

Niara Sudarkasa

University president
Born August 14, 1938, Fort Lauderdale, Florida

"I think that as a woman president, I bring an obvious maternal side—if you want to call it that—a caring sense that I am here to help nurture and mold students in a more direct and involved way than I think a male president would."

n October 1987 Niara Sudarkasa was inaugurated president of Lincoln University, one of the oldest and most prestigious black colleges in the United States. Lincoln's graduates have included many world-famous figures, including U.S. Supreme Court Justice Thurgood Marshall and President Kwame Nkrumah of Ghana.

Sudarkasa's appointment was exceptional in that she was the first woman to be president of Lincoln, a university that was closed to women during its first century of existence. Yet the selection committee had no doubt about Sudarkasa's qualifications. At her inaurugation ceremony, a member of the committee said, "When we looked around to find the best man we could for this position, we discovered that he was a woman."

Started college at the age of fourteen

Niara Sudarkasa took her African name in the 1970s. Her first name, Niara, means "a woman of high purpose." She was born Gloria Marshall, the daughter of Rowena Marshall, a silk finisher, and George Marshall, a soldier in the U.S. Army. After her parents divorced, Sudarkasa gained a stepfather, Alex Charlton, who owned a cocktail lounge in Fort Lauderdale.

Sudarkasa attended Dillard High School in Fort Lauderdale, along with her three brothers. Striving to show she was as good as her brothers, she was an exceptionally hardworking student, and when only fourteen she won a Ford Foundation Early Entrant Scholarship to Fisk University in Nashville, Tennessee.

During her junior year at Fisk, Sudarkasa did a semester at Oberlin College, and she decided to transfer there for her final year. At Oberlin she came across an article written by a Nigerian that caused her to notice similarities between Caribbean and African culture. Sudarkasa's grandparents were from the Caribbean, but she had never before realized how much of its culture had been inherited from Africa. Fascinated by this discovery, she determined to visit Africa to learn more about the history of its people. But first she had to complete her university course.

After graduating from Oberlin College with a bachelor's degree in sociology in 1957, Sudarkasa enrolled at Columbia University, New York, where she earned a master's degree in anthropology in 1959. She then won a Whitney Opportunity Fellowship to study for a Ph.D., and the following year she also won a Ford Foundation Foreign Area Training Fellowship to study the Yoruba language of Nigeria. During the next three years Sudarkasa studied Yoruba in England, at the University of London School of Oriental and African Studies, and then in Africa itself, where she made a particular study of the language and role of the Yoruba women in the markets of Nigeria. Back home in 1964, she completed her thesis and was awarded her Ph.D. in anthropology.

Acclaimed anthropologist and university president

Sudarkasa embarked on her academic career as an assistant professor at New York University, where she taught for three years. She then moved to the University of Michigan, where she spent the next twenty years—as assistant professor (1967–70), associate professor (1970–76), and then professor of anthropology (1976–87). She was the first black woman to be a full professor in the division of arts and sciences. In 1984 she took on an additional responsibility when she was appointed associate vice-president for academic affairs.

During these years Sudarkasa maintained her interest in Africa and the African American connection. She was so enthusiastic about black culture that she gained a reputation as a scholar-activist on campus. "I was very politicized about Africa," she has recalled, "so I was a vocal spokesperson for all the things that the students were advocating in those days, the early seventies: black studies, more black and minority students in the universities. I became the activist I had not been in the sixties." Sudarkasa's activities, together with her involvement in African American studies, caused her to be appointed director of the Center for Afro-American and African Studies in 1981.

Sudarkasa returned to Africa several times on research trips, visiting Ghana, Nigeria, and Benin. The research led to more than 30 scholarly papers, which brought Sudarkasa an international reputation as an anthropologist. She is particularly known as an authority on Yoruba woman traders, West African migration, and the African and African American family. Sudarkasa's husband, contractor and sculptor John L. Clark, also has a broad knowledge of Africa, having accompanied her on many of her trips. Her son, Michael, has been there too and currently works for the African Development Bank in the Ivory Coast.

Both husband and son were immensely proud when Sudarkasa was appointed president of Lincoln University. For the inaugura-

Niara Sudarkasa

tion ceremony she wore a gown that symbolized her ties with Africa. It was royal blue, trimmed with a piece of blue and gold kente cloth which her mother had obtained during a visit to Ghana. "Something told me to use the kente in the robe," Sudarkasa recalled. "I saw it as a way of having my mother always with me. I also reflected on the connections of the kente with Ghana and Kwame Nkrumah, that country's first president and one of Lincoln's greatest sons. Having the kente on my robe was a magnificent coming together of many things."

As president, Sudarkasa has strengthened Lincoln's ties with Africa. The university has a large collection of African paintings, jewelry, and other art objects, which form the basis of an African museum. African studies are encouraged, though not to the exclusion of other subjects. Lincoln University has a strong reputation in the sciences, and Sudarkasa is determined to maintain and, indeed, increase it.

695

She wants to ensure that her students have the necessary expertise in science, math, and engineering so that they can compete successfully in a technologically sophisticated world.

Referred to as Madame President, Sudarkasa is popular with the students, who find her so approachable that they have been known to give her a friendly hug or kiss. "I bring an obvious maternal side—if you want to call it that," she says, "a caring sense that I am here to help nurture and mold students in a more direct and involved way than I think a male president would." She especially hopes to imbue her students with a sense of service: "Unless a sense of service and duty is instilled, our upward mobility will only be measured by cars and styling."

Henry Ossawa Tanner

Painter, photographer
Born June 21, 1859, Pittsburgh, Pennsylvania
Died May 25, 1937, Paris, France

"His success in Paris was unprecedented for a Negro artist and gave hope and confidence to younger, less privileged Negroes seeking recognition in art."—Marcia M. Mathews

Henry Ossawa Tanner was the first African American painter to gain an international reputation. During his lifetime, he was best known for his paintings of biblical themes, but his early work included black genre paintings. These sensitive portrayals of African American life are now considered among his best works.

Although Tanner lived most of his adult life in France, his fame spread across the Atlantic, bringing him recognition in America too. His success was a great encouragement to younger black artists, though the American art world tended to classify him as a "Negro artist," thereby placing him outside the mainstream. Not until the 1960s did Tanner receive full recognition as one of the handful of artists who established American art as a distinct art form, separate from European art.

The bishop's son

Tanner's choice of religious themes for many of his paintings was partly the result of his upbringing as the son of an elder of the African Methodist Episcopal Church. His father, Benjamin Tanner, was appointed rector of Bethel Church in Philadelphia in 1866 and was later made a bishop. Tanner's mother, Sarah (Miller) Tanner, was the granddaughter of a white plantation owner, but like Tanner's father she had been raised in freedom.

The Tanners had seven children, of whom Henry Ossawa was the eldest. His second name was given him in memory of abolitionist John Brown's raid on Osawatomie, Kansas, in 1856. Tanner said that he first became fascinated by art at the age of twelve, when he watched an artist sketching in Fairmont Park, Philadelphia. On returning home he borrowed fifteen cents from his mother to buy paints and brushes. His parents encouraged his efforts, though they tried to dissuade him from making a career as an artist. They knew how difficult this would be for an African American. When Tanner was seventeen he went to work in the flour business, but he soon became ill, and by the time he had recovered he had persuaded his parents to agree to his choice of an art career.

For the next four years Tanner perfected his skills, painting portraits, landscapes, and seascapes, and making pictures and clay models of the animals at the Philadelphia Zoo. Yet he was aware that he needed professional training, and in 1880 he enrolled at the Pennsylvania Academy of the Fine Arts. There he came under the influence of the realist painter and sculptor Thomas Eakins, who taught Tanner how to improve his technique and how to express mood by the contrast of light and shadow in his paintings.

The struggling young artist

After two years at the academy, Tanner left in the hope of earning enough money to study in France. But during the next few years his drawings and paintings barely brought in enough to live on. Hoping to do better as a photographer, he opened a studio in Atlanta in 1888, but this proved to be a disaster, and he was glad to accept the offer of a family friend, Bishop Joseph Hartzell, to teach art at Clark University in Atlanta.

Before beginning to teach at Clark, Tanner spent several months in North Carolina, sketching the people and the landscape. He later worked up these sketches of black life into the finished paintings that now represent his black genre period. The paintings so impressed Bishop Hartzell that he arranged for an exhibition of Tanner's work at the end of Tanner's first year of teaching. When no one bought any of the pictures, Hartzell purchased them all himself. This money enabled Tanner

to fulfill his long-standing dream of studying in Paris, and he sailed for Europe on January 4, 1891.

Tanner enrolled at the Academie Julien in Paris, where he studied on and off for the next five years. During his second year in France he came down with typhoid fever and returned to Philadelphia to recuperate. While at home, he completed two of his best-known black genre paintings, *The Banjo Lesson* (1893) and *The Thankful Poor* (1894). As a scene from everyday life, *The Banjo Lesson* is in the tradition of the French artist Jean-François Millet, but as a picture of a wise old man teaching an innocent young boy, it makes a warm statement about the dignity of African American culture. Similarly, *The Thankful Poor* portrays with dignity the sparse mealtime gathering of a poor black family, conveying an impression of spiritual strength.

The Thankful Poor was the last of Tanner's black genre paintings. From 1894 on, most of his works were on biblical themes, though his first two successes in France were European-style genre painting. Entitled *The Music Lesson* and *The Sabot Maker,* they were accepted for exhibition at the prestigious Paris Salon in 1894 and 1895, respectively.

Acclaimed painter

During Tanner's time in the United States in 1893–94, he had found the racial atmosphere appalling after the relaxed attitude of France, and from then on he made only occasional trips home. In 1896 his painting *Daniel in the Lion's Den* won him an honorable mention at the Paris Salon, and in 1897 his *Raising of Lazarus* won him a medal. The latter painting was bought by the French government, which previously had purchased the work of only two other American artists—John Singer Sargent and James McNeill Whistler.

To gain authentic background material for his paintings, Tanner visited Palestine and Egypt in 1897 and again in 1898. The results were evident in such paintings as *The Annunciation* (1898), which was the first of Tanner's works to be bought by an American museum—the Philadelphia Museum of Art. Tanner's model for *The Annunciation* was Swedish-born Jessie Olssen, whom he married in 1899. Their child, Jesse Ossawa Tanner, was born four years later.

The early 1900s were a peak time for Tanner as he turned out a succession of paintings in an increasingly masterly style. A respected member of the "American Colony" in Paris, he was honored throughout Europe and was gradually winning recognition in the

Henry Ossawa Tanner

United States, too. In 1905 he was the first African American to have his paintings hung in the annual exhibition at the Carnegie Institute, and in 1908 he had his first one-man show in New York.

The outbreak of World War I brought many disruptions; Tanner remained in France throughout the war and worked for the American Red Cross. After the war, new styles of art, which Tanner did not find appealing, began to gain popularity. Nevertheless, his traditional paintings still found an audience, and in 1923 he was awarded the Legion of Honor by the French government. In the United States he was elected a full member of the National Academy in 1927.

Despite the prestige he enjoyed, the 1920s were not good years for Tanner. His wife died in 1925, leaving him so stricken with grief that he ceased painting for a while. Soon afterwards, his son suffered a nervous breakdown, from which he took years to recover. These tragedies affected Tanner's paintings, which became far more mystical. He was working on a painting called *Return from the Crucifixion* at the time of his death in 1937.

After Tanner's death, he was soon forgotten. The up-and-coming young painters considered his representational style old-fashioned, and as a black artist who had spent most of his working life abroad, he was easily overlooked. Although a few admirers of his work made sporadic attempts to bring it to public notice, the full range of his talents was not appreciated until he was given a large one-man show at the Smithsonian Institution in 1969. Another major exhibition of his work was given by the Philadelphia Museum of Art in 1991. He is now fully recognized not only as a pioneering African American artist, but as a significant influence in the development of American art.

Mildred Taylor

Writer
Born September 13, 1943, Jackson,
  Mississippi

"The dream of writing in part stemmed from the storytelling tradition of my family and the need to show black people as I saw us."

Mildred Taylor is the author of a series of highly acclaimed children's books about the Logan family of Mississippi and their experiences in the 1930s and 1940s. Taylor grew up listening to the tales of her many relatives from Mississippi, from whom she gained a picture of African American life that was warm and strong—very different from the demeaning portrayal of blacks given in her school books. One of the reasons Taylor wanted to become a writer was so that she could spread this true picture of black life to the world at large.

"The dream of writing in part stemmed from the storytelling tradition of my family," she said, "and the need to show black people as I saw us." The characters in her books are based on friends and relatives she knew or has been told about: "They were people who lived in Jackson or in my father's or my mother's rural community. The land, the house, the school, the history are all drawn from that community of lives as I remember them … and as I remember the stories told."

Taylor's books have won numerous awards, including the Newbery Medal and the Coretta Scott King Award, and more than one of her novels has been named Outstanding Book of the Year by the *New York Times*. She has also been a finalist for the National Book Award.

Cherished her storytelling family

Although Mildred Taylor is from a Mississippi family, she left the South when she was a few months old. Her father, Wilbert Taylor, suddenly decided he could no longer stomach the racism, and one day he just took off, heading north. A week later, having found a factory job in Toledo, Ohio, he called for his family to join him. His wife, Deletha (Davis) Taylor, then gathered up their two daughters—Mildred and her older sister, Wilma—and boarded the train for Ohio.

In Ohio the Taylors moved into a large duplex which had room for the many family members who came to stay. Like Taylor's father, other relatives soon decided to leave the South. But many stayed behind, living on land that had been in the family for generations. The land was south of Jackson, Mississippi. Taylor came to know it well, for she often spent holidays there during her childhood, staying in the house her great-grandfather had built at the turn of the century.

These holidays were a mixed pleasure, for the drive South was always an ordeal because of the segregation laws. The moment the family crossed the border from Ohio into Kentucky they began to see the "white only" signs. Restrooms at gas stations were for whites only, and so were the restaurants along the way. Even the motels would not admit black customers. When the Taylors needed to stop for the night, they pulled off the road into a grove of trees.

Nevertheless, Taylor came to love the South. "There were two sides of the South I saw," she said. "The one of racism, of oppression and segregation, filled me with fear and anger. But the other South, a South of family and of community, filled with warmth and love, opened to me a sense of history and filled me with pride.... Once we were in the rural community where my father had grown up, once we were on the family land, my mind stepped back into another time."

This was easy because the place had not changed much over the years, and the early days still seemed part of the present. Many a night Taylor sat on the porch, listening to the recollections of an uncle or aunt or to stories told by her grandparents. When Taylor returned to Ohio after the holidays, she took a whole world of memories with her.

Worked in Ethiopia for the Peace Corps

Taylor attended integrated schools in Ohio where there were few black children and in some classes Taylor was the only one. As a result, she tried to do extra well so as not to let down her race, especially considering the negative view of African Americans given in her school books: "The history books talked of blacks as a docile, subservient, almost moronic people, content and happy with slavery. They talked of a people content with their way of life still, a people with no past except slavery and not much future."

In elementary school Taylor tried to explain to her white classmates and teacher that this wasn't what black people were like, but nobody believed her. "By the time I entered high school," she said, "I had a driving compulsion to paint a truer picture of Black people.... I wanted to show a Black family united in love and pride, of which the reader would like to be a part."

By then Taylor knew she wanted to be a writer, but she was worried that she did not have the talent. The essays she wrote for her English classes at Scott High School usually brought more criticism than praise. This was partly because she was modeling her style on such white writers as Ernest Hemingway rather than following the storytelling tradition of her heritage. Only when she started writing in the first person did she find her true voice and begin to write well.

On graduating from high school Taylor enrolled at the University of Toledo's School of Education. Her parents had persuaded her to train as a teacher so that she could always get a job. They did not imagine she could ever support herself as a writer. In the 1950s there were far fewer black writers and journalists than there are today, and none seemed to be operating in Toledo. Taylor saw the sense of her parents' advice, but she went on writing. Throughout her college years she sent in stories to magazines and entered contests for young writers. Although she never won, she gained valuable practice.

Meanwhile, Taylor was also working toward another longstanding ambition—to visit

Africa. The desire had grown in her over the years, and on earning her B.Ed. degree in 1965 she set off for Ethiopia, where she spent two years teaching as a member of the U.S. Peace Corps. After another year working for the Peace Corps back home, she enrolled as a graduate student in journalism at the University of Colorado. There she became an active member of the Black Student Alliance (BSA) and helped create a black studies program and a black education program.

After earning her M.A. in 1969, Taylor continued to work for BSA programs. It was during these years that the stories about the Logan family of Mississippi began to take shape in her mind. She wrote the first one in the early 1970s, a period that also saw her brief marriage to Errol Zea-Daly, from whom she was divorced in 1975.

Prize-winning novel adapted for television

Taylor's first story about the Logans was the novella *Song of the Trees,* which was based on an incident her father had told her about his family's land during the Depression. Taylor wrote the story in the first person—it is told by eight-year-old Cassie Logan. While Cassie's father is away working on the railroad, a white neighbor tries to buy some trees on the Logan land. The plot focuses on the efforts of Cassie, her brothers, and other family members to save the trees.

On completing the manuscript in 1973, Taylor entered it in a competition of the Council on Interracial Books for Children and won first prize in the Afro-American category. At last she had made her breakthrough as a writer.

As a result of the prize, the story was published by Dial Books in 1975. That same year the *New York Times* named *Song of the Trees* Outstanding Book of the Year.

Taylor's next book, *Roll of Thunder, Hear My Cry* (1976), was a full-length novel, which again was based on true stories told by her father and other relatives. As before, the story is told by Cassie, who is now nine years old. The events she describes take place in one year, between 1933 and 1934. *Roll of Thunder, Hear My Cry* gives far more detail than *Song of the Trees,* presenting a strong and enduring picture of the Logan family as they face the ever-present racism and all the problems that go with it. The book was enormously successful from the moment of its publication, winning the Newbery Medal and other awards and later being adapted for television. It is considered a classic and has been published in eleven countries.

Mildred Taylor

Taylor continued her saga of the Logans in *Let the Circle Be Unbroken* (1981), which begins with the trial of a black family friend, a minor character from her previous book. Her next story, *The Friendship* (1987), is again about the Logans, but *The Gold Cadillac* (1987) describes a childhood experience of Taylor and her sister—the hostility shown by whites when the Taylors drove through the rural South in their splendid new car. In 1990 Taylor brought out two more Logan books: *Mississippi Bridge,* which is told by a ten-year-old white boy who wants to be friends with the Logan children, and *The Road to Memphis,* which is told by Cassie and is set in 1941.

Taylor's books are especially powerful because of their straightforward yet shocking accounts of racist events and behavior. It is because of this approach that in 1988 Taylor was honored by the Children's Book Council "for a body of work that has examined significant social issues and presented them in outstanding books for young readers." Taylor plans to write more books about the Logans, and these too will undoubtedly explore social issues while telling a gripping story about this inspiring and courageous family of African Americans.

Susan Taylor

Editor, television host
Born January 23, 1946, New York, New York

"There is little to remind us daily of how powerful and capable we are, so we must do that for ourselves and for each other."

As editor-in-chief of *Essence* magazine, vice-president of Essence Communications, and former host and producer of its television program, Susan Taylor has considerable influence as well as great style and charm. She uses all these qualities to help African Americans cope with the daily problems and frustrations that can seem so huge and insurmountable.

Taylor feels that with determination and plenty of encouragement, most members of the black community have a chance of living happy, rewarding lives. She sees proof of this all around her. "Something so delicious is happening in Black America," she says. "We're only 120 years up from slavery, and we are doing incredibly well if we look at the fact that the people we're comparing ourselves with have been in this race for 400 years with all of the assets, all of the support. We've been running that same race with shackles on our ankles trying to hold us back."

Encouragement built her confidence

Susan Taylor knows what it is like to be poor and has experienced frustration and lack of confidence. Raised in Harlem, where her father was a shopkeeper, Taylor had few luxuries during her childhood. As she grew older, she became interested in acting and performed occasionally with the Negro Ensemble Company, but she decided to pursue a practical career and trained as a beauty specialist, becoming a licensed cosmetologist.

In her early twenties Taylor tried her hand at writing beauty and fashion articles, and when *Essence* was founded in 1970 she was taken on as a free-lance beauty writer. Taylor became a full-time member of the *Essence* staff the following year when she was appointed beauty editor. Despite this achievement, 1971 was not a good year for her. She had recently given birth to a child—her daughter, Shana—and she faced all the problems of being a single mother. "I … didn't believe in myself," she later told the *Los Angeles Times*. "I had no money, no man. My car was broken. I was making $500 a month working at *Essence* and paying $368 a month for rent. I could not see tomorrow."

Taylor was helped through this difficult period of her life by a minister who encouraged her to believe in herself. Nobody before had ever built up her confidence in this way, and it motivated Taylor to give others similar encouragement through her work at the magazine. "There is so little to remind us daily of how powerful and capable we are," Taylor

Susan Taylor

has said, "so we must do that for ourselves and for each other."

In 1972 Taylor's responsibilities at *Essence* were enlarged to include fashion as well as beauty. She loved her work at the magazine and approached it with total dedication. Only two years old, *Essence* was the first life-style magazine devoted to black women. Taylor regarded that as an immensely important breakthrough. As she later explained to a white journalist: "Imagine yourself as a white women wanting to buy a magazine and seeing black faces on every cover. Wouldn't you feel isolated and ignored?"

Award-winning magazine executive

When Taylor started work at *Essence* it was just a small journal with a limited circulation. Today it has a readership of more than 50,000 and brings in revenues of about $20 million a year. Since 1981 Taylor has been editor-in-chief, and as part of her duties she writes its popular editorial feature, "In the Spirit." These editorials cover a wide range of subjects: practical advice on health matters, philosophical and religious musings, hair-styling tips, vacation advice, discussions of drug abuse, abortion, and other controversial subjects—and always plenty of advice to help readers build pride in themselves and in their African American heritage.

In addition to her editorials, Taylor often writes feature articles for the magazine. She may interview personalities—such as television's Oprah Winfrey or South Africa's Winnie Mandela—or she may write on current affairs. Many of Taylor's current affairs articles inform her readers about life in Africa, and others focus on issues of concern in the United States.

Taylor copes with her busy and challenging schedule because of her deep religious faith. "My day starts with quiet time about 6 a.m.," she told an interviewer. "I meditate. It's not any formal kind of meditation. It's just getting centered. I try to tap into that spiritual side of me. Because when I go out without that intact, I get crazy, befuddled, and depressed. I read some psalms or the Lord's Prayer just to affirm some things for myself—that I'm going to move through this day from the highest perspective, that I'm going to be a problem solver and not fall victim to the things I see."

In 1986 Taylor added further responsibility to her schedule when she was appointed vice-president of Essence Communications in charge of producing and hosting Essence's television show. This program was the first nationally syndicated magazine show produced for a black audience, and it was such a success that it ran for four seasons in more than sixty countries. Taylor designed the tele-vision show to have a different purpose from the magazine: "The magazine is a hands-on, how-to vehicle for helping black women move their lives forward," she said. "The television show is aimed at everyone to project a positive image of black Americans. People tend to have negative views of what black people are all about."

Taylor combats this negative view among whites and within the African American community itself. Meanwhile, she has practiced what she preached by taking some positive steps in her own life. During the late 1980s Taylor made time to study for a bachelor's degree at Fordham University in New York

City, and in 1990 she graduated in social science and economics. Shortly afterwards Taylor married Kephera Burns.

Over the years Susan Taylor has used her position as a successful career woman and an eloquent voice in the media to promote a wide range of charitable causes, including the Edwin Gould Services for Children, an adoption and foster-care agency. She has been honored with numerous awards, including the Women in Communications Matrix Award, and in 1988 Lincoln University gave her an honorary doctorate of humane letters.

Susie Baker King Taylor

Activist
Born August 5, 1848, Isle of Wright, Georgia
Died October 6, 1912, Boston,
   Massachusetts

"In this land of the free we are burned, tortured, and denied a fair trial, murdered for any imaginary wrong conceived in the brain of the negro-hating white man. There is no redress for us from a government which promised to protect all under its flag.... No, we cannot sing, 'my country is of thee, Sweet land of Liberty!' It is a hollow mockery."

Although Susie Baker King Taylor was born a slave, she managed to learn to read and write and displayed abilities usually denied one of her status. She joined a regiment during the Civil War as a nurse and taught soldiers to read and write. After the war, she helped form a Women's Relief Corps and compiled a list of war veterans living in Massachusetts. Her greatest accomplish was writing, *Reminiscences of My Life in Camp,* a book that documents the successes of African Americans from the Civil War to the turn of the century despite racism and discrimination.

Learned to read and write in hiding

Taylor was born on August 5, 1848, and she spend her early years with her mother, Hagar Ann, on the Grest farm on the Isle of Wright in Liberty County, Georgia. Her father was Raymond Baker, and while it is not clear if he was a slave, it is known that his wife and children were held in bondage. When Taylor was seven, Mr. Grest allowed her maternal grandmother, Dolly Reed, to take her and a younger sister and brother to nearby Savannah to live. Although it was against the law, Reed sent Taylor and her brother to a free woman's home to learn to read and write. In 1860 Taylor began an informal education, occasionally learning from neighboring white children. Her first illegal tutor was Katie O'Connor, who volunteered to teach her if she did not tell her father. The two met each evening for a four-month period until O'Connor entered a convent. Reed's landlord, James Blouis, was Taylor's second tutor until he was conscripted into the Civil War in 1861.

During the war, Reed attended meetings and discussed current affairs with other concerned citizens. Taylor would often accompany her and began to develop her own opinions. She decided to help by writing passes for slaves and free blacks. Her contributions ended abruptly when police raided a suburban church meeting; Reed was arrested and handed back to her master. Taylor was sent back to her mother on the Grest farm on April 1, 1862.

With Union soldiers winning battles in the area, Taylor, an uncle, and several other family members escaped to St. Catherine Island. Union troops protected them and thirty other blacks for two weeks, before they were shipped to St. Simon's Island. During the trip Taylor talked with several Union soldiers, and they passed the message to Commodore Goldsborough that she could read and write. Goldsborough convinced her to operate a small school on the island. She agreed to teach forty children during the day and a handful of adults at night.

As the Civil War continued, Union officers deemed that the outpost on St. Simon's Island was not secure. In the late fall of 1862, the black residents, including Taylor, were relocated to Camp Saxton in Beaufort, South Carolina. The school was closed, and Taylor worked as a laundress for the First South Carolina Volunteers, an all-black unit led by white officers and the first black regiment formed in the South. Although morale was high, conditions were poor. Taylor reported that despite the support of their commanding officers, the black troops were ill-clad, were not paid for eighteen months, and were given a lower salary than white troops.

Regimental nurse

Taylor stayed with the regiment until the war ended. Several members of her family also joined the regiment. She learned how to care for and use a rifle, and during her spare time she would cook meals for the wounded and teach those interested how to read and write. As the war continued, her duties increased. Besides caring for the uniforms, bandages, and other supplies, she assisted the surgeons. She became an unofficial camp nurse—soothing the sick and helping with other tasks assigned by the doctors. She donated the majority of her time to these tasks. She was an excellent nurse and the soldiers continually thanked her. When her kindness was noted, she replied, "You are all doing the same duty, and I will do just the same for you."

While in the regiment, Taylor met Sergeant Edward King, who also had lived in the city. After escaping from his master, he joined the regiment. Taylor and King became close friends and eventually married.

Taylor did not receive any pay or certificate of service during the war. Since she was not credited as a Union nurse, she did not

Susie Baker King Taylor

receive a post-war pension. When the war finally ended, she and her husband went to Savannah, where Taylor settled in as a housewife. Her husband took a job as a longshoreman, although he was trained as a boss carpenter. Since there was no school for blacks in the community, Taylor established one in her home. She had twenty day students and several night students, whom she each charged a dollar per month.

On September 16, 1866, Taylor's husband was killed in an accident while unloading vessels at the pier. Not yet twenty, Taylor was an expectant mother and a widow. In December her condition and the establishment of a free school, Beach Institute, forced her to stop teaching. Shortly after her son was born, she resumed her work at a country school in Liberty County, but she resigned her position within a year.

Returning to Savannah, Taylor ran a night school with help from her brother-in-law. The next year the school was forced to close because the Beach Institute started another free evening program. She placed her son with her mother and applied for her husband's army pension of one hundred dollars. After receiving the money, she placed some of it in the Freedman's Bank, only to lose it when the bank collapsed.

Taylor found work as a laundress for Mrs. Charles Green, and in 1873 the Greens relocated to Rye Beach for the summer, taking Taylor along as their cook. It was her first trip to the North, and she made frequent trips to Boston. In 1874 she returned to Boston in the employ of James Barnard. She made several trips back to the South, but Boston became her home. In 1879 she met and married Russell L. Taylor.

Organizes the Corps of Sixty-seven

In 1886 Taylor helped organize the Corps of Sixty-seven, Women's Relief Corps, auxiliary to the Grand Army of the Republic. She served as a guard, secretary, treasurer, and in 1893 as president. Three years later she was involved in another war-related venture; she compiled a list of war veterans living in Massachusetts, locating both white and black soldiers.

Taylor finished her manuscript, *Reminiscences of My Life in Camp,* in 1901. The book was not only an autobiography, but it also highlighted the achievements of African Americans from the Civil War to the turn of the century. The first half of the book documented black accomplishments, but the second half was devoted to the legacy of racism and discrimination. Taylor believed that racism was a national problem, but it was more prominent in the South. She published the manuscript in 1902, but there were no reviewers of the work or records of its sales. Most of the purchases were probably made by fellow clubwomen and their families.

Little is known about Taylor after her book was published. She probably continued as a domestic and spent time with war organizations. Her husband died before the book was published, and she spent her remaining years alone. On October 6, 1912, the landlady found her body slumped near her bed. Taylor was buried in Boston's Mount Hope Cemetery with an unmarked headstone. The local newspapers did not carry an obituary or funeral notice for her.

Mary Church Terrell

Educator and social activist
Born September 23, 1863, Memphis, Tennessee
Died July 24, 1954, Washington, D.C.

"I will not shrink from undertaking what seems wise and good because I labor under the double handicap of race and sex."

During her long and distinguished career as a teacher, lecturer, and social activist, Mary Church Terrell worked in many different ways to improve conditions for African Americans, especially African American women. Her activities continued into her old age, when she led the fight to get Washington, D.C., desegregated—and won the battle at the age of ninety, just a year before her death.

Terrell's success as a social activist was achieved largely by working within the system—giving lectures and speeches and serving on boards and associations. She was one of the organizers and first president of the National Association of Colored Women and one of the founders of the National Association for the Advancement of Colored People. For many years she was an active member of the Republican party, and she attended both the International Congress of Women in Berlin (1904) and the International Peace Conference (1919).

An author as well as a lecturer and activist, Terrell recounted the story of her life in the book *A Colored Woman in a White World* (1940). She wrote the book, she said, "to show

Mary Church Terrell

what a colored woman can achieve, in spite of the difficulties by which race prejudice blocks her path, if she fits herself to do a certain thing, works with all her might and main to do it, and is given a chance."

Followed a professional calling, against her parents' wishes

Mary Church Terrell was the eldest child of Louisa and Robert Church, both of whom had been slaves. When Mary was three, her father was shot in the head during the Memphis riots. But he survived, and over the next twenty years he invested in real estate, doing so well that he became a millionaire—the wealthiest black man in the South. However, it was Mary's mother who supported the family during the early years. She ran a fashionable hairdressing salon in Memphis.

While Mary was still a young child, her parents divorced, and Mary and her brother Thomas were placed in the care of their mother. Having started school in Memphis, Mary was sent north to Yellow Springs, Ohio, at the age of six so that she could get a better education than was available for black children in the South. In Yellow Springs she boarded with a black family and attended Antioch College Model School for two years before moving on to the public school. In eighth grade she transferred to the high school in Oberlin, from which she graduated in 1879.

At all these schools the majority of students were white, as were most students at Oberlin College, where Mary studied for the next few years. She decided to study classics, which did not please her parents. They said it would ruin her chances of finding a husband: "Where will you find a colored man who has studied Greek?" Mary was the only woman in a Greek class of forty young men, yet she suffered no discrimination either as a woman or as an African American. Indeed, she thoroughly enjoyed college life, took part in the various debates, joined the literary society, edited the *Oberlin Review,* and graduated in 1884 as one of the first African American women to earn a bachelor's degree. She was also one of the first to earn an M.A., which she was awarded four years later.

On graduating from Oberlin, Mary was expected to return to Memphis to act as her father's hostess. Although her parents believed in education, they did not think it proper for their daughter to follow a profession. When Mary accepted a teaching position at Wilberforce College in Ohio in 1885, her father was so angry he did not speak to her for a year.

After two years at Wilberforce, Mary accepted a position as Latin teacher at the

Colored High School in Washington, D.C. There she met Robert Terrell, a fellow teacher and the person her parents had said did not exist—"a colored man who has studied Greek." Mary married Terrell in 1891 on her return from a European tour. Her father, having made up his quarrel with her, had treated her to two years in Europe. Typically, Mary took advantage of the tour to enlarge her education. As well as attending concerts and plays, she studied the languages of the countries she stayed in and became fluent in both French and German.

Influential in desegregating Washington, D.C.

One year after her marriage, Mary Church Terrell began her career as a social activist. She was spurred into action by the lynching of Tom Moss, a family friend from Memphis, who was murdered because his grocery store was doing better business than the white stores in town. Shocked by Moss's death, Terrell wrote to the President of the United States, urging him to speak against such vicious racism, but President Harrison took no action.

That same year, 1892, Terrell helped organize the Colored Women's League, a local women's group, and in 1896 she amalgamated her group with other black women's organizations to form the National Association of Colored Women (NACW). She was elected first president of the organization, a role she filled so capably that she was twice re-elected and then made honorary president for life.

During her years with the NACW, Terrell tried to deal with every issue that affected black women—not only major civil rights issues such as getting women the vote, but practical things like setting up day-care centers for working black mothers. In pursing these aims she cooperated with other like-minded organizations, such as white women's suffrage groups and international women's groups, and she lectured widely and published numerous articles on social issues.

In 1904 Terrell was invited to speak at the International Congress of Women held in Berlin. The only black delegate, she was determined to make a good impression and delighted her hosts by giving her speech in German. She then amazed the audience by repeating it in French and in English. In 1919 Terrell again had an international audience when she addressed the delegates at the peace conference in Switzerland, and in 1937 she represented black American women at the meeting of the World Fellowship of Faiths, held in London, England.

For about fifteen years Terrell served on the District of Columbia School Board, one of the first black women in the country to be appointed to a district school board. She was invited to join many other boards and associations, for she could be relied upon to take action as well as to speak her mind. In one of her final actions she led a group of African Americans into Thompson's Restaurant in Washington and then sued the restaurant when it refused to serve her group. Terrell won the lawsuit in 1953 and so set in motion the desegregation of all public facilities in the nation's capital. She died the following year at the age of ninety-one.

Clarence Thomas

Supreme Court justice
Born June 23, 1948, Pin Point, Georgia

"I am of the view that black Americans will move inexorably and naturally toward conservatism when we stop discouraging them; when they are treated as a diverse group with differing interests; and when conservatives stand up for what they believe in rather than stand against blacks."

When the civil rights champion Thurgood Marshall retired from the U.S. Supreme Court in June 1991, he said he hoped that President George Bush would not replace him with "the wrong Negro." Bush replaced him with conservative judge Clarence Thomas, and in Marshall's opinion, this was indeed "the wrong Negro."

Thomas's appointment caused one of the greatest furors ever known over a judicial appointment. The controversy centered on the allegations of a black law professor, Anita Hill, who said that Thomas had sexually harrassed her some years earlier, when she was working for him at the Equal Employment Opportunity Commission. The nation was riveted to the televised Senate hearings investigating the charges during the fall of 1991. The issues of racism and sexism raised were far larger than the matter at hand—whether Thomas was suitable for a position on the Supreme Court.

Even before this, Thomas was known as a controversial figure, and his actions had lost him the support of many civil rights activists. His critics accused him of being two-faced, of advancing his career by accepting jobs offered just because he was black—while at the same time declaring that he would make his way on merit alone. They also objected to his extreme stand on such matters as abortion. Thomas's admirers, on the other hand, praised him for speaking out against abortion. They agreed with many of his views and were pleased that an African American from such humble origins should take his seat among the greatest in the land. Thomas often stressed his "humble beginnings," and indeed he had come a long way since his birth in the tiny coastal hamlet of Pin Point, Georgia.

Grandfather's influence

Thomas and his brother were reared mainly by their grandfather, Myers Anderson. Their father deserted the family when the boys were toddlers, and their mother Leola—who was only eighteen when Thomas was born—then married a man who didn't want to be bothered with children; so she handed over her two sons to her father and left her daughter with an aunt.

While living with their mother, the children had been crowded into a one-room hut near the marshes. Their living conditions were improved and their lives were considerably more regulated with Grandfather Anderson. A devout Catholic, Anderson was a strong influence on Thomas. He believed in doing things for himself, and instead of taking low-paying jobs, he created his own fuel oil business in Savannah—no easy accomplishment in the racist South of the 1950s.

Anderson paid for the boys' education at St. Benedict the Moor, an all-black grammar school. They were taught by white nuns who insisted on hard work and strict discipline. On graduating from St. Benedict in 1962, Thomas spent two years at St. Pius X High School before his grandfather moved him to a white Catholic boarding school called St. John Vianney Minor Seminary. Here, for the first time, Thomas was the butt of personal racism, which he had been shielded from at his segregated schools. He also found the atmosphere unpleasantly racist when he enrolled at Immaculate Conception Seminary in Conception, Missouri. He had intended to study for the priesthood, but he left the seminary in disgust in 1968, having heard a fellow student rejoicing over the assassination of civil rights leader Martin Luther King, Jr.

During the next three years, Thomas studied for a degree at Holy Cross, a Jesuit college in Worcester, Massachusetts. Here he became something of an activist, joining the Black Student Union, which agitated for improved conditions for black students. However, he was far more conservative than most of his colleagues and remained true to the tenets taught him by his grandfather and the nuns.

On graduating in 1971, Thomas married a fellow student, Kathy Ambush. Their son, Jamal, was born two years later while Thomas was a law student at Yale University. Thomas had entered Yale through the university's affirmative-action program, which arranged for the enrollment of students from minority groups. Although he was glad to be studying at so prestigious a college, he could not help wondering whether he had been accepted only because he was black. From this experience grew Thomas's distrust of what he calls "handouts," and he was often to speak against them. Meanwhile, he worked hard to prove to himself that he had been chosen because of his abilities, not because of his color.

Ambitious lawyer

When Thomas graduated from Yale Law School in 1974, he avoided the stereotypical role of civil rights lawyer. Instead, he specialized in tax law, joining the staff of John Danforth, attorney general of Missouri. When Danforth, a Republican, was elected to the U.S. Senate in 1977, Thomas became legal counsel for the huge chemical company, Monsanto Corporation. Two years later, he moved to Washington to become Danforth's legal assistant, working mainly on energy and environmental issues.

Thomas's career took off in a big way as soon as Ronald Reagan was elected president in 1980. As a black lawyer who held extremely conservative views, Thomas was looked on favorably by the Reagan administration, and in 1981 he was made assistant secretary for civil rights under the secretary of education. Ten months later, he was put in charge of the Equal Employment Opportunity Commission (EEOC), an agency in charge of enforcing civil rights laws.

Why Thomas accepted these positions is unclear, since they were the type of "black" appointment he had so often spoken against. He had never been part of the civil rights movement, and his activism, such as it was, had ended after his first few years at college. Since then Thomas had become increasingly

Clarence Thomas

conservative, proclaiming that the poor should do more to help themselves. He had publicly criticized his sister for depending on welfare, though she was no longer on welfare when he spoke out against her—she was working double shifts in a nursing home for about two dollars an hour.

Inevitably, Thomas had a stormy time as head of EEOC. He was going through a difficult period in his personal life, having separated from his wife, and he often lost patience with the civil rights leaders, complaining that they moaned and whined. For their part, they accused him of using his position to settle petty scores, and they said he was inconsistent in his policies—one minute speaking in favor of hiring minorities and another time against it. Most of all, they felt he was not rooting out civil rights abuses vigorously enough.

Meanwhile, Thomas gained increasing approval from ultra-conservative groups such as the Heritage Foundation, especially when

he made public statements against abortion and about people's "God-given rights." Consequently, in 1990, President George Bush nominated Thomas to the federal appeals court—a traditional stepping-stone to the Supreme Court. The next year came Thomas's nomination to the Supreme Court, whereupon the usual Senate committee was formed to decide whether to confirm or reject the president's nominee.

Supreme Court controversy

Even before Professor Anita Hill came forward with her allegations, there was a groundswell of opposition to Thomas's nomination. The National Association for the Advancement of Colored People (NAACP) came to the regretful decision that it must oppose the nomination, explaining that "Judge Clarence Thomas's judicial philosophy is simply inconsistent with the historical positions taken by the NAACP." Civil rights leader Jesse Jackson put it more bluntly: "He is a prime beneficiary of our work ... yet he stood on our shoulders and kicked us in the head." In both cases, it was the record of Thomas's performance with the EEOC that stood against him, even though both Jackson and the NAACP would have liked an African American to be appointed. Ironically, Thomas was being treated as he had always demanded—by merit rather than color.

Other critics honed in on his lack of judicial experience and the fact that he was "not a brilliant legal scholar." Bruce Shapiro, writing in *Nation,* said that Thomas was "among the more scantily qualified Supreme Court candidates in recent memory." Nevertheless, President Bush stood staunchly behind his candidate, basing his support largely on Thomas's character.

When Hill's allegations were made public, the emphasis of the controversy changed, bringing in racial and sexist elements. Thomas claimed that he was being victimized as a black man—that the Senate hearings were a "high-tech lynching"; meanwhile, women's groups rushed to support Hill, claiming that she was being vicimized as a woman. Thomas gained considerable emotional support by declaring that Hill's televised statements about his sexual advances created a terrible ordeal for himself and his wife (he had married a white woman, Virginia Lamp, a few years earlier). Many black viewers supported Thomas, swayed by his arguments and by Republican assertions that Hill was part of a Democratic campaign to smear him.

When the hearings ended, the all-male Senate committee voted to support Thomas, and the Senate approved his nomination by a vote of 52 to 48. Yet the issues did not go away. Despite his appointment to the highest court in the land, a shadow was cast over the career of Clarence Thomas, so that he is still faced with the same challenge he had in his youth—to prove himself worthy of his position through the quality of his work.

Jean Toomer

Writer
Born December 26, 1894, Washington, D.C.
Died March 30, 1967, Doylestown,
  Pennsylvania

"I am of no particular race. I am of the human race, a man at large in the human world, preparing a new world."

When Jean Toomer's novel *Cane* was published in 1923, the writers of the Harlem Renaissance were ecstatic. Here was a new talent and an exceptionally brilliant one—a black poet-novelist who had captured the atmosphere of the South and transformed it into literature. No other writer at that time had written about the African American experience with such eloquence. Yet the book sold only about five hundred copies and was not reprinted until 1951. Meanwhile, Toomer's literary career quietly faded. He never published another major work.

Until the end of the 1960s, Toomer was largely forgotten—regarded as a very minor literary figure. But then there was a resurgence of interest in *Cane,* which led to new editions of the book, along with the publication of Toomer's other writings, including his poems.

Cane is now considered one of the best African American novels ever written, and Toomer himself is regarded as a major poet— the most important black poet, in some people's view. As the critic Kenneth Rexroth has said, "Toomer was the first poet to unite folk culture and the elite culture of the white avante-garde." He was able to do this because he had a foot in both worlds.

A racially mixed childhood

Much of Jean Toomer's work centers on a search for identity, a subject that preoccupied him because of the question of his own racial

Jean Toomer

identity. He was neither black nor white, and yet he was both, a mix of "Scotch, Welsh, German, English, French, Dutch, Spanish, with some dark blood," as he once said. His full name was Nathan Eugene Toomer—like that of his father, Nathan Toomer, a planter in Georgia. His mother, Nina (Pinchback) Toomer, came from a fair-skinned family that was proud to claim black ancestry and had played an important role during Reconstruction.

When Toomer was less than a year old, his father deserted the family, and his mother took him to live with her parents, who had a house in a wealthy white neighborhood in Washington, D.C. Around 1906, his mother married a white man, so Toomer continued to live in a white environment. Not until 1910, when he was back with his grandparents after his mother died of appendicitis, did he live in a black neighborhood. His grandparents had

moved to a less wealthy part of Washington, having experienced financial troubles.

During the years he had lived among whites, the fair-complexioned Toomer had been accepted without any problems, and now the same thing happened when he was living in a black environment. By the time he was twenty, he decided he would not think of himself as black or white; he would simply consider himself an American. In the meantime, he attended the black M Street High School in Washington and then went on to college—several colleges, since he toyed with the idea of studying agriculture, but stayed nowhere long enough to get a degree. At length, in 1919, he decided to become a writer.

The author of *Cane*

At the time of his decision Toomer had been a student at the City College of New York for two years, studying the works of Henrik Ibsen, George Bernard Shaw, and other socially aware authors. Toomer began by writing short stories, poems, and articles, but he was not satisfied with any of them. He felt he had not yet found a way of expressing his feelings about race and the other issues that troubled him.

Toomer found the answer during the summer of 1921, when he served as temporary superintendent of a small, rural, black school near Sparta, Georgia. There he lived among the local people and became fascinated by their folk culture and overwhelmed by the beauty and the power of the land. He heard spirituals sung by the men and women as they went about their daily work. He saw the poverty and hardships they endured, and he saw how their culture gave them strength.

On the train returning north in November, Toomer began to write the pieces that became the first section of *Cane*. The book is organized into three sections. The first section is set in Georgia and consists of twelve poems and six sketches about southern women—five black women and one white. The second section, which is also a mix of verse and prose, focuses on city life in the North and its effects on black people who have moved there from the South. The third section, a long prose piece, returns to Georgia, as seen through the eyes of Ralph Kabnis, a black northerner. As a whole, the novel is about being black in America, about the search for one's identity as an African American, and the search for one's roots. In the course of this search, the book reveals the strength and beauty of the African American culture.

On its publication in 1923, *Cane* caused great excitement among the young writers of Harlem; Arna Bontemps said that he "went quietly mad" when he first read book. Toomer's masterly skill with words, the symbolism in his stories, the pastiche manner in which he presented them—plus, of course, the subject matter itself—all combined to cause the black literary world to proclaim Toomer a brilliant new black writer.

Few authors have had such a promising beginning, but Toomer's style was so innovative and creative that he did not gain a large following among the general public. Nor did he team up with the writers of the Harlem Renaissance. Toomer did not like being hailed as a black writer. He wanted to be thought of as an American writer who was concerned with other matters in addition to the African American experience. After 1923, he consciously turned away from black America and focused his attentions in new directions.

The philosopher

In 1924, Toomer became interested in the teachings of George I. Gurdjieff, the Greek-Armenian spiritual philosopher. Gurdjieff promised his disciples "internal harmony," which was basically what Toomer had always been seeking. After visiting Gurdjieff in France during the summer, Toomer became a teacher of the Gurdjieff philosophy and established small groups of followers in New York and Chicago.

One member of Toomer's groups was the white novelist Margery Latimer. They were married in 1932, but less than a year later, she died giving birth to their daughter. In 1934, Toomer embarked on a second marriage, again to a white woman, Marjorie Content, who was from a wealthy New York family. They settled on a farm in Doylestown, Pennsylvania, and Toomer gave up his Gurdjieff teaching. The philosophy had not brought him the internal harmony he sought, though it had provided a new outlet for his writing.

Toomer continued to write throughout his life, and occasionally he had a poem or short story printed in a literary journal, but most of his writings were rejected by the publishers. They tended to be dull, pushing the Gurdjieff philosophy and lacking the literary genius that had been so obvious in *Cane*.

Collections of Toomer's writings have been published in recent years, most notably *The Wayward and the Seeking* (1980), which includes some of his more interesting autobiographical pieces, and *The Collected Poems of Jean Toomer* (1988). There have also been critical assessments and new editions of his masterwork, *Cane,* which remains one of the very best novels of the African American experience. It stands alongside such classics as Richard Wright's *Native Son* and Ralph Ellison's *Invisible Man.*

Jackie Torrence

Storyteller
Born February 12, 1944, Chicago, Illinois

"There is a new breed of storyteller—the professional—who chooses to make a living travelling throughout the nation spinning tales to all who will listen."

J ackie Torrence was the reference librarian who came to the rescue when a children's librarian fell ill and could not read a story to an assembly of children. The children were so impressed with her storytelling gifts that they wanted to hear the story again and again. As her popularity grew, Torrence eventually left the library to become a full-time storyteller. She knows several thousand characters and dozens of sound effects like creaking doors and howling ghosts. In one story she can play a high-spirited, five-year-old girl, a ninety-eight-year-old woman, and a thirty-eight-year-old woman. Torrence has traveled across the globe and delighted thousands with her gifts.

A family of storytellers

Torrence was born on February 12, 1944, in Chicago, Illinois, but spent much of her childhood on Second Creek, near Salisbury, North Carolina. She was raised by her grandparents, who often had relatives stop by and tell stories. Her grandfather, Jim Carson, was a particularly good storyteller, and when her grandmother baked bread in an old cookstove, Torrence would often listen to her stories.

When she was ready for school, Torrence moved to Salisbury and lived with her unmarried Aunt Mildred. She had few opportunities to make friends, and many classmates made fun of her speech impediment. In *Homespun: Tales from America's Favorite Storytellers,* Torrence recalled, "I was a fat child, had no daddy, and felt unattractive.... In the fifth grade, I realized I didn't talk like everyone else. I had a speech impediment [and] ... whenever I began to talk, it sounded as though I had rocks in my mouth, and the other kids laughed at me. I was shattered."

Her teacher, Pauline Pharr, encouraged her to write stories that Pharr would then read to the class. Together, these two shared her creative talents with the other children, and, for once, Torrence gained in popularity.

After she was accidently struck in the mouth by a thrown bottle, it was discovered that Torrence had a dental abnormality. She had impacted teeth—an extra set of teeth in her mouth that prevented her from speaking correctly. With the help of her English teacher, Abna Aggrey Lancaster, Torrence began to

Jackie Torrence

make progress. In *I Dream a World*, Torrence stated Lancaster was "one of the most incredible people I have ever met, says that in me she found an eagle among her chickens. She worked with me day and night and Saturdays to change my speech. She will tell you that she never taught school, she taught students."

Lancaster gave Torrence the courage to stand in front of an audience and to say what she wanted to say. She read the Scriptures in the school assembly programs to nurture her ability to perform before an audience.

After completing her secondary education, Torrence matriculated at Livingstone College. Since sororities were too expensive, she became a member of the Drama Club, where she starred in the play, *A Raisin in the Sun*. Although she was successful at college and wanted to continue, she did not finish her college education. She met and married a ministerial student, and for eight years they traveled from one impoverished southern church to another throughout Georgia, Mississippi, Arkansas, Oklahoma, and Texas. While in Little Rock, Arkansas, Torrence filled in for her husband, reading the Scriptures, praying, and usually relating a Bible story. In *Homespun,* she said, "When I told the congregation a Bible story, I thought I was teaching. I didn't know—didn't have no idea under the sun—that I was storytelling."

With her marriage ending in failure, Torrence returned to North Carolina, where she left her daughter, Lori, in the care of her mother in Granite Quarry. She became an uncertified reference librarian in the public library.

Becomes library storyteller

In 1972 the children's librarian fell ill, and the library director asked Torrence to tell the assembled children a story. Since she had never done such a task before and felt she probably could not do it, Torrence told the director that she was too busy. The director told her she could take an extra hour off, so she reluctantly agreed. She read Richard Chase's *The Grandfather Tales* to five children who insisted that she read it a second and a third time. "It was those kids," she told the *Wall Street Journal*. "The bug bit me. I've been in love with storytelling ever since."

For the next few weeks, Torrence delighted the library's children with stories. She eventually became the full-time storyteller and was known as "the Story Lady." As her reputation spread and her confidence grew, huge crowds began appearing at the library to hear her. Soon neighboring communities were clamoring for her. Torrence had to make a decision: either confine her storytelling to the library or try to make it a full-time job. Although she was worried about the future, Torrence decided to resign from the library.

Torrence need not have worried. She has been such a successful storyteller that she has traveled throughout the United States, Canada, England, and Mexico. She has given presentations in schools, colleges, and universities, as well as through radio, television, and recordings.

Her stories cover a variety of topics and come from many sources. She is well-known for her retelling of tall tales, ghost stories, African American tales, and Appalachian lore. Some have criticized her use of Uncle Remus stories (as recorded in heavy dialect by Joel Chandler Harris) as racist, but Torrence feels these stories are a part of American lore.

In *Horn Book,* she wrote: "As a teaching tool, the tales implied great morals when they told of the sly ways the slaves had outsmarted the master; they were warning devices and were used as signals to those who were hiding—needing information about people who could and would help....

"Why do we resent them now? The fact that the tales came from the evil days of slavery could be a major reason. We also seem to be uncomfortable with the dialect and with their overall ideals. Whatever the reason, we are making a grave mistake. These stories are important to the black as well as to the white heritage of America."

To learn a story, Torrence reads it five times, but does not memorize it so she can add something fresh to every performance. The first reading is to see if she likes the story. The second time she tries out personalities for the characters. The third time she memorizes key phrases. The fourth time she polishes the characters, and the last time she reads it is to reassure herself that she knows the story.

Torrence believes storytelling transports its listeners to distant times and places, and can be used as a tribute to the black race. In *I Dream a World,* Torrence said, "If it had not been for storytelling, the black family would not have survived.... I wish you could see all my uncles and aunts when we get together and the stories come out. They are storytellers on a higher level than I will ever be."

Toussaint-Louverture

Slave insurrectionist
Born 1743
Died 1803

For years blacks living on the small island of Saint Domingue (now called Haiti) suffered from the cruelty of their French masters. Stern, autocratic governors-general held absolute power over thousands of slaves who produced raw materials to be used overseas. This cruelty gave rise to the first strong black leader in the New World—François-Dominique Toussaint. With Toussaint at the vanguard of a popular uprising, his troops smashed through French forces and burned their homes to the ground. His stunning victories won him the nickname Louverture, meaning "The Opener," and the title of General of Saint Domingue for life. He later became known as the Deliverer for conquering the

French stronghold of Cap François. He eventually became governor-general of the island and restored it to prosperity before the French attempted to retake the island.

Under French control

In 1630 French forces seized control of the island of Saint Domingue and began shipping a steady stream of sugar, cotton, and indigo (a blue dye made from plants) back to France. The French held absolute control over the island, keeping most of its black population in slavery. When the French Revolution broke out in 1789, mulattoes (those born of mixed races), who could own land but had no social standing, revolted. France responded by allowing mulattoes to have seats in the new colonial assembly.

While mulatto concerns may have been addressed, black slavery continued as harshly as ever. At this time the island was inhabited by 30,000 whites, 24,000 free blacks and mulattoes, and 452,000 black slaves. As the French Revolution gained momentum, the blacks also became interested in freedom. They gathered in the forest at night and plotted an uprising. One of those meetings took place on August 1, 1789, when Boukmann, a voodoo priest whose name and reputed deeds terrified the slaves, gathered the island's black leaders. Among them was Toussaint-Louverture, who was known for his wisdom and respect for learning.

Eight days later the French woke up to the sounds of hundreds of drums. The blacks swept from village to village, killing any whites they could find and burning their houses. The sky glowed with flames as more

Toussaint-Louverture

than six thousand coffee plantations and two hundred sugar refineries were destroyed. The French finally mustered a counteroffensive and captured Boukmann at Cap François. His head was impaled on a pole as a warning to any black who joined the uprising.

Toussaint-Louverture quickly became the new leader of the blacks, many of whom had taken refuge in the forest. He unsuccessfully attempted a peace treaty with the French. At the same time, France declared war on Spain and England, and since Spain controlled a part of Saint Domingue, Toussaint-Louverture joined forces with the Spanish, who provided the blacks with firearms. Toussaint-Louverture led his forces from the northern and eastern portions of the island. With Spanish assistance, Toussaint-Louverture's army drove the French forces from these areas. France sent three thousand reinforcements, but they were soon overcome either by the blacks or by a fever that was sweeping across the island.

France realized the war was going against them and proclaimed an end to slavery.

Toussaint-Louverture routs the French

Toussaint-Louverture did not trust the French. He abandoned his Spanish allies and routed the French in every town he passed. He eventually conquered the French stronghold of Cap François, ending their rule over the island. Toussaint-Louverture became a hero to his people.

With all former French territory under his control, Toussaint-Louverture proclaimed himself governor-general. He turned his attention toward rebuilding the island by developing its natural resources and foreign trade. Saint Domingue began to prosper. Toussaint-Louverture even decided to renew trade relations with France. He felt the uprising was based on hatred of slavery, rather than of the French. To prove there was no longer any animosity, he sent his two sons to school in Paris.

Toussaint-Louverture imposed a system of forced labor that some regarded as being only slightly better than the slavery they had just escaped. The island was divided into districts, each under a general, and everyone was forced to work. Those who did not were buried alive, sawed between two planks, or made to suffer death or punishment in other horrible ways. Toussaint-Louverture justified his decisions by saying that his army needed these resources to resist Napoleon's attempt to recapture the island.

During Napoleon Bonaparte's efforts to create a French empire and conquer most of Europe, he turned his attention also to Saint Domingue. Napoleon regarded Toussaint-Louverture as an obstacle to his plan to create a great French empire in the New World. With Louisiana in his hands and with Saint Domingue as a key point in the Caribbean area, he could dominate the entire Western Hemisphere, or at least a large proportion of it. He felt the only reason the blacks were able to force the French out of Saint Domingue was because of their superior numbers.

In February 1802, French Captain-General LeClerc arrived in the waters around Saint Domingue with eighty-six ships and twenty-two thousand soldiers. Its main force was directed at Cap François, and the other ships were stationed around the island to await the attack. LeClerc sent word to Henri Christophe, a former general in Toussaint-Louverture's army who was now governor-general of Cap François, to prepare for his formal reception. Not having the approval of Toussaint-Louverture, Christophe refused LeClerc's entry.

The French forces attacked, and Christophe's forces put up a valiant, but ultimately unsuccessful, fight. Many peasants did not join the fight, partly because they were becoming complacent from their army's previous successes. Realizing his forces were in a fight they could not win, Christophe decided to leave Cap François a smoldering ruin. He began by setting his own fabulous palace on fire and then leading his troops to the hills. LeClerc seized command of the Cap and immediately decreed that all plantations be returned to their previous French owners, and that slavery be reinstituted for all blacks. These decrees frightened the peasants, and they rushed to join Christophe.

Toussaint-Louverture dies in French jail

LeClerc realized he made a mistake and declared all blacks free forever. He offered Christophe a generalship in the French army, which he accepted. Toussaint-Louverture , now an old man and unable to sustain a new uprising, retired with honor. But LeClerc was never sincere. On the pretext of having Toussaint-Louverture meet with the French to discuss the final disposal of his troops, LeClerc had him captured and taken to France, where he died in prison in 1803.

With Toussaint-Louverture disposed of, LeClerc planned to destroy Jean Jacques Dessalines, Toussaint-Louverture's second-in-command. A maid overheard LeClerc's plot and told Dessalines the details in African sign language in the presence of his enemies. News of the attempt on Dessalines's life set off a new revolt, and Saint Domingue was once again the scene of burnings and killings. This time the mulattoes joined the blacks and drove the French off the island. Saint Domingue was proclaimed a republic and given the Indian name of Haiti. Dessalines was named governor of Haiti for life, and his first act was to have all Frenchmen on the island put to death.

These events had an important impact on American history. A historian once said that Toussaint-Louverture "rose to leadership through a bloody terror, which contrived a Negro 'problem' for the Western Hemisphere, intensified and defined the anti-slavery move-ment, became one of the causes, and probably the prime one, which led Napoleon to sell Louisiana for a song, and finally, through the interworking of all these effects, rendered more certain the final prohibition of the slave-trade by the United States in 1807."

Robert Townsend

Film director, actor
Born February 6, 1957, Chicago, Illinois

"We haven't seen even one movie where the hero is black and he's talking to everybody. I just want one to cheer for. Like I cheer for Terminator, I cheer for Rambo, I cheer for James Bond."

R obert Townsend is a black filmmaker who—rather than concentrating on issues that are specific to the black community—wants to move beyond color to portray characters who are neither "black" nor "white." In his latest film, *The Meteor Man* (1993), he plays a superhero—an alien with superhuman powers. "People need inspiration, especially black people," he says, and he sees no reason why the mythical heroes should always be white.

All Townsend's movies attack black stereotyping in some way or other. He considers it immensely important to give both blacks and whites a more balanced view of the black community, presenting African Americans as they really are—widely diverse in character yet having the same hopes, dreams, and ambitions as anyone else.

Townsend is fully aware of the strong influence films can have. "They affect the way we dress, comb our hair, even the way we decorate our living rooms," he says. "That's powerful stuff, and you have to treat it accordingly." His hope is that his films will influence Americans to get past their racial barriers and see people simply as people.

Discovered he was better at acting than at basketball

Robert Townsend is the son of Robert and Shirley (Jenkins) Townsend, who divorced when he was a small child. He owes much of his success to his mother, who worked in the post office to support her four children. She set them an example of self-confidence and independence and taught them to believe they could achieve anything they really wanted. "Because of that, I never believed in limitations," Townsend has said.

As a child growing up on the west side of Chicago, Townsend's first ambition was to be a basketball player. But although he made the team, his main contribution was his habit of amusing his teammates by doing comic impersonations—much to the annoyance of his coaches. Realizing that comedy was more in his line than basketball, Townsend joined the Experimental Black Actors Guild when he was sixteen. Still a high school student, he was by far the youngest member of the group. Yet he knew this was the world he wanted to be in. Throughout his childhood he had been an avid television viewer, a fan of stars as varied as comedian Red Skelton and celebrated black actor Sidney Poitier. More than anything, Townsend wanted to join their ranks.

At the Experimental Black Actors Guild, Townsend was given some basic training in acting and directing, and he also studied with the comedy troupe Second City. When he was eighteen he gained his first movie role, a small part in *Cooley High* (1975). Graduating from high school that year, he was all set to carry on with his career as an actor, but his mother insisted that he attend college first. He studied radio and TV communications at Illinois State University and then transferred to William Patterson College in New Jersey. In New Jersey, Townsend commuted to New York City to work with the Negro Ensemble Company and study with the famed dramatic coach Stella Adler. He completed his studies at Hunter College, New York, and he performed in several Off-Broadway plays and also did stand-up comedy routines in various clubs.

Combated Hollywood stereotyping with his credit cards

In 1982 Townsend headed for California with dreams of becoming a film star, but he was soon disillusioned. As a young black actor, almost the only parts he was offered were roles as servants, slaves, or criminals. The most noted films he appeared in were *Streets of Fire* (1984), *A Soldier's Story* (1984), *American Flyers* (1985), *Odd Jobs* (1985), and *Ratboy* (1986). These were mainstream films, but many of the movies Townsend appeared in were designed solely for an African American audience.

There seemed to be two separate worlds in Hollywood. There was the main film business, in which white directors made movies to be distributed throughout the world, and then there was the black film business, in which black directors and actors made movies aimed principally at black audiences. Townsend objected strongly to this unrealistic apartheid. As he pointed out, the issues dealt with in "black" films were common to everyone: "Whites sit down after dinner and say, 'Hey honey, let's go see a black film tonight.' The problem is that the films made by black filmmakers cross the spectrum, just like all other films do. We need to be looked at in that way. Until then, the money will be spread thin to the various films. We will all lose."

Townsend set out to break this pattern with *Hollywood Shuffle,* the first film he produced and directed. He co-wrote the script with his friend Keenen Ivory Wayans (creator of the hit comedy television series "In Living Color"), and he paid for the production largely out of his own savings. Although the film was made on a shoestring, costing only $100,000— a pittance by Hollywood standards— Townsend used up his savings long before the shooting was finished. When he ran out of money he used credit cards, and when he could not pay his actors he filled up their cars with gas on his charge accounts.

By the time *Hollywood Shuffle* was completed, Townsend was about $40,000 in debt. He had taken a big risk, but it paid off. Having held a screening to show the movie to every distribution company in Hollywood, he obtained a contract with Goldwyn studios, which settled all his debts as part of the deal. Neither Goldwyn nor Townsend lost on the agreement. When the movie was released in 1987, it grossed $850,000 in the first month, and it eventually earned more than $10 million.

Part of the success of the film lay in the fact that it attacked stereotyping. The story centers on Bobby Taylor (played by Townsend) who works at a hot dog stand and keeps missing work to attend film auditions in the hope of becoming an actor. But the only role he is ever offered is that of a jive-talking hustler. Bobby has nightmares about his predicament, as well as a number of reveries that are both ironic and very funny. For example, he imagines himself being a student at a Black Actors School, where classically trained black actors are given courses in Jive Talk and Shuffling, and are taught to play pimps and hustlers. As the reviewer David Denby observed in *New York,* "The movie's comic range derives from the strength of such bitterness— Townsend's disbelief over the grotesque choices open to black actors."

Acclaimed director and producer

The success of *Double Shuffle* brought Townsend new opportunities. He was chosen as the director of Eddie Murphy's concert film, *Raw* (1987), and he also directed the HBO comedy special, *Partners in Crime* (1987–88). He also had occasional acting jobs, as in *The Mighty Quinn* (1989). Meanwhile, Townsend was also attending to other business. As well as marrying Cheri Jones in 1990, he was at work producing and directing his second feature. Titled *The Five Heartbeats,* it was released in 1991 after four years in production.

The Five Heartbeats again attacked stereotyping, though in a less obvious way than *Double Shuffle.* The movie follows the fortunes of a fictitious rhythm and blues singing

Robert Townsend

group, but not the "typical" group of popular imagination. As Townsend described it: "The story is a positive look at five young black men with an attempt to break away from any of the negative stereotypes that are tagged to us through the media. Each character is totally different from the other. One might be what most people expect from the black male, while the others take you in completely different directions. I want to show people something they haven't seen before."

Townsend is also showing people what they haven't seen before in his 1993 movie, *The Meteor Man*. This time he has dreamed up something completely new, a black superhero—or, rather, a superhero who just happens to be black. For that is the whole point of the movie—that here is a universal hero being portrayed by a black actor. The hero, played by Townsend himself, is an alien with superhuman powers who is disguised as an inner-city high school teacher.

Townsend feels that the movie business is long past due for this "first." As he points out, "We haven't seen even one movie where the hero is black and he's talking to everybody. I just want one to cheer for. Like I cheer for Terminator, I cheer for Rambo, I cheer for James Bond. I just want one.... He doesn't have to be super, just a hero."

William Monroe Trotter

Civil rights leader, journalist
Born April 7, 1872, Chillicothe, Ohio
Died April 7, 1934, Boston, Massachusetts

"Trotter was one of the twentieth century's first important Negro leaders in the militant tradition."—Stephen R. Fox

O f all the early civil rights leaders, William Monroe Trotter was by far the most militant. As publisher of the *Guardian* newspaper, which he founded in 1901, he continually pressed for full civil rights, while also keeping up a long-standing feud with celebrated black educator Booker T. Washington. In Trotter's view, Washington was a sellout because he placed more emphasis on jobs than on civil rights and because he behaved in a conciliatory manner toward whites.

In 1905 Trotter founded the Niagara Movement with fellow civil rights activist W. E. B. Du Bois, but he later disagreed with Du Bois, whom he regarded as insufficiently radical. Trotter would not compromise. Firm in his beliefs and committed in his aims, he expected others to follow where he led and to meet his standards.

Thrived in his abolitionist family

Trotter showed little sign of being difficult during his childhood and seems to have made friends easily. He and his two sisters were raised in a white suburb of Boston and grew up in a comfortable middle-class environment. Their father, James Trotter, had been a well-known figure in the antislavery campaign and was highly regarded in Boston, where his family was welcomed into many white homes. At the time there was a more relaxed racial atmosphere in Massachusetts than in most parts of the United States, and Trotter suffered little racism as he was growing up. At his high school, where he was the only African American in his class, he was elected class president.

Trotter's mother, Virginia, was extremely religious, and Trotter followed her example, becoming so active at the white Baptist church that he was urged to train as a minister. However, his father was against this, since a black minister would be permitted to serve only a black congregation, and such segregation was against his principles.

In 1891 Trotter entered Harvard University, where he had four happy years, working hard, enthusiastically taking part in sports, and gaining considerable popularity. He made Phi Beta Kappa in his freshman year, the first African American to be so honored at Harvard.

After graduating from Harvard, Trotter went into real estate, working for a white firm run by friends of his father. In 1899, after learning the business thoroughly, he set up his own company. That same year he embarked on what was to be a supremely happy marriage to Geraldine Pindell, "a fine forthright woman, blonde, blue-eyed and fragile." Pindell's family, like Trotter's, had a history of antislavery campaigning.

Trotter's real estate business did not prosper, however. It was difficult for a black man to compete in a traditionally white business, especially as Boston became more racist. Trotter sensed a "growth of caste feeling and caste laws." The urge to do something about the situation caused him to plunge into civil rights activity, which preoccupied him for the rest of his life.

Founded the *Guardian* and demanded full civil rights

In 1901 Trotter founded the *Guardian* newspaper to campaign for racial equality. The paper, which was extremely outspoken, was an immediate success, gaining a circulation of 2,500 within its first eight months. Initially Trotter had a co-editor, George Washington Forbes, who was a librarian at the Boston Public Library, but Forbes left the paper after a couple of years because its aggressive stance endangered his job.

By then Trotter had mounted a full-scale attack on Booker T. Washington—a daring action, since Washington was highly regarded by blacks as well as whites. In the pages of the *Guardian* Trotter attacked Washington on three fronts: first, for saying that racial conditions were improving when in fact they were getting worse; second, for maintaining that jobs were more important that political rights, a hypocritical stance, since Washington him-

William Monroe Trotter

self proudly boasted that he had been given the vote; and third, for limiting the prospects of the students at Tuskegee Institute, the college founded and run by Washington, which only offered manual and agricultural training.

In 1903, when Washington came to Boston to speak in favor of segregation, Trotter went to the meeting to argue with the famous educator—and by so doing caused a riot. Washington then sued Trotter, who spent a month in jail as a result. During his absence his wife, Geraldine, took over as editor of the *Guardian*.

Trotter's imprisonment caused W. E. B. Du Bois (who was also anti-Washington) to join forces with Trotter in the campaign against racist policies, and in 1905 they formed the Niagara Movement. This movement condemned the conciliatory approach of Washington and called for full civil rights to be granted immediately to all African Americans. The

partnership between Trotter and Du Bois lasted barely two years, for Trotter was far more radical than Du Bois. There were continual quarrels, and Trotter became so difficult that a member of the Niagara movement complained, "It is impossible for a man with ideas and opinions of his own … to get along with Trotter."

Lobbied to include racial equality clause in Treaty of Versailles

In 1909 both Trotter and Du Bois attended the founding meeting of the National Association for the Advancement of Colored People (NAACP), but Trotter did not join the organization. This was partly because Du Bois assumed a prominent role in the NAACP, but Trotter also objected that the NAACP was funded by whites and largely led by whites. To offer black activists an alternative, Trotter formed his own group, the National Equal Rights League, which he described as "an organization of the colored people and for the colored people and led by the colored people." His league attracted quite a large number of followers who wanted immediate action and were uncomfortable with the white presence in the NAACP.

Over the years Trotter threw his support behind various presidential candidates, switching between Democrat and Republican according to their racial attitudes. In the 1912 elections he supported Woodrow Wilson, since Wilson seemed the least racist candidate. But once Wilson became president, he showed little concern for the plight of African Americans and even approved a number of segregation laws and other discriminatory measures. Trotter was so incensed that in 1914 he led a delegation to the White House and argued vehemently with the president. The following year he again attracted notice when he was arrested in Boston for trying to prevent the screening of the film *The Birth of a Nation.*

In 1919, following the end of World War I, Trotter made plans to attend the peace conference at Versailles, France, intending to get the conference to pass a measure outlawing racial discrimination. When the American authorities heard of this plan, they revoked Trotter's passport, but with typical ingenuity Trotter managed to get over to France anyway—by hiring out as a cook on a ship. His bid to get a racial equality clause included in the Treaty of Versailles failed.

Trotter's last years were marred by unhappiness, for his beloved wife died in the influenza epidemic that swept the world after World War I. Trotter carried on with his civil rights efforts and with the *Guardian,* but Geraldine had been his most faithful supporter as well as his closest companion, and he became increasingly dejected without her. He died, apparently of suicide, on his sixty-second birthday.

Although Trotter was clearly a difficult person and too extreme for some people to tolerate, he was a man of strong principles who acted courageously on his beliefs. Both as an activist and as a leader of nonviolent protest, he made a unique contribution to the early civil rights movement and set an example that others would follow later in the century.

Sojourner Truth

Abolitionist, reformer
Born about 1797, Ulster County, New York
Died 1883

"I think that 'twixt the niggers of the South and the women at the North all talking about rights, the white men will be in a fix pretty soon."

Born into slavery, Sojourner Truth was offered few opportunities in life. Her brothers and sisters were sold at an early age, and she was maltreated by several masters. Truth finally ran away to find a better life in New York City. A deeply religious woman, she believed herself chosen by God to preach His word and to help with the abolitionist efforts to free her people. Truth travelled across the country, and as her reputation as an orator grew, she was greeted by large crowds wherever she went.

A controversial figure for most of her life, Truth is recorded in the history books for two unusual court cases. She was the first African American to win a slander suit against prominent whites, and she was the first black woman to test the legality of the segregation of Washington, D.C., streetcars.

During the Civil War she gathered supplies for soldiers and helped newly freed slaves find work and housing. After the war she continued her speaking tours for the Lord and against racial injustice, even when old age and ill health restricted her activities.

Lived in master's cellar

Truth was born Isabella Baumfree in Ulster County, New York, to an African named Baumfree (after his Dutch owner) and a woman named Elizabeth. Both parents were slaves of Charles Hardenbergh, a wealthy landowner, and all but one of Truth's brothers and sisters were sold before her birth. Truth was called Bell while she was growing up, and she lived with her family and other slaves in a damp cellar beneath their master's house. When Truth was nine years old, Hardenbergh died, and she was sold at an auction for one hundred dollars to a storekeeper, who mistreated her. She was eventually purchased by a tavern owner, who sold her in 1810 to John J. Dumont, a well-to-do landowner of New Paltz, New York, for three hundred dollars. A short time later she married an older slave named Thomas. Over a ten-year period she gave birth to five children, although only a son, Peter, and three daughters, Diana, Elizabeth, and Sophia, survived. Her master, Dumont, may have fathered several of her children.

New York State adopted a law in July 1817 requiring all slaves over the age of forty to be immediately freed, and all others to be freed by 1828. Dumont promised to free Truth a year early, but he reneged. Truth grabbed her infant daughter and fled; she was taken in by Isaac and Maria Van Wagener of New York City, who eventually purchased her freedom for twenty dollars.

Truth stayed with the Van Wageners as a servant. She discovered that her son had been sold out of state—in contravention of New York law—and with the assistance of Quakers, she successfully pressed the court for his re-

Sojourner Truth

turn. It was one of the first cases of a black woman successfully bringing suit against a white man.

In 1829 Truth and her two children went to Manhattan, where she worked as a servant. She became interested in religion after she had a vision of Jesus shielding her from the anger of God. She attended a Methodist church and then the Zion African Church, where she met her brother who had been sold as a child. She made the acquaintance of Sarah and Elijah Pierson, a wealthy and deeply religious couple, who preached in crime-ridden areas. Truth eventually moved in with them, working as a servant and missionary.

Robert Matthews, who called himself Matthias, approached the Piersons in the spring of 1832 claiming to be God the Father. A cult developed around him, which included the Piersons and Truth. She gave him her life savings to help establish a commune in Sing Sing (now Ossining), New York, called Zion

Hill. Truth worked at the commune as an unpaid housekeeper. Matthias and Pierson began to fight over control of the commune, until 1835 when Pierson died suddenly from arsenic poisoning. Matthias was arrested, tried, and found not guilty. Ben Folger, a cult member, suggested that Truth was involved in the murder, but she was never formally charged. She responded by suing him for libel and was awarded $125.

An itinerant preacher

Truth returned to New York City and renewed her membership in the Zion African Church. In June 1843, she took the name Sojourner Truth and set out on foot as an itinerant preacher. She slept wherever she could find shelter and worked when she needed food. She sang and gave sermons at camp meetings, in churches, and on town streets. Her message was: God is loving, kind, and good, and all men should love one another.

In 1843 Truth stayed at a communal farm and silk factory founded by George W. Benson. Here she had her first contact with the abolitionist movement, and she met Benson's brother-in-law William Lloyd Garrison, a leader in the abolitionist movement, and abolitionist Frederick Douglass. When the communal association ended in 1846, Truth continued to work in Benson's household. She made periodic tours across New England to speak against slavery.

Truth was considered a powerful orator. At nearly six feet tall, with an imposing bearing and a direct gaze, she brought skeptical audiences to attention. Many of her speeches began with, "Children, I speak to God and God speaks to me." She became a leader in the women's rights movement after speaking at a feminist convention in Worcester, Massachusetts, in 1850. A year later she made a historic speech at the National Woman's Suffrage Convention at Akron, Ohio. In response to male speakers who said women should be denied rights on the grounds that women are physically and intellectually weak, Truth said: "That man over there says that women need to be helped into carriages, and lifted over ditches, and to have the best place everywhere. Nobody ever helps me into carriages, or over mud puddles, or gives me any best place, and ain't I a woman? Look at me! Look at my arm! I have plowed, and planted, and gathered into barns, and no man could head me—and ain't I a woman?"

While in Ohio, Truth set up headquarters at the office of the Salem *Anti-Slavery Bugle.* She maintained herself by selling her book, *The Narrative of Sojourner Truth,* which was written by Olive Gilbert and published in 1850. Truth headed east in 1852 and spent several days in Andover, Massachusetts, with abolitionist Harriet Beecher Stowe, who spread Truth's fame in an *Atlantic Monthly* article in April 1863. White supremacists often tried to disrupt her meetings, and she was clubbed in Kansas and mobbed in Missouri. The *St. Louis Dispatch* mistakenly reported that Truth was a man, and the rumor stuck. Once at a women's rights convention in Indiana, she bared her breast to prove that she was a woman.

Supplies soldiers during Civil War

In 1857 Truth moved to the spiritual community of Harmonia, Michigan, near Battle Creek, where her daughters and their families soon settled as well. When the Civil War broke out, she nursed Union soldiers, lobbied for better sanitary facilities in army camps and travelled through Michigan seeking contributions of food and clothing for black volunteer regiments. On October 29, 1864, she was received by President Abraham Lincoln at the White House. Truth remained in Washington for more than two years to assist freed slaves, who were not yet admitted to full citizenship and were living in refugee camps and slums. In December 1864, the National Freedmen's Relief Association presented her with the title "counsellor to the freed people" at Arlington Heights, Virginia. This work gave her a new idea, the "Negro State," which she presented to President Ulysses S. Grant in the form of a petition in 1870. The idea was that the government should settle African Americans on public land in the West, rather than supporting refugee camps. The concept never really caught fire, but many African Americans migrated to Kansas and Missouri partly because of her efforts. Truth visited African American settlements in the Midwest and lectured them to "Be clean! Be clean! For cleanliness is godliness." While in Washington, she conducted some of the first sit-in protests against segregated streetcars and eventually tested the legality of segregation in the courtroom.

Truth spent time giving speeches from Washington to Boston and in the West to Iowa. During these speaking tours she sold her book and photographs of herself and stated her message of mystic but benevolent religious sentiments, African American rights, and women's suffrage. Her audiences ranged from "small"

to "good size." Her appearance was still noted in newspapers, but as time passed, the stories were mixed with ridicule.

In 1867 Truth became active in the newly formed American Equal Rights Association, whose goal was the extension of voting rights in New York State to women and blacks. Eight years later her grandson and constant companion, Sammy Banks, fell ill, so Truth returned to Battle Creek to stay with him. She continued to lecture through the North and Midwest. Truth suffered from poor health during her final years, and she died in Battle Creek in 1883 at about the age of eighty-six. She was buried in Oak Hill Cemetery in Battle Creek.

Harriet Tubman

Underground Railroad guide
Born 1820, Dorchester County, Maryland
Died March 10, 1913, Auburn, New York

"On my Underground Railroad, I never run my train off the track and I never los' a passenger."

H arriet Tubman was the heroine of the Underground Railroad—the network of people who helped slaves from the South escape to the northern free states and to Canada. This was a dangerous occupation for the whites involved in the operation, but it was especially dangerous for Tubman, who was herself an escaped slave. At one point, a reward of $40,000 was offered for her capture.

Between her own escape in 1849 and the outbreak of the Civil War in 1861, this small, sturdy woman returned to the South time and again to bring groups of slaves to safety. She was known as the Moses of her people because, like the prophet Moses, she led her people out of bondage. More than three hundred slaves escaped to freedom with her help.

A childhood of slavery

Looking back on her childhood, Tubman said, "I grew up like a neglected weed, ignorant of liberty, having no experience of it." She was born in the slave quarters of a Maryland plantation, one of the eleven children of Benjamin and Harriet Ross. Although the Rosses were allowed to live as a family, the children were hired out as soon as they were old enough to work. Tubman was first hired out when she was six, living with various families for whom she did housework or minded the babies. Like most slave children, she was punished for the slightest fault. One of the women she worked for whipped Tubman so often and so viciously that her neck was crisscrossed with scars that remained visible for the rest of her life.

Tubman first helped a slave escape when she was thirteen, at great cost to herself. The young man, who was fleeing from his overseer, tried to hide in a local store. But the overseer found him there and called to Tubman to hold the man so that he could bind and whip him. Nobody ever dared disobey the overseer, but instead of moving in to help, Tubman just stood there in the doorway, allowing the young man to duck past her and get away. In fury, the overseer hurled a heavy iron weight after him, but it missed its mark and hit Tubman on the head, knocking her to the ground. The wound was so severe that she was expected to die, and she lay for months in

her family's cabin being nursed back to health by her mother.

The blow on the head had a lasting effect on Tubman, causing her to fall asleep suddenly in the midst of activity—an obvious disadvantage for the fugitive she was to become. It also left a deep scar, which made her easily recognizable. Despite this, she grew up to be an exceptionally strong young woman.

After her recovery, Tubman was hired out to a builder who already employed her father. Although only five feet tall, she became so muscular that she could easily handle heavy work, carrying loads, cutting down trees, and hauling logs. She enjoyed working in the woods because it gave her a sense of freedom, and during the next few years she proved to be such a good worker that the builder allowed her to earn money.

Escape

In 1844, she married a free black, John Tubman, and went to live with him, though she remained a slave. Her family had expected to be freed on the death of their master a few years earlier, but instead had acquired a new master. After her marriage, Tubman hired a lawyer to look into the records, and she discovered that her mother had officially become free years ago, long before Tubman was born. No one had informed her, so she had remained a slave.

This discovery preyed on Tubman's mind, for it meant that she should have been born free. Worse still, it seemed very likely that she would soon be sold to a slaveowner in Georgia. In recent years, the plantation where her family lived had not been doing well, and the

Harriet Tubman

owner had been raising money by selling off his slaves. Harriet knew that because of her sudden sleeping spells, she could not possibly survive in the chain gang on the journey south. If she wanted to stay alive, she would have to escape.

Tubman hoped her husband would come with her, but he was strongly opposed to the whole idea and threatened to report her if she tried to leave. This was a problem she had not expected, but when she learned for sure that she was going to be sold, she realized she had no choice. Slipping away one evening, Tubman made for the house of a white woman who had once offered her help. The woman gave her food and told her of another safe house a little farther north. In this manner, Harriet Tubman made her way up the Underground Railroad, moving from shelter to shelter, hiding in the woods by day and often sleeping outdoors at night. At last, one morning in 1849, she crossed into the free state of Pennsylvania. "I had crossed the line of which I had so long been dreaming," she said. "I was free."

Conductor on the Underground Railroad

Tubman began her life as a free woman by working as a cook in Philadelphia. There she visited the offices of the Vigilance Committee, an organization that helped escaping slaves and passed on news of their families. Through the committee Tubman learned that one of her sisters was about to be sold. Immediately, she decided to go back to Maryland and bring her sister to safety.

On this first journey as a "conductor," Tubman brought out her sister, her sister's husband, and their two children. She later brought out the rest of her family, including her elderly parents. More often, she conducted people she did not even know. Sometimes, she made several trips in a year, heading back into slave territory almost as soon as she arrived in Pennsylvania.

It was always dangerous work, and it became more dangerous as Tubman's fame spread; posters were circulated offering a reward for her capture. Since it was safer to travel in small groups, she usually took only two or three people at a time, though she once had a party of eleven. She always traveled with a rifle, with which she threatened anyone who lost heart and wanted to go back. "Go on—or die!" she would say. It was not safe to let any slaves return, because their masters would force them to reveal where they had sheltered and who had helped them. Already, troopers were raiding Quaker homes in the hope of catching escaped slaves. Many participants in the Underground Railroad were Quakers, though others were simply people who were strongly against slavery.

In the early 1850s, escaped slaves were no longer safe in Pennsylvania and other northern states, because the newly enacted Fugitive Slave Law permitted them to be captured there and returned to their former owners. After this had happened a couple of times, the Underground Railway spread its network farther north, taking escaped slaves all the way to Canada.

Tubman made her first trip into Canada in 1851, and for the next few years her home base was the small town of St. Catharines in Canada West (now Ontario). Safely on the other side of the border, it was the place where Tubman stayed and worked between trips and where she housed her parents when she brought them north. However, her parents so disliked the cold Canadian winters that she decided to risk settling them in New York State, and in 1857 she bought a small frame house for them in the community of Auburn, near Syracuse.

War heroine and social worker

By 1860, many people in the North were ignoring the Fugitive Slave Law, and it was safe for Tubman to appear in public. She was much sought after as a guest speaker at antislavery meetings, where she thrilled the abolitionists with accounts of her dangerous journeys.

When the Civil War started, she offered her services to the Union army and became a scout, a spy, and a nurse. For much of the time, she was stationed on Port Royal, one of the Sea Islands off the coast of South Carolina, where many escaped slaves had taken refuge. Her main role was to nurse those who were sick, but from time to time she was sent into Confederate territory, and in 1863 she took part in a raid to help bring more slaves to safety on the island.

After the war, Tubman retired to Auburn, where in 1869 she married Nelson Davis, who was more than twenty years younger. Despite this, she outlived him by many years. As she grew older, she remained very active, concerning herself with local affairs, raising funds for schools for former slaves, and helping the poor and disabled. In 1903, she bought a large piece of land next to her house, where she established the Harriet Tubman Home for Aged and Indigent Colored People. Tubman spent the last two years of her life in the home, and on her death the town of Auburn erected a bronze plaque in her memory.

Nat Turner

Leader of slave insurrection
Born October 2, 1800, Southampton
  County, Virginia
Died November 11, 1831, Jerusalem
  (Courtland), Virginia

"Because Turner's motive was a desire for liberty, he may be regarded as cast in the same mold as the American patriots who fought the Revolutionary War.... No less than Patrick Henry, Turner believed that 'give me liberty or give me death' must be man's guiding philosophy."—Lamont H. Yeakey

Nat Turner has long been honored as the "Black Spartacus" because, like the Roman slave and gladiator, he led a slave revolt to free his people from bondage. Turner's insurrection of 1831 was the most successful of all the risings against slavery in the United States. Although it did not succeed in liberating the slaves, it gave great impetus to the abolition movement, which was then getting underway and which did succeed in making slavery illegal some thirty-four years later. There had been many uprisings before Turner's—far more than the slaveowners liked to admit—but none had been so quick growing and ferocious. The rebellion spread through Southampton County, Virginia, like a brushfire, leaving a climate of terror in its wake. For weeks afterward, until Turner was captured, the mere rumor of his approach sent people fleeing for safety. This one man had struck fear into the hearts of slaveowners not only in Virginia but throughout the South.

The young visionary

The seeds of rebellion had been sown during Turner's childhood, for both his parents sought freedom in their own ways. His mother had considered murdering him at birth to prevent him from suffering the misery of slavery. His father actually did find freedom, for he escaped when Turner was a small boy and was never recaptured. He is thought to have joined the many fugitives who lived in the Dismal Swamp, which covers six hundred square miles of southern Virginia and northern North Carolina.

Turner was an exceptionally bright child, a natural leader, but as soon as he was old

Nat Turner

enough he was put to work as a field hand. Nevertheless, he taught himself to read and made a careful study of the Bible. As he grew older, he became deeply religious and on Sundays he preached to his fellow slaves, many of whom viewed him as a prophet, for Turner seemed to have supernatural powers. He said he had seen visions and heard "voices" that told him he had a special mission in life. He had no doubt what this mission was—he was convinced he had been called by God to free his people.

Turner's reading of the Bible had made him acutely aware of the great gulf between the way Christians were supposed to act and the way the whites did in fact act in Southampton County. How could these slaveowners call themselves Christians when their conduct was so contrary to the teachings of the Bible? Turner pointed this out in his sermons, urging the local slaves to fight for justice and resist their owners. When he was twenty-one, he attempted his own form of resistance by escaping, and he stayed free for a month. But Turner did not feel he was doing right. His conscience troubled him, and he decided it was his duty to return.

Turner's master died the following year and Turner was sold to a neighboring planter, Thomas Moore. In 1830, he was moved again and became the slave of Joseph Travis, who had married one of the Moore women. The Travis family was the first to be killed when, the following year, Turner launched his rebellion.

Nat Turner's rebellion

Turner believed that God would tell him when to make his strike for freedom, and he prayed constantly that he would be given a sign. In February 1831, there was an eclipse of the sun—a strange phenomenon for those knowing nothing of astronomy—and Turner took this to be the sign he had been waiting for. He made his plans, choosing July 4 as the day of action. This year, he said, Independence Day would indeed bring independence. But as it turned out, he had to delay the revolt because he fell sick.

On August 13, there was another strange sign in the sky. The sun seemed to have a peculiar bluish-green tinge. Once again Turner made ready to act. He told his plans to as few people as possible, for there was the danger of betrayal if too many shared the secret. Nine years earlier, Denmark Vesey's insurrection had been betrayed before it could get started because too many people knew about it.

Nobody gave warning of Nat Turner's rebellion, which began on Sunday, August 21, 1831. Around the middle of the day, Turner met secretly with five fellow slaves—Hark, Henry, Nelson, Jack, and Will. All were trusted friends, committed to the utmost secrecy, and they arranged to meet again at midnight. Soon after midnight they attacked the home of Turner's owner, Joseph Travis, killing Travis and four others. Then they set off across the country, gathering recruits as they went. At every plantation, they killed the whites, though they spared a family of poor whites who owned no slaves. Their quarrel was against slaveowners, not against fellow workers.

As Turner moved from plantation to plantation, he was joined by between sixty and eighty slaves, most of them on horseback. By Monday evening they had killed between fifty-five and sixty-five men, women, and children and were within three miles of Jerusalem, the county seat (now the city of Courtland). So far, they had met little resistance and had suffered few casualties, but the authorities were hastily mustering their forces—summoning the state militia and federal troops, and as many volunteers as they could find.

Some of the militia routed a small group of rebels on Monday evening, but when they came up against Turner with the main rebel force, they retreated to Jerusalem. Since Turner's forces had suffered some losses and since most of his men were exhausted, he did not press on and attack Jerusalem that night. This was a mistake, because the town had a large stock of guns and ammunition, which his men could well have done with, for they were not well armed. Moreover, the delay gave the authorities time to rush reinforcements to the area. By Tuesday morning, some three thousand federal soldiers and state militia were in Jerusalem, ready to strike at Turner and his sixty or so followers.

In the face of such odds, Turner's small, courageous band never had a chance. They were easily routed on Tuesday morning. Turner managed to escape, and for two months he hid in a cave. Meanwhile, rumors of his whereabouts spread panic throughout Virginia, for many believed he would suddenly appear at the head of another, much larger army. Determined to find him at all costs, Governor John Floyd of Virginia offered a $500 reward for Turner's capture and circulated the following description: "Nat is between 30 and 35 years old, 5 feet 6 or 8 inches high, weighs between 150 and 160 pounds, rather bright in complexion, but not a mulatto, broad shoulders, large flat nose, large eyes, broad flat feet, rather knock-kneed, walks brisk and active, hair on top of head very thin, no beard, except on the upper lip and the top of the chin, a scar on one of his temples, also on the back of his neck, a knot on one of his bones of right arm, near the wrist, produced by a blow."

While the troops were searching for Turner, they were also conducting a general massacre. It is estimated that about two hundred black people were slaughtered in Southampton County before the panic died down. Turner's wife was beaten frequently in an attempt to get her to say where Turner was hiding.

The aftermath

Turner was discovered by accident on October 30 and taken prisoner. For the next three days, he was interviewed by the court attorney, Thomas Gray, who later published the text of Turner's so-called *Confessions*. When Gray tried to get Turner to admit to having done wrong, Turner refused outright. Rising from his prison cot, he said, "Was not Christ crucified?" Nevertheless, when brought to trial on November 5, he was found guilty and sentenced to death. Six days later he was hanged.

Yet Nat Turner's legend lived on. His story encouraged others to make a bid for freedom, and the next few years saw a number of plots and small uprisings throughout the South. At the same time, slaveowners clamped down with brutal new restrictions. In Virginia, laws were passed making it illegal for slaves to be taught to read or write or to hold religious meetings without a white person present. Such measures outraged more moderate whites and added fuel to the antislavery movement.

Over the years, Nat Turner's story has inspired artists and writers as well as freedom fighters and civil rights activists. In 1967, writer William Styron dramatized the tale in his best-selling novel *The Confessions of Nat Turner*. As Lamont H. Yeakey of the Black Economic Research Center has so aptly pointed out, Turner was not only an African American hero. He was in the true tradition of American heroes: "Because Turner's motive was a desire for liberty, he may be regarded as cast in the same mold as the American patriots who fought the Revolutionary War.... No less than Patrick Henry, Turner believed that 'give me liberty or give me death' must be man's guiding philosophy."

Mario Van Peebles

Actor, director, writer
Born c. 1957, Mexico City, Mexico

"I grew up seeing a black man in charge, so I didn't have a color chip on my shoulder.... It never occurred to me that I couldn't do it because of my color."

Mario Van Peebles

One of the new generation of young black filmmakers, Mario Van Peebles has already made his mark as both actor and director. As an actor he has shown impressive versatility in the wide range of roles he has played in television and movies. As a director, he first drew attention with the movie *New Jack City* (1991), a low-budget film which earned millions for its studio.

The son of actor-director Melvin Van Peebles, Mario could have ridden to fame on the coattails of his celebrated father, but he made his own way to the top through hard work and determination. Nevertheless, his movie director father inspired confidence. "I grew up seeing a black man in charge," he said, "so I didn't have a color chip on my shoulder.... It never occurred to me that I couldn't do it because of my color."

"Work like a dog and advertise"

The eldest of three children, Van Peebles had an unusual childhood because his family was so often on the move, living wherever his parents' work took them. "We were always broke. My room was usually a hotel closet.

Mom was my schoolteacher," he told a reporter for *Ebony* magazine. Born in Mexico, he lived in France, Morocco, and Denmark before settling with his mother in San Francisco after his parents' divorce. His mother, Maria, was a professional photographer, and because his parents remained on good terms after the divorce, Van Peebles was never cut off from his father.

When Van Peebles was about fourteen, he was given a small part in the movie *Sweet Sweetback's Baadasssss Song,* which his father wrote and directed. But later, when he graduated from high school, his father made a point of not helping him get into acting. "I'm going to give you some free advice," his father told him. "Early to bed, early to rise, work like a dog and advertise." This was not the type of response Van Peebles had been hoping for, but he later realized that it was his father's way of making him learn how to stand on his own feet. "Though it didn't seem like it then, it was the greatest gift he could have ever given me. So many kids of famous people never learned the value of *earning* something, or how sweet it is to have accomplishments to call your own."

Van Peebles's father also pointed out that the film business was indeed a business and involved knowing how to manage money. Taking this lesson to heart, Van Peebles enrolled at Columbia University, where he majored in economics. After graduating in 1978, he gained practical experience by working as a budget analyist for the City of New York.

Starred as Clint Eastwood's sidekick

In 1981 Van Peebles acted in a small part in the Broadway play *Waltz of the Stalk,* which was written and directed by his father. But he realized he still had a great deal to learn, and after the play closed he took acting lessons and supported himself by modeling. Van Peebles continued these lessons for the next few years, determined to make the grade as an actor, though he could more easily have pursued a career as a male model. With his handsome looks and slim figure, he was just what the agencies wanted, and his picture appeared frequently in *Gentlemen's Quarterly, Essence,* and other magazines.

During his spare time, Van Peebles wrote screenplays and hoped to seel them to a film studio. Clearly, he was following his father's advice to "work like a dog," and before long his efforts paid off. After handling a few small stage roles in the early 1980s, Van Peebles was given roles in three movies in 1984: *The*

Cotton Club, Delivery Boys, and *Exterminator II.* Meanwhile, he also made his way into television and was a regular in the daytime TV drama *One Life to Live.*

Van Peebles continued to do well the following year, in which he again landed three movie roles, but his big break as an actor came in 1986 when he appeared with Clint Eastwood in *Heartbreak Ridge.* Van Peebles's performance as the marine recruit Stitch Jones, Eastwood's right-hand man, brought him wide attention—and a large number of fans. More movie roles followed: *The Last Resort* (1986), *Jaws: The Revenge* (1987), and *Hot Shot* (1987).

Nineteen eighty-seven was also the year that Van Peebles was given the lead role in the comedy *Sonny Spoon,* an hour-long television movie. He played a private detective who frequently worked in disguise, posing as a wide range of characters. Commenting on the diversity of roles which the part allowed him to play, Van Peebles explained, "One of the things I wanted to show was that here you have this young black guy in the lead and he's able to cross every line. This guy's going to go from the church lady to the blond yuppie. They have me speaking French in the show, Spanish."

Proves his mettle with *Posse* and *New Jack City*

Van Peebles's involvement in television soon gave him the opportunity to try his hand as a director. He began by directing episodes of "Wiseguys," "21 Jump Street," and an afternoon special for children, "Malcolm Takes a Shot." Having proved his abilities on television, he was then approached by Warner

Brothers to direct the movie *New Jack City.*

Van Peebles approached the project in his customary businesslike manner and surprised the studio by the speed with which he made the movie. The shooting was completed in a mere 36 days. This greatly reduced the cost of production, yet the quality of the movie was not affected. When *New Jack City* was released in 1991 it was given excellent reviews and was an immediate success. Conceived as an anti-drug and anti-violence film, its theme was the exploitation of black youngsters. Wesley Snipes starred as the villain of the piece, playing Nino Brown, a Harlem gangster and drug king, while Van Peebles played the part of the police officer who was in charge of the undercover operation against Brown.

New Jack City was designed to show the ruthlessness of the world of gangsters and drugs, but its anti-violence message seemed to be lost when riots broke out at several theaters. It soon became clear, however, that these disturbances were the result of overbookings. The film was so popular that some theaters sold too many tickets, and fighting erupted when frustrated moviegoers could not get in to see the movie. As more theaters began to show the film, the violence subsided.

Having proved himself as a gifted and thoroughly businesslike movie director, Van Peebles went on to score an even greater success with his next movie, *Posse* (1993). A smash hit from the day it opened, *Posse* brought in more than $11 million in the first two weeks and quickly became one of the successes of the year.

Posse was hailed as Hollywood's first major black western, but Van Peebles objected to it being called a "black" western. "We have more white people in *Posse* than *Unforgiven* [Clint Eastwood's recent western] had black people, but they didn't call that a *white* western," Van Peebles protested. Nevertheless, he had deliberately used the film to spread the message of black involvement in the history of the West.

"There were a lot of things I wanted to do with *Posse*," he told a reporter. How many people know that one out of every three cowboys was black, or that of the forty-four first settlers in Los Angeles twenty-six were black? How many people know the very name 'cowboy' came from the fact that slave hands used to take care of the livestock, and they'd call them 'Boy'?"

As with *New Jack City,* Van Peebles gave himself a part in the movie, and he also gave his father a part. In recent years, father and son have acted together on several occasions.

Sarah Vaughan

Jazz singer
Born March 27, 1924, Newark, New Jersey
Died April 3, 1990, Hidden Hills, California

"Her control of her voice is phenomenal.... I know of no one who can move from a whisper to full volume in the course of a few notes and make the move sound less affected than Sarah Vaughan."—Martin Williams

W ith her rich, powerful voice, which extended over more than three octaves, Sarah Vaughan could have been an opera star, but instead she chose to sing jazz and pop songs—in her own unique way. Vaughan had a superb sense of music, and she used her voice like an instrument, singing around the main melody and improvising differently each time. She was the first female jazz singer to adapt to the improvising bebop style.

Writing in the *Saturday Review,* Martin Williams described the distinctive Vaughan style most aptly: "She can take a note at the top of her range and then bend it or squeeze it; she growls and rattles notes down at the bottom of her range; she can glide her voice over through several notes at mid-range while raising dynamics, or lowering, or simply squeezing." This type of experimental singing thrilled Vaughan's audiences.

During her forty-seven-year career, Vaughan received numerous awards, including an Emmy and a Grammy. Her most popular hits included "Misty" and "Broken-Hearted Melody." Another legendary jazz great, Ella Fitzgerald, called Vaughan "the greatest singing talent in the world today."

The young jazz fan

Sarah Lois Vaughan was the only child of Asbury Vaughan, a carpenter, and Ada (Baylor) Vaughan, a laundress. Both her parents were musical. Her father played the piano and guitar, and her mother sang in the choir at Mount Zion Baptist Church in Newark. Sarah joined her mother in the choir as soon as she was old enough, though she developed her unique singing style as a result of learning the piano and organ. "I learned to take music apart and analyse the notes and put it back together again," she later explained.

Sarah Vaughan

By the time Sarah was fourteen, she was a keen jazz fan and used to sneak into the bars in Newark to listen to the performers. At eighteen, just for the fun of it, she entered an amateur talent contest at the Apollo Theater in Harlem, singing her own rendition of "Body and Soul." To her surprise, she won first prize, which was ten dollars and a week's performance at the theater. During this week, she was heard by Billy Eckstine—who at the time was a singer with jazz pianist Earl Hines's band— and he recommended her to Hines. Thus, in 1943, at the age of nineteen, Sarah Vaughan began her career in show business. She had entered the jazz world so easily and so quickly that it took her some time to get used to the idea and develop from a shy teenager into a confident performer.

The road to success

Vaughan spent only a year with the Hines band, because in 1944 Billy Eckstine formed his own band and asked her to join it. In both bands Vaughan worked with trumpeter Dizzy Gillespie and saxophonist Charlie Parker, whose playing she began to imitate in her singing. Although she never had singing lessons, she was eager to learn phrasing and other skills, and she did so by listening to the players she most admired. Both Gillespie and Parker were impressed by her singing and did what they could to help her. It was through Gillespie that she obtained her first recording contract as a soloist, and in 1945, with Gillespie and Parker, she recorded "Lover Man," which brought her to national attention. Two other early successes were the singles "Don't Blame Me" and "I Cover the Waterfront."

In 1947, Vaughan married the trumpeter George Treadwell, who then became her manager and booked her to sing in New York and Chicago clubs. Treadwell spent several thousand dollars turning Vaughan into a polished and sophisticated soloist—buying her expensive gowns as well as arranging singing lessons and working on her musical arrangements. As a result of his efforts, Vaughan began to perform in the better clubs and soon gained a large number of fans. Every year from 1947 to 1952, she won *Downbeat* magazine's award for best female singer. Meanwhile, her record sales were averaging 3 million a year.

Nevertheless, Vaughan had the same problems as other black performers, especially on tour, when she could spend hours looking for a hotel or restaurant that would admit her. Often, white clubs did not provide her with a dressing room, and in one Chicago theater she was pelted with tomatoes because the audience had expected a white soloist.

The divine one

In 1953, Vaughan began to record pop songs as well as jazz, and over the next five years she had almost a dozen hits, including "C'est la Vie," "The Banana Boat Song," "Mr. Wonderful," "Smooth Operator," and "Passing Strangers." Her first million seller was "Broken-Hearted Melody," which was all the rage in 1959. During the same period, her most celebrated jazz recordings were "Lullaby of Birdland" and "April in Paris."

During the 1950s, Vaughan also had a brief film career, appearing in *Murder, Inc.* (1950), *Disc Jockey* (1951), and *Harlem Follies* (1955). As her fame grew during the 1960s, she appeared frequently on television and toured in Europe as well as the United States. In the 1970s, she toured South America, Japan, Africa, Australia, and England. Her fans called her "the Divine One."

Although Vaughan had personal problems in the course of four marriages, her professional life moved from strength to strength. While spending much of her time touring and playing in nightclubs, she also made guest appearances with the National Symphony Orchestra, the Los Angeles Philharmonic, and other prestigious orchestras. She performed privately for more than one president and was as popular at the White House as she was at jazz festivals.

One of Vaughan's greatest talents was her continuing inventiveness. Each time she sang a song, it seemed slightly different. It was this brilliance at improvisation that had first won her praise in her youth, and she was still surprising her audiences with her vocal experiments when she was in her sixties. As Will Friedwald pointed out, "It wasn't her staying power that amazed.... Rather, Vaughan amazed by continuing to find inspiration, while doing the same songs and the same routines year after year."

Denmark Vesey

Leader of slave insurrection
Born around 1767, West Africa
Died July 2, 1822, Charleston, South
  Carolina

"Vesey's example must be regarded as one of the most courageous ever to threaten the racist foundations of America."—Sterling Stuckey

R emember Denmark Vesey of Charleston!" was the battle cry of the first black regiment formed to fight in the Civil War. The war achieved what Vesey had so desperately striven for—the abolition of slavery. He had planned his own "war of liberation" in 1822, but his plans were revealed before the uprising could take place.

Vesey's actions were particularly courageous because by the time he planned his rebellion, he had already gained his freedom and was making a good living. But he had seen too much suffering—he hated slavery and slaveholders—and he was determined to free his people from the terrible oppression and cruelty. Like others who rose against the

system, Vesey was condemned to death and hanged. Yet his opponents could not kill his spirit. Vesey became a symbol in the struggle for freedom and an inspiration for later abolitionists, including John Brown.

The young slave

Denmark Vesey is thought to have been born in West Africa, where he was captured and taken as a slave to St. Thomas in the Danish West Indies. In 1781, when he was about fourteen, he was bought by a slaver called Captain Joseph Vesey, who was struck by his good looks and intelligence. Denmark, as he was called, was one of 390 slaves whom Captain Vesey brought from St. Thomas to Haiti, then a French colony called Saint-Dominigue. There the boy was sold and put to work in a sugar plantation.

Cutting and pulping sugar cane is hard and exhausting work even for a grown man, but Denmark did not remain at it for long. One day, he surprised his fellow slaves and annoyed his new master by falling to the ground in an epileptic fit. A slave who suffered from epilepsy was of little use on a plantation, so Denmark's master returned him to Captain Vesey when the captain next called at Saint-Dominigue. The boy was "unsound goods," he said.

Since Denmark was not suited to heavy labor, the captain made him his personal servant, and during the next two years Denmark saw many of the horrors of the slave trade as he sailed with the captain on his voyages between Africa and the West Indies. When in 1783 the captain decided to give up his slaving voyages and settle in Charleston, South

Carolina, Denmark went with him. He remained the captain's slave for the next seventeen years.

As a personal slave, Denmark Vesey lived a comparatively comfortable life—far better than slaves working on plantations—and he had a certain amount of freedom to come and go as he pleased. Nevertheless, he was still a slave, subject to the whims of his master, and his first thought when he won $1,500 in a lottery in 1800 was to buy his freedom. He paid his master $600, and with the rest of his winnings he set up a carpentry shop.

Planning the war of liberation

Vesey proved to be a highly skilled carpenter, and his business did so well that he grew quite wealthy. He became a minister of the African Methodist Church and, with his growing family of children and his comfortable house in Bull Street, he was viewed as a respectable member of the community. And so he was. But he had other things on his mind, too.

Since living in Saint-Dominigue in his youth, Vesey had followed the events there with interest, and he was thrilled when he heard about the great uprising of slaves in 1791. He was even more thrilled when the slaveowners fled and the black people of the former colony took control. In 1804, Saint-Dominigue became the independent nation of Haiti.

Here was a success story to fire the imagination. If the slaves of Saint-Dominigue could triumph over their masters, why not the slaves of South Carolina? Why not those throughout the South? Vesey was aware that previous attempts at rebellion had been put down mer-

cilessly, but the events in Haiti gave him new hope. As he thundered from the pulpit each Sunday, he began to sow the seeds of rebellion. He urged his congregation to break free from slavery, and he quoted verses from the Bible to give them encouragement. He spoke to workers in the plantations and on street corners, reading aloud from antislavery pamphlets written by whites. He even argued with whites who supported slavery—an activity that always drew an admiring and awestruck black audience.

As Vesey traveled from place to place spreading his message, the black people of the Charleston area began to look on him as a savior, and he had no difficulty gathering recruits when he started to organize his war of liberation. By 1822, he had a carefully arranged plan of battle and had chosen four dependable lieutenants: Ned and Rolla Bennett, who were slaves of the governor; Peter Poyas, a ship's carpenter; and Gullah Jack, who was widely believed to be bulletproof. Vesey had also gathered a supply of weapons, which he obtained from supporters in Haiti.

Vesey chose Sunday, July 14, as the day of the uprising, because the plantation hands could come to town on a Sunday without arousing suspicion. By the end of May, he and his four lieutenants had recruited a secret army of slaves and free blacks that numbered about nine thousand. They planned to strike at midnight, when they would seize the guardhouse and other key points, and block all the bridges. Meanwhile, a group of horsemen would gallop through the town killing whites to prevent them giving the alarm. Every detail was carefully worked out, and Vesey felt they stood a good chance of taking over Charleston.

The end of a dream

Knowing how loyal household slaves could be to their masters, Vesey had ordered that none should be included in the plot. But some house slaves did hear about it, and one of them told his master. The authorities immediately were on the alert. Vesey responded by pushing the date of the rising forward to mid-June, but no sooner had he informed his followers than this date was betrayed too. Suddenly, Charleston was bristling with soldiers, with patrols roaming the streets and guards at every bridge.

When Vesey realized that nothing could be done, he burned all lists of names and sent his followers home, but too many people knew who the leaders were. During the next few weeks, hundreds were rounded up, including Vesey, who was captured after a two-day search. He was condemned to death and was publicly hanged before an enormous crowd early in the morning of July 2. Although some of his followers were released, forty-three were deported and thirty-five were hanged.

The immediate effect of Vesey's insurrection was that life became far worse for the black population of South Carolina. In a panic, the State Assembly passed strict new laws limiting the movements of slaves and preventing free blacks from entering the ports. Yet the seed Vesey had sown did not die. A martyr in the cause of liberty, he inspired others to continue the struggle, and their efforts eventually did result in the abolition of slavery and the hope of a brighter future.

Charleszetta Waddles

Humanitarian
Born October 7, 1912, St. Louis, Missouri

"It's not me that's doing the good, it's God."

In Detroit, a dedicated woman declared a personal war on poverty. Since founding the Perpetual Help Mission in 1956, Mother Charleszetta Waddles has improved life for countless people, inspiring them with new hope and optimism as well as seeing to their material needs.

Back in the 1950s, when Mother Waddles first opened her mission, it was a very small operation centered in her basement, where she collected food to distribute to the hungry. Today, from her headquarters at 12479 Grand River in Detroit, she assists hundreds of thousands of people each year. Perpetual Help now includes ten urban missions, two of which are in Africa; and they not only offer food, they provide whatever type of assistance is needed—such as job training, counseling, arrangements for health care, or coping with an emergency by helping with the utility payments.

Despite the years of effort she has put into the mission, Mother Waddles believes that she herself is not the source of its good work. An ordained Pentecostal minister, she gives all the credit to her Maker. "It's not me that's doing the good, it's God," she says.

Born to help others

Even as a child, Mother Waddles was exceptionally thoughtful and caring. She was born

Charleszetta Lena Campbell, the oldest in a family of seven. Her lifelong commitment to helping others came partly from seeing the way her father, Henry Campbell, was treated when he was out of work. Having lost his job as a barber because he had not realized one of his clients had impetigo, he was then deserted by most of his friends.

Waddles has never forgotten the way people behaved when misfortune struck her family: "I watched the people in our church go from saying 'Come here, darling,' to 'Not now, I'm in a hurry.' And, boy, I felt that. I saw my dad go stand on corners, for hours at a time. And so many, many times, I saw my mother cry. When my father died, there weren't hardly any of those people from the church at his funeral."

Although Waddles was only twelve when her father died, she immediately left school because her mother, Ella (Brown) Campbell, had a heart condition and could not cope on her own. Waddles cheerfully took on the role of mother's help and principal wage earner. "It just didn't bother me," she said. "I had started doing little chores in the neighborhood and washing windows for people when I was nine years old and I would take food to the fair."

When Waddles was fourteen she had her own baby to look after, having married the teenaged Clifford Walker. Five years later Walker died, leaving his nineteen-year-old widow without support. By the age of twenty-one Waddles had married again, but although her second husband was much older, he proved to be very unstable. It was during this second marriage that Waddles moved to Detroit, where her husband found work. Although she returned to St. Louis to nurse her dying mother, she settled back in Detroit after her mother's death. By then she had nine children but no husband, for the marriage had broken down.

This could have been a gloomy time for Waddles as she and her children subsisted on welfare, but she remained cheerful and outward looking, thinking of others more than herself. Because of this attitude, and because of her deep religious faith, this difficult time in her life marked the beginning of something very wonderful.

Perpetual Help Mission

Waddles believes that she was called by God to set up her mission. In 1948, when she was thirty-six, she had a vision directing her to "create a church that had a social conscience, that would feed the hungry, clothe the naked, and take folks in from outdoors."

Charleszetta Waddles

At the time she was living in the basement of a friend's house and was already helping others through her local church. She was at a barbecue raising funds for the church when she met her third husband, Payton Waddles. "He got not only the barbecue," she recounts, "he got me and my nine children." Payton later gave her a tenth child, and until his death in 1980 he provided the support and love that made it possible for Waddles to run her mission. She believes Payton was sent by God to help her carry out her work.

Her work had a practical slant from the beginning. All who attended the prayer meetings she held in her basement were asked to bring a can of food from their shelves, and the food was given to families in need. In 1950 Waddles opened a "35 cent restaurant," where anyone could have a full meal for only 35 cents. The wealthy were welcome as well as the poor, and they too could eat for 35 cents, though they could pay more if they wished— and most did. Some people dropped in just for a cup of coffee and paid as much as three dollars. Whether the customers were poor or affluent, all were offered the same choice of food and the same elegant service: a menu, a flower on the table, a napkin, and silverware. Although Waddles had assistants to serve the food, she herself did all the cooking and laundry.

In 1956 she found a home for her mission in a store that was up for lease and was offering two months' free rent. Thus was the Perpetual Help Mission officially formed. From the first, it focused on taking an active role in solving people's problems, whether the problem was hunger, unemployment, personal worries, or even drug addiction. "I wanted a black, religious, charitable church, one that tended to the earthly things as well as to the heavenly things," Waddles has stated.

Over the years the mission has attracted thousands of supporters who have given everything from small cans of food to large donations of money. Waddles herself has been able to contribute some of the money because of the two best-selling cookbooks she has written. She has also written a book of philosophy and has published many of her weekly sermons, and the proceeds from them go toward the mission too.

Waddles's sermons stress such principles as the dignity of hard work and the belief that if people have a positive outlook they can do much to help themselves. She tries to instill this positive outlook along with the food and practical assistance her mission provides. "We've got to help them to help themselves," she says.

In 1989 the Public Broadcasting Service made a thirty-minute television documentary about Waddles titled *Ya Done Good*. She has also been the subject of articles in major magazines, including *Life,* which carried a story about her titled "A One-Woman War on Poverty." Others have shown their appreciation by bestowing honors on her. Waddles has received more than 300 awards and tributes, including the Humanitarian Award, presented by President Richard Nixon. Yet she still thinks of herself as a very simple person who is merely doing what is needed, in accordance with God's wishes. "I guess I'm just a nobody trying to tell somebody I'm somebody who loves everybody," she says.

Alice Walker

Writer
Born February 9, 1944, Eatonton, Georgia

"Black women are called 'the mule of the world,' because we have been handed the burdens that everyone else—everyone else—refused to carry."

With the publication of her third novel, *The Color Purple*, in 1982, Alice Walker gained wide recognition as one of America's most celebrated women writers. The book won the Pulitzer Prize for fiction and the American Book Award, and in 1985 was made into a film, which won several Academy Awards.

Since having her first poetry book published in 1968, Walker has produced a wide selection of work including novels, short stories, poems, essays, and literary criticism. She regards herself as a "womanist"—a black feminist—and much of her work focuses on the pain and problems women face in a sexist and racist society. Her unflattering portraits of men have drawn criticism from some quarters, but Walker maintains that she is committed to preserving "the wholeness of entire people, male and female." As her writings show, she is also strongly committed to preserving black culture.

Early life

Much of Walker's fiction is set in the South that she knows so well from her youth. She was the youngest of the eight children of Willie and Minnie (Grant) Walker, who were struggling sharecroppers in Georgia. Growing up in the small town of Eatonton, Walker was surrounded by the violence and racism that pervaded the South, where black people like her parents worked for a pittance in the fields while whites had control over virtually everything.

When Walker was eight, one of her brothers accidentally shot her with a BB gun, blinding her in one eye. The ugly scar tissue that formed over the eye made her feel self-conscious and shy, so that she became withdrawn and very much aware of other people's behavior. Going off to the fields by herself, she took to recording her observations in a notebook and spent many hours reading and writing poetry. Although Walker had an operation at the age of fourteen that successfully removed the scar tissue, the experience left a permanent mark on her character, and there

Alice Walker

was always the fear that she might somehow lose the sight in the other eye.

At school, Walker was a hard-working student, and in her final year she was chosen to be class valedictorian. Because of her partial blindness, she received a scholarship for handicapped students that enabled her to attend Spelman College, the prestigious college for black women in Atlanta. Arriving there in 1961, she was soon caught up in the civil rights movement and enthusiastically joined with other students in demonstrations and marches. But Walker found the rules at Spelman uncomfortably restrictive, and at the end of her sophomore year she moved to the more liberal Sarah Lawrence College in the Bronx, New York.

Poet and novelist

At the end of her first year at Sarah Lawrence, Walker went to Africa for the summer. That year, she also discovered that she was pregnant. She began writing the poems that formed her first book while she was desperately trying to decide what to do—whether to bring shame on her family with an illegitimate baby or to bring them misery by killing herself. With the help of friends, Walker was able to get an abortion, and from then on she wrote with renewed vigor, turning out poem after poem as she celebrated the fact that she was still alive and the crisis was over. The poems were on various subjects—Africa, the civil rights movement, love, and death—and they were published four years later as the book *Once* (1968).

After graduating with a bachelor's degree in 1965, Walker returned to the South, deter-mined to take an active part in the civil rights movement, which at the time was concentrating on voter registration. She spent the summer of 1965 in Mississippi, helping impoverished African Americans register to vote. In the course of her work she met Melvyn Leventhal, a Jewish civil rights lawyer, whom she lived with for a year in New York City and married in 1967. That fall they moved back to Mississippi, where they set a precedent by being the first legally married interracial couple in the city of Jackson.

Walker lived in Jackson for the next seven years, working briefly for a Head Start program, but spending most of the time writing. Her first novel, *The Third Life of Grange Copeland,* appeared in 1970. This story of male violence in three generations of a poor Southern family dealt with the two themes that dominate so much of Walker's writings— the effects of racism on family life and the suffering of women at the hands of men. Walker's first collection of short stories, *In Love and Trouble* (1973), explored similar themes, but her second novel, *Meridian* (1976), took a slightly different approach. Set against a background of the civil rights movement, this book was largely concerned with the role of black women as mothers. This was a subject very much on Walker's mind, since her daughter Rebecca was born just three days after she finished writing the novel.

In addition to these works of fiction, Walker brought out three books of poems during the 1970s, as well as writing a children's biography of Langston Hughes and compiling an anthology of the writings of Zora Neale Hurston, the Harlem folklorist. These were busy and exciting years for Walker. In 1972, she moved to Boston, having accepted a position as a lecturer in literature at Wellesley College and the University of Massachusetts. Then, in 1974, she and her husband moved back to New York City, where she became a contributing editor for *Ms.* magazine. However, her marriage was no longer running smoothly, and she and Leventhal were divorced in 1976.

The Color Purple

By the time Walker began work on *The Color Purple,* she was a very practiced writer, having produced ten books and contributed to numerous anthologies and magazines. She started writing the novel in New York City, before her divorce, and completed it the following year, after she had moved to San Francisco.

Told in a series of letters written in authentic Southern folk speech, *The Color Purple* tells the story of Celie, a Southern black woman who, as a teenager, is beaten and raped by her stepfather and who later marries a man who beats her simply because she is his wife. Yet this is an account of female strength as well as victimization, for Celie manages to overcome her degrading circumstances, having been given great support by her sister and a female friend.

When the book was published in 1982, it had tremendous impact. Peter S. Prescott in *Newsweek* called it "an American novel of permanent importance," and feminist Gloria Steinem announced, prophetically, that its publication "could be the kind of popular and literary event that transforms an intense repu-

tation into a national one." Walker did indeed become a nationally acclaimed figure. Even before she was awarded the Pulitzer Prize or the American Book Award, her novel topped the best-seller lists, and it remained on the *New York Times* best-seller list for six months. Meanwhile, Warner Brothers bought the movie rights for $350,000.

The following year saw the publication of *In Search of Our Mothers' Gardens: Womanist Prose,* a collection of essays that Walker had written during the previous fifteen years. While many of these pieces touch on personal matters about her own life, they are concerned with some of the same themes as *The Color Purple.*

Recent works

In 1988, Walker brought out *To Hell with Dying,* a book for young people based on the very first story she ever had published. It was about an old man who was saved from death many times by the love of his neighbor's children. That same year, Walker also published a collection of prose pieces, *Living by the Word,* and the following year saw the appearance of another novel, *The Temple of My Familiar.* This novel was rather different from her other books in that it went far back into history, exploring the relationship of species, races, and sexes. Walker described it as "a romance of the last 500,000 years."

As the years passed, Walker's interests have widened, moving from black women to the problems faced by all women, and from racism in the South to racism throughout the world. Similarly, her activism on behalf of civil rights developed into activism over world problems such as nuclear weapons. In 1982, she gave a powerful speech against nuclear weapons at a benefit held for the Women's Party for Survival.

Although Walker has long been in great demand as a speaker, she continues to devote much of her time to writing, and she began the 1990s with two more books: a collection of poetry, *Her Blue Body Everything We Know* (1991), and the novel *Possessing the Secret of Joy* (1992). While her work has drawn criticism for its controversial material, it has also received great praise, especially for the powerful portrayals of sexism and racism, political vision, and experimentation with dialogue. With the publication of each new book, Alice Walker continues to play an important role in the development of African American literature.

Madame C. J. Walker

Entrepreneur, philanthropist
Born 1867, Louisiana
Died May 25, 1919, Irvington, New York

"The girls and women of our races must not be afraid to take hold of business endeavors. I started in business eight years ago with one dollar and fifty cents. (Now I am) giving employment to more than a thousand women."

I t has been said that only in America can a cottonpicker become a millionaire, and occasionally you'll find someone who fits this saying. A case in point is Madame C. J. Walker. Born on a plantation, she spent her early years picking cotton and later juggled her career as a domestic with being a single parent. Faced with a life of few prospects, she turned to producing and selling hair preparations in the hope of becoming a businesswoman.

A short time later, Walker was a success. Blacks across the country bought her hair products, and at one time she had five thousand commissioned salespeople on hand. Walker demonstrated to other black women that they too could be successful if they took charge of their own lives.

Life on the plantation

Sarah Walker was born in 1867 in Louisiana to former slaves, Owen and Minerva Breedlove. She lived in a run-down shack with her parents on the Burney family plantation in Delta, Louisiana. Her parents worked as sharecroppers on the plantation until they died. Walker also toiled in the cotton fields, having sharp cotton bolls prick and cut her fingers as she worked from sunrise to sunset.

When she returned home from the field, things were no better. The house had only one door, no water, no toilet, and a dirt floor. After her parents died she moved to Mississippi with her sister Louvenia and her husband. Her brother-in-law began to abuse her, so at age fourteen she married Moses McWilliams and moved away. In 1885 they had a daughter, Lelia, and two years later, when Walker was twenty, her husband was killed by a lynch mob.

Since blacks had the best chance for employment and education in urban areas, Walker moved to St. Louis, Missouri, where she had relatives who helped her find work as a cook and a laundress. Although Walker couldn't read or write, she decided an education would be a top priority for Lelia. She sent her to Knoxville College, a private black college in Knoxville, Tennessee.

Her daughter was now looked after, but Walker suffered other troubles. She experienced hair loss because of the stressful wrap and twist method commonly used to straighten the hair of blacks. Walker used patented medicines and her own secret ingredient (supposedly sulfur) to stop her hair loss. Her hair quickly grew back, and her friends, seeing the results, became enthusiastic customers.

Black people needed methods for handling hair since most had no running water, supplies, or equipment. They usually carried in water from outdoors and had to place their body in an awkward position to shampoo it.

Madame C. J. Walker

Feeling there was a market, Walker developed a hot comb and her "Wonderful Hair Grower" solution. She decided to give up her life as a domestic and laundress and take a chance on becoming a businesswoman.

Hair preparation formula sells

Walker moved to Denver, Colorado, to live with her sister-in-law and her four nieces. She had one dollar and fifty cents in her pocket and used that to start her own hair preparation company. Her formula seemed to work well, so Walker and her relatives began filling jars and stashing them in the attic of their home. Six months after moving to Detroit, she married C. J. Walker, a newspaper man who knew how to market her product through advertising and mail order.

She had many disagreements with her husband because he felt she should be satisfied with making ten dollars a day. Walker was convinced that her hair preparations would fill a market need, and she eventually left her husband to further her dream of successfully operating her own business. Although they divorced, she continued to use the initials of his name. At this time whites called all black women by their first names, so black women frequently kept their first names a secret. That is why she was referred to as Madame C. J. Walker rather than Sarah Breedlove Walker.

Although many of Walker's inventions were not original ideas, they were improvements over existing models. She was the first woman to organize supplies for black hair preparations, develop a steel comb with teeth spaced to comb the strands of blacks' hair, send the products through the mail, organize commissioned salespeople, and develop her own beauty school.

Her daughter, Lelia, soon became her chief asset. She assisted in the manufacturing, helped with business decisions, and travelled across the country to sell the products. In 1906 Lelia was placed in charge of the mail-order operation, and she introduced the products to parts of the South and the East. In 1908 mother and daughter moved to Pittsburgh, Pennsylvania, and set up a beauty school. Lelia looked after production and the beauty school, while Walker continued to sell the products door-to-door. In 1910 she stopped in Indianapolis and decided its central location made it the ideal spot for the company's headquarters. At that time her company had five thousand black agents selling her products on a commission basis. They made over one thousand dollars a day, seven days a week, which was a large amount in those days. She continued to expand her distribution by recruiting and retaining her sales force of black women. Her agents taught other women to establish beauty shops in their homes and to learn techniques of book-keeping. By 1919, twenty-five thousand women called themselves Walker agents.

Overcomes illiteracy

Perhaps Walker's biggest challenge was to fight her own illiteracy. She surrounded herself with educators and lawyers to assist in her business transactions. For a while she wrote her name in an illegible script on checks and bank documents. When she became successful, she hired tutors to teach her to read and write. Her handwriting became so legible that the bank called her in to see if the signature was really hers.

Walker built a huge mansion on the Hudson River in Irvington, New York, which she named Villa Lewaro. There she entertained leaders of the black community with socials, soirees, and dinners. She never forgot her upbringing and contributed thousands of dollars to black charities and educational institutes. She also promoted the idea of black economic self-help, believing that if blacks could develop their own businesses, they could manage their lives. Due to these efforts, Walker became a source of inspiration, and all black women who were Walker agents were proud of her and of themselves. She gave hope for employment to many people and provided dignity to people concerned with their appearance. She helped open the door for black women to think of careers other than domestic work.

Walker died on May 25, 1919. Funeral services were held in the Villa Lewaro by the pastor of her church. She was buried in Woodlawn Cemetery in the Bronx.

Maggie L. Walker

Bank president
Born July 15, 1867, Richmond, Virginia
Died December 19, 1934, Richmond,
  Virginia

"If our men are so slothful and indifferent as to sleep upon their opportunities, I am here today to ask the women of North Carolina to awake, gird their armour and go to work for race uplift and betterment."

With less than fifty dollars in the bank and less than eighteen hundred members, the Independent Order of Saint Luke was facing insolvency until Maggie L. Walker became president. She turned the African American self-help organization's finances around, so much so that they eventually founded their own bank. Besides serving as the bank's president and later chair of the board, Walker was also editor of *The St. Luke Herald* and was active in many organizations that promoted black interests.

Education and encouragement

Walker was born on July 15, 1867, in Richmond, Virginia, to William and Elizabeth Mitchell, ex-slaves who worked in the Van Lew mansion. Walker was given a good education and was encouraged to pursue her own ventures. Her father decided there would be better opportunities in downtown Richmond, so he moved the family to a small clapboard house there.

William Mitchell found work as the head waiter at the Saint Charles Hotel before mysteriously disappearing. Five days later they dragged his body out of the James River, apparently a victim of robbery and murder. Walker's mother increased her laundry business, while Walker herself carried laundry for her mother's clients and looked after her brother. She grew up as one of two women who supported the family, and all her life she realized the virtues of her black sisters. In 1909 she spoke about this appreciation: "And the great all absorbing interest, this thing which has driven sleep from my eyes and fatigue from my body, is the love I bear women, our Negro women, hemmed, circumscribed with every imaginable obstacle in our way, blocked and held down by the fears and prejudices of the whites, ridiculed and sneered at by the intelligent blacks."

Walker led her class at Armstrong Normal and High School, a segregated institution in Richmond's public school system. She joined the Old First Baptist Church and became very active in the Thursday night Sunday-school meetings. She met a young contractor, Armstead Walker, at these meetings, and the two eventually married. She soon took charge of the Sunday school class and often spoke at churches.

At fourteen, Walker had joined the Independent Order of Saint Luke (IOSL). In 1886 when she married Armstead Walker, she stopped teaching to devote herself to her new family and also increased her activities in the order. Although it was basically an insurance company started by Mary Prout in 1867 in Baltimore, Maryland, the IOSL was created by blacks to help the sick and bury the dead during the post–Civil war period. It also encouraged self-help and racial solidarity. The order was a natural outlet for Walker's energies. She rose through the ranks from secretary of a Good Idea Council to a delegate to the annual convention in Petersburg, and finally to Grand Sentinel.

Right Worthy Grand Secretary of the IOSL

In 1890 the Magdelena Council, Number 125, was named in Walker's honor. Eventually she became Right Worthy Grand Secretary, succeeding William T. Forrester in 1899. She took over an organization in a tough economic situation. There was only $31.61 in the bank, a stack of unpaid bills, and only eighteen hundred members. Walker increased memberships through the formation of a department store and a bank. The *Richmond Times Dispatch* stated on August 23, 1924, that the IOSL had collected $3,480,540.19. But the order was more than just a financial success, the *Encyclopedia of Southern Culture* stated, "the Order demonstrated a special commitment to expanding the economic opportunities within the community in the face of racism and sexism."

With IOSL funds, Walker established *The St. Luke Herald* on March 29, 1902, to provide increased communications between the order and the local community, and to discuss black concerns. "The first issue espoused lofty ideals and came out foresquare against injustice, mob law, Jim Crow laws, the curtailment of public school privileges and the enactment of laws that constricted the roles of blacks in Virginia politics," explained Daniel Jordan in *Commonwealth*. Walker served as editor of the weekly for three decades.

In 1903 Walker decided the IOSL needed a bank to house the funds from its expanding operations and to help black people finance their own homes. By 1920, 645 black homes were paid for because of help from the bank, greatly improving the living conditions of blacks in Richmond. Walker was president until poor health caused her to retire in 1932, at which time she became board chair. She helped invent the bank's slogan,, which reflected her intention of keeping black people's money in black people's pockets: "Bring It All Back Home."

Walker encouraged children to save their money by providing small cardboard boxes in which to save pennies. When the pennies reached a dollar, the children were praised for opening bank accounts. Walker said in *Women Builders*, "Numbers of children have bank accounts from one hundred to four hundred dollars. They sell papers, cut grass, do chores, run errands, and work in stores on Saturdays."

Besides the IOSL, Walker was involved in other organizations that promoted racial improvement and education. She helped establish and maintain a community house in Richmond, secured a visiting nurse for blacks, and advised the Piedmont Tuberculosis Sanitorium for Negroes in Burkeville. She was active in many organizations to promote black interests, serving as founder and presi-

Maggie L. Walker

dent of the Council of Colored Women, cofounder of the Richmond branch of the National Association for the Advancement of Colored People (NAACP), vice-president of the Negro Organization Society of Virginia, and board member of several organizations, including the national NAACP, Colored Women's Clubs, National Urban League, and the Virginia Interracial Committee. She served in various groups, including the State Federation of Colored Women, the International Council of Women of the Darker Races, and the National Association of Wage Earners.

Walker also joined with other women in the community to fight for women's suffrage and voter registration. She was involved in the formation of the Virginia Lily-Black Republican Party, a splinter faction of the Virginian Republican party. They had their own platform and nominated their own candidates. Walker unsuccessfully ran for state superintendent of public instruction. She was also active in the National League of Republican Colored Women and handled their funds.

In 1907 Walker fell on the front steps of her home and severely damaged the nerves and tendons in her knees. During her last ten years she spent most of her time in an upstairs suite and on a window-enclosed porch from which she would greet neighbors. In 1915 Walker's husband died after one of their sons mistook him for a prowler on the porch and shot him. As her health deteriorated, Walker was confined to a wheelchair in 1928. Six years later, she died of "diabetes gangrene," according to her death certificate. Walker was buried on December 19, 1934, in the family section of Evergreen Cemetery.

Sippie Wallace

Blues singer and songwriter
Born November 1, 1898, Houston, Texas
Died November 1, 1986, Detroit, Michigan

"I would just be thinking it over in my mind, child, and it would just come to me to make a song about what was troubling me."

One of the leading blues singers of the 1920s, Sippie Wallace was known as "the Texas Nightingale." She had a smooth, strong voice, well suited to blues music, and could perform light, breathless pieces as movingly as sad, earthy laments. One of her specialities was the "shout," in which the singer repeats two lines of a song and then improvises a third.

Wallace composed most of her own songs, many of which are still popular. Like many other blues artists, she fell out of fashion in the 1940s and 1950s before experiencing a comeback in the 1960s. Since then, as a new generation of young people has discovered blues music, Wallace's songs have once again been popular and several have been hits.

Worked as assistant to the snakedancer

Sippie Wallace was born Beulah Belle Thomas, the fourth child of George and Fanny Thomas. When she was a small child, her brothers and sisters nicknamed her Sippie "because my teeth were so far apart and I had to sip everything." Sippie's parents were strict Baptists who did not approve of ragtime mu-

Sippie Wallace

sic, so her musical education centered on the local Baptist church in Houston, where she sang in the choir and played the organ.

By the time Sippie was a teenager, she was singing popular music, despite her parents' disapproval. Her older brother George planned to be a musician, and he often played ragtime and blues on the family piano while Sippie hummed along. George wrote his own songs, and Sippie joined him in his efforts, composing the lyrics for his pieces.

In 1912 George went to New Orleans to launch his musical career, and soon afterwards Sippie followed him. About two years later, when she was barely seventeen, she married Frank Seals—a mistake, she soon realized. While trying to get over the marriage, Sippie wrote "Adam and Eve Had the Blues," which she and George set to music. She later had a more successful marriage with Matt Wallace, though that too had its problems because of

his gambling. In the meantime, Sippie concentrated on breaking into show business.

The easiest way to get into show business at that time was by joining one of the traveling vaudeville troupes that performed throughout the South. This Sippie did, though she could not get taken on as a performer. She began her road show career as a maid and stage assistant to Madam Dante, a snakedancer. But whenever there was the opportunity, she sang at social gatherings so that she gradually became known as a singer. This tactic worked so well that before Wallace was twenty she was touring with the tent shows and was gaining wide fame as "The Texas Nightingale."

Rode a crest of popularity

While Wallace toured the small towns of the South building her reputation as a singer, her brother George was making his mark in Chicago as a composer and music publisher. In the early 1920s George sent for Wallace to join him so that they could write and record music together. Their younger brother Hersal also arrived in Chicago. Although Hersal was only about fourteen, he was already an accomplished pianist, and he often acted as Wallace's accompanist.

Working together, Wallace and her brothers soon produced a fine selection of blues numbers, including "Muscle Shoals Blues," which was a hit in 1922. Wallace then began to record with Okeh Records. From the first she had tremendous success, achieving several hits, including the singles "Shorty George" and "Up the Country Blues," which sold more than 100,000 copies.

Over the next few years Wallace recorded "Special Delivery Blues" (1926), "The Flood Blues" (1927), and other highly popular numbers. She was recognized as one of the top blues singers in the business and performed with such jazz greats as trumpeter Louis Armstrong. Splendid in her sequined evening gowns, Wallace could charm any audience, whether performing in a large theater or on a makeshift stage. People flocked to hear her, for her recordings had brought her a large number of fans throughout the South.

Yet all was not smooth sailing. Blues songs often tell of unhappiness, and Wallace had plenty. While she was at the height of her popularity in the 1920s, her success was blighted by personal tragedy. First, one of her sisters died. Then, in 1926, her younger brother Hersal died of food poisoning, and in 1928 her brother George was killed when he was run over by a streetcar.

In 1929 Wallace moved to Detroit, where she recorded "You Gonna Need My Help" and one of her most popular numbers, "I'm a Mighty Tight Woman." This was the last record she was to make for a long time. With the onset of the Great Depression, the small record companies went out of business or limited themselves to very few recordings. Moreover, blues was giving way to other forms of popular music. Wallace's stage bookings dwindled and then petered out, and by 1932 her career seemed to be over.

Wallace received a further blow a few years later when her husband died. But rather than giving up, she focused her energies in other directions—on family and church affairs. For the next thirty years she wrote and performed church music, taught her choir the songs she had written, and led them in spirituals and gospel songs. Meanwhile, she raised the three orphaned daughters of one of her nieces. Although Wallace was out of the public eye, she was not out of action.

Wowed audiences again—well into her eighties

In the 1960s blues made a comeback in the wake of rock and roll as the younger generation discovered the music of the 1920s. By this time Sippie Wallace was a senior citizen, but she had not lost touch with the music of her youth. During her years out of the limelight she had given the occasional nightclub performance, and she had also recorded a couple of singles. Friend and fellow blues singer Victoria Spivey now persuaded Wallace to come out of retirement and sing at the folk-blues festivals that were being held throughout the country.

Although Wallace was far older than most of her fellow performers, she was a tremendous success, and in 1966 she traveled to Europe with the American Folk Blues Festival. Her performance was as dramatic as ever. "Sippie Wallace astonished by the breadth of her singing," enthused one reviewer. That same year Wallace released the album *Sippie Wallace Sings the Blues,* in which she gave new renditions of several of her old classics, including "Trouble Everywhere I Roam," "Special Delivery," and "I'm a Mighty Tight Woman."

In 1971 Wallace's popularity received a further boost when the young white singer and guitarist Bonnie Raitt featured two of Wallace's songs on her debut album. Wallace then toured and recorded with Raitt as well as continuing to tour on her own. She kept up this schedule throughout the 1970s and into the 1980s. In 1982, when she was more than eighty years old, she made her last album, *Sippie*. She gave her last concert when on tour in Germany in 1986, just a few months before her death at the age of eighty-seven.

One of the highlights of this late-life career was Wallace's performance at the Lincoln Center's Avery Fisher Hall in New York City in 1980. Commenting on her tumultuous reception at the concert, the reviewer for *New York Times Magazine* wrote: "It's one of the program's bittersweet ironies that, of all the performers, it's probably the aging Sippie Wallace who's best known to audiences under thirty.… And yet it shouldn't be surprising that a young audience appreciated her—the blues, after all, is the root of both jazz and rock and roll."

Booker T. Washington

Educator
Born April 5, 1856, near Hale's Ford,
  Franklin County, Virginia
Died November 14, 1915, Tuskegee, Alabama

"Education ought to do more for a person than merely teach him how to read and write."

T he Tuskegee Institute, the world-famous center for agricultural research, was founded in 1881 by Booker Taliaferro Washington, who served as its principal for the next thirty-four years. During these years, Tuskegee grew from a tiny training school for black teachers to a busy campus that taught hundreds of students agriculture and manual skills.

Widely regarded as the black leader of his day, Washington took a conciliatory attitude toward civil rights, believing that well-paying jobs were more important than social equality. He believed that if blacks proved themselves to be industrious workers and law-abiding property owners, whites would of their own accord grant equality. While this attitude offended many black intellectuals, it was popular with whites, with the result that Washington was able to get the funding he needed to build Tuskegee into a thriving educational institution.

Born into slavery

When Booker T. Washington was four years old, he was listed by his owner, James Burroughs, as "1 negro boy, Mulatto" worth $400. Washington's father was a white man—probably one of the Burroughs family—and his mother, Jane, was a slave on the plantation. He was the middle of his mother's three children. He had an older brother, John, and a sister, Amanda.

As a child, Washington swept the yards and took water to slaves working in the fields, and he also carried the schoolbooks of one of the Burroughs children. He wished that he, too, could learn to read, and this became such an obsession that his mother scraped together the money to buy him a second-hand spelling book.

During the Civil War, Washington's mother married Washington Ferguson, who had also been a slave of the Burroughs family, and when they were freed in 1865, they settled in Malden, West Virginia. There, for the first time, Booker had the opportunity to attend school. But he was a student for only a few months before his mother died, and he had to get a job to help support the family. He found work in the salt furnaces and then in a coal mine, taking classes in the evenings. He was determined to get educated.

Washington had his first bit of luck in 1870 when, at the age of fourteen, he was taken on as a houseboy by the mine owner's wife, Viola Ruffner, who was a firm believer in education. She allowed him time for study. Mrs. Ruffner was to be a lasting influence on Washington, for she instilled in him her own strict beliefs about the importance of discipline, cleanliness, and the dignity of labor, all of which later became part of the educational system that Washington established at Tuskegee.

Student and teacher

While working for the Ruffners, Washington heard about the Hampton Institute, a school for blacks that had been established by the Virginia legislature. Intent on studying there, he gathered together his small savings and in 1872 set off on the 500-mile journey. Although only sixteen, he walked much of the way, taking odd jobs to help spin out his money. When eventually he arrived at Hampton, he had just fifty cents left.

During the next three years, Washington at last had the satisfaction of being a full-time student, though he also worked as a janitor to pay for his room and board. An exceptionally hard worker, he graduated with honors in 1875. He then spent two years teaching in Malden and one year studying at the Wayland Seminary in Washington, D.C., before returning to Hampton as a teacher.

It soon became apparent that Washington was a talented teacher. With his great enthusiasm for learning, he found it easy to inspire his students. His main work was with American Indian students, for whom he organized a program of training, but he also found time to set up a night school. He was the obvious choice when the head of the Hampton Institute was asked to recommend a teacher to be principal of the new normal school that the Alabama legislature was establishing for black students. The school was to be located at Tuskegee, Alabama, and called the Tuskegee Normal and Industrial Institute.

Booker T. Washington

Principal of Tuskegee Institute

When Washington arrived at Tuskegee in 1881, he found that no preparations had been made for the school. Although the legislature had promised a grant of two thousand dollars, the money had not yet been provided and consequently no land had been bought. There were thirty students to teach, but no building to house them in. Washington gave his first classes in a shanty donated by a black church.

Soon he was able to rent some land, and bit by bit the classrooms were built—often by the students themselves. Over the years, Washington had to spend a great deal of time on fund-raising, but he succeeded in persuading Andrew Carnegie and other rich industrialists to make generous donations. As a result, Tuskegee Institute grew and prospered. By the time of Washington's death in 1915, it was a well-endowed college with two hundred staff members, some two thousand regular students, and another two thousand students taking extension courses.

From the first, Washington stressed the importance of practical training. Students learned math and building skills by figuring out the cost of a building and then actually constructing it. This emphasis on manual skills met the approval of the industrialsts who were funding Tuskegee and who wanted well-trained workers. They also approved of the way Washington emphasized obedience and discipline.

Washington was no social reformer, and therefore whites were comfortable recognizing him as a spokesman for black Americans. He was in great demand as a speaker, his most memorable speech being one in Atlanta in 1895, at the opening of the Cotton States and International Exposition. By stating his view that blacks should not demand equality but should be content simply to be earning good money, he drew the wrath of many black intellectuals, though he pleased the whites in the audience. In fact, Washington did want equality, but he believed that it would come in due course, and he was not prepared to rock the boat to get it.

This was not the only time Washington found himself involved in a dispute. At Tuskegee, he was very much a "one-man band," insisting that everything be done his way. Some of the staff left, unable to submit to his dictatorial attitude; others stayed for many years. One of his greatest successes was in luring the renowned scientist George Washington Carver to Tuskegee as director of agriculture. Carver's pioneering work greatly added to the reputation of the institute.

Washington the man

Washington outlived two wives and was married to his third wife at the time of his death. All of his wives were closely involved in the running of Tuskegee. Although his lack of activism over civil rights has been criticized by later generations, he did what he thought best for the times. He could not have built up the institute so successfully if he had not had the trust of so many influential whites. As well as gaining the support of powerful millionaires who poured money into Tuskegee, he helped set up the National Negro Business League, which had the backing of Theodore Roosevelt and other presidents.

Washington was also greatly respected by his students, many of whom were given their start in life at Tuskegee. When Washington died, they built him a brick tomb overlooking the Tuskegee Institute.

Denzel Washington

Actor
Born 1954, Mt. Vernon, New York

"I enjoy acting. This is when I feel most natural. This is really my world. I was obviously destined to get into this, and I decided to get into this, and I guess I have the equipment to do it."

There are very few black, romantic leading men in Hollywood, but Denzel Washington may be on the verge of changing that. As an actor blessed with good looks and a wide range of talent, Washington has forged a solid career of highly regarded performances. His characters have varied from the smoldering Private Peterson in *A Soldier's Story* to the cooly understated Steve Biko in *Cry Freedom* to the screen-dominating *Malcolm X*. His performances have earned him an Academy Award and an Obie Award, and great respect among his peers.

High school in upstate New York

Washington was born in Mt. Vernon, New York, and grew up on the edge of the Bronx. His father was a pentecostal minister and his mother was a beautician. Washington was a good student and had friends from many different ethnic backgrounds. His parents divorced when he was fourteen, and it was a difficult transition for him. He began getting into fights. A guidance counselor suggested that he apply to a private boarding school in upstate New York. Although the school was mainly for very rich whites, Washington applied and received a full scholarship. After graduating, he entered the pre-med program at Fordham University in the Bronx. Finding pre-med unsatisfactory, he drifted through several majors including biology and journalism. He also took an acting workshop, but wasn't convinced that acting would be his career.

During the summer recess Washington worked as a counselor at a YMCA-sponsored camp. One night he organized a talent show and someone told him he was a natural actor and that he should consider becoming a professional. He liked the idea, and when he returned to Fordham in the fall, he auditioned for the university's production of Eugene O'Neill's *The Emperor Jones*. He won the part over a number of theater majors and went on to star in several more dramas at the university, including Shakespeare's *Othello*.

Robinson Stone, a retired actor, was Washington's drama instructor at Fordham. In an interview with the *Chicago Tribune* he said, "He was thrilling even then. Denzel was from the Bronx campus—not even a theater major—and he got the lead role in the school production of *Othello*. He was easily the best Othello I had ever seen, and I had seen Paul Robeson play it. I remember Jose Ferrer came to look at it. He and I agreed that Denzel had a brilliant career ahead of him. He played

Denzel Washington

Othello with so much majesty and beauty but also rage and hate that I dragged agents to come and see it."

Lands a role in *Wilma*

Word of Washington's ability spread, and he was offered a small role in the television drama, "Wilma," which was based on the life of runner Wilma Rudolph. After he received his degree, he worked on a variety of film, television, and theater projects. Early in his career, Washington appeared opposite George Segal in *Carbon Copy,* a comic movie, and later played a role in the television mini-series "Flesh and Blood." Soon afterward he was cast as Dr. Philip Chandler in the television drama "St. Elsewhere," a role he played for five years to good reviews. *Washington Post* writer Megan Rosenfeld said Washington's role gave him "the kind of popular recognition that is both the boon and the curse of serious actors. Chandler is an intelligent and

ambitious young man, portrayed not as a black paragon, but as a human being with all the flaws and problems of anyone else."

Early in the 1980s, Washington returned to the stage to play the role of Private Peterson in *A Soldier's Play.* He received an Obie Award for his off-Broadway performance, and he was invited to portray Pederson in the film version. Washington took a break from "St. Elsewhere" to play the role. Washington turned in a solid performance as the young private goaded to murder by an abusive drill sergeant. Bob Thomas, a *Chicago Tribune* writer, stated Washington was "one of the most versatile of the new acting generation."

Good reviews, coupled with his good looks, dignified personality, and his ability to look at ease despite being in a comedy or drama, seemed to augur well for his future. Unfortunately, his race limited the number of roles he received. Even after he appeared in the Oscar-nominated role of activist Steve Biko in *Cry Freedom,* he did not receive many job offers. In 1989 he told the *Washington Post* that he found himself, "waiting for an opportunity to come [my] way but realizing there's no group of people like [me] who are successful, who can give you the faith to say, 'well, if I wait, it will come.' So you end up taking [roles] ... that are not necessarily the best, that aren't optimum."

The role of Trip

When Washington was first approached with the role of Trip, a runaway slave in the film *Glory,* he considered it less than optimum. The original screenplay concentrated on Robert Gould Shaw, a Civil War general who led the first black regiment into battle and died with them in an unsuccessful assault. Washington requested that the screenplay be rewritten to explore the life of the black foot soldiers. He accepted the revised script and took the role of Trip. He studied the history of the Civil War and slavery in the South, and decided to portray his character as a man in a fit of controlled rage. His performance earned him an Academy Award for best supporting actor in 1990. It was his second nomination and only the fifth Oscar ever won by a black actor.

After winning an Oscar, he began receiving more leading-man roles. He appeared in dramas such as *For Queen and Country*, and Spike Lee's *Mo' Better Blues*, and in such comedies as *Heart Condition*. He also received critical acclaim in the 1993 movie *X*, in which he portrayed slain activist Malcolm X. Kathy Huffhines, a *Detroit Free Press* movie critic, says Washington has "the knife's edge intensity that makes quick, deep impressions. Usually, actors begin with comic, romantic or action roles, then move toward seriousness. Washington is taking that trip in reverse, keeping serious roles while trying to move toward romance, action and comedy."

It is difficult to predict if Washington will receive romantic leading-man roles, since Hollywood seems reluctant to offer such roles to black men. He has had few roles in love stories to date, but as a dynamic and riveting actor, he should win more. If he does, he could become a groundbreaking star who paves the way for future black actors.

Despite his public career, Washington likes to keep his private life private. He avoids the Hollywood party circuit, preferring to stay at home with his family. He married Pauletta Pearson, an actress, in 1983, and they have two children, John David and Katia. He told the *Washington Post* that "acting is just a way of making a living. Family is life. When you experience a child, you know that's life."

Faye Wattleton

Organization executive, reproductive rights activist
Born July 8, 1943, Saint Louis, Missouri

"The women who came to my hospitals under less than dignified circumstances were not affluent. That girl in Harlem who died was not affluent.... That's when I became aware of the political significance of these people. If they really cared about equity and fairness in life they would say that as long as abortion is legal in this country, poor people should have the same access as the rich."

As a young nurse, Faye Wattleton saw first hand the importance that access to abortion meant for young, poor women. Many of these women disfigured or even killed themselves in back alley abortions because they could not afford a legal abortion. These experiences caused Wattleton to join the Council of Planned Parenthood Federation of America (PPFA). In time she became its president, seeking equal access to abortion for poor women, lobbying for mandatory sex education programs, and struggling to keep family planning on the national agenda. Wattleton is now viewed as one of the most influential black American women in the field of reproductive rights.

Aimed national spotlight on reproductive issues

Wattleton was born on July 8, 1943, in Saint Louis, Missouri, to George, a factory worker, and Ozie, a seamstress, Wattleton. Her family was very poor but stressed the importance of helping those less fortunate. At sixteen she entered Ohio State University Nursing School in Dayton, Ohio, and two years later she received a college degree. Her first job was as a maternity nursing instructor for the Miami Valley Hospital School of Nursing in Dayton, Ohio.

In 1966 Wattleton moved to New York to study at Columbia University, and a year later she received an M.S. in maternal and infant health care, with certification as a nurse-midwife. While a student, she interned at Harlem Hospital, where she came across a beautiful seventeen-year-old girl who died after her mother tried to induce her to abort by inserting a Lysol douche into the girl's uterus. Later that year Wattleton moved to back to Dayton to become a consultant and assistant director of Public Health Nursing Services in the City of Dayton Public Health Department. She joined the local Planned Parenthood board and at the age of twenty-seven became its executive director.

During her tenure the number of clients tripled and the budget increased from less than $400,000 to just under $1 million. In 1973 Wattleton married Franklin Gordon, a social worker who was raised in Roxbury, Massachusetts. Two years later she was not only a

mother but was also the chairwoman of the national executive director's Council of Planned Parenthood Federation of America (PPFA). Three years later she became PPFA president. She was the first black, first woman, and youngest person ever to head the organization.

Wattleton's first task was to bring PPFA back onto the national agenda. By this time Planned Parenthood had lost most of its attraction among middle and upper-class women. Most of the clients were poor or blue collar workers. Wattleton attempted to rally support for the cause by appearing on radio and television talk shows, including "Good Morning America," "World News Tonight," "Today Show," and "Nightline." Talk show host Phil Donahue called her "a talk show host's dream guest" because she got to the point and was always well informed.

Fighting the Hyde Amendment

One of her toughest battles was against the Hyde Amendment, passed in 1977 to "prohibit the use of any federal funding for abortion, unless the life of the mother was endangered." This decision meant that hundreds of thousands of women could no longer have their abortions paid for by Medicaid. Wattleton argued that poor people, like the rich, should have access to a full range of health care services.

"The women who came to my hospitals under less than dignified circumstances were not affluent," she told *New York Times Magazine.* "That girl in Harlem who died was not affluent.... That's when I became aware of the political significance of these people. If they really cared about equity and fairness in life they would say that as long as abortion is legal in this country, poor people should have the same access as the rich."

Under Wattleton's leadership, Planned Parenthood began a series of newspaper and television advertisements geared towards educating teens, parents, and public school officials on the financial and human costs of runaway teen pregnancy. She also coauthored the book *How to Talk to Your Child about Sex,* which sold more than 30,000 copies. Another issue she fought was the fact that by 1989 no major television network would accept contraceptive advertising, and only seventeen states and the District of Columbia required sex education in their schools. Wattleton saw these messages as contradictory: television often promotes sexual promiscuity, yet school systems and network programs do not educate teenagers on its hazards.

As she increased her time PPFA activities, Wattleton's personal life began to slide. Even though she commuted from New York to Dayton on weekends to be with her husband, Franklin Gordon, and their daughter, her marriage began to dissolve. In 1981 the two divorced, but Wattleton maintained a calm and rational demeanor. It is these qualities that Wattleton has used to inspire supporters and disarm opponents. John Willke, a medical doctor and president of the National Right to Life Committee, told *Savvy Woman* that Wattleton was "an attractive and articulate spokesman for her cause." Journalists have also commented on her appearance. The *New York Times Magazine* described her "immaculately tailored, carefully maintained surface" and

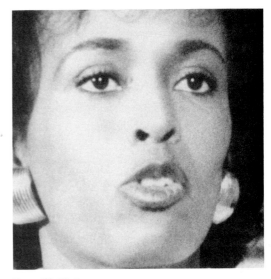

Faye Wattleton

went on to state that she "wears a pale mauve leather suit with a deep purple silk tank top. Her fingernail polish matches her suit."

Furious over recent Supreme Court decision

Wattleton has won many awards for her activities. In 1980 *Savvy* named her one of the country's outstanding nonprofit organizations. Four years later she was named to the Young Presidents' Organization. In 1986 she received the American Humanist Award, the World Institute of Black Communication's Excellence in Black Communications Award, and the Women's Honors in Public Service from the American Nursing Association. She has also received the Independent Sector's 1987 John Gardner Award, the 1989 Congressional Black Caucus Humanitarian Award, the Better World Society's 1989 Better World Population Medal, and the American Public Health Association's 1989 Award of Excellence.

Wattleton belongs to many organizations, including the National Academy of the Sciences' Institute of Medicine's Study Committee on the Role of State and Local Public Health Departments, the advisory committee of the Women's Leadership Conference on National Security, and the President's Advisory Council on the Peace Corps. She is also a board member of the Ohio State University Alumni Association and the National Urban Coalition.

The PPFA has grown to 21,000 volunteers and staff across the country. With a $300 million budget, the organization provides medical and educational services to nearly 4 million Americans through 178 affiliates in 47 states and the District of Columbia. It also serves an additional 4 million people in the developing world through its international division, Family Planning International Assistance.

The biggest challenge to PPFA is the Supreme Court's decision on July 3, 1989, that gave states the right to limit access to abortion. Although the decision may have caused many leaders to admit defeat, Wattleton told the *New York Times Magazine* that "my commitment and my determination is in no way diminished. I am furious as can be."

In a *Savvy Woman* interview in mid-November, Wattleton stated she was unsure of how long she would remain as president. She said, "Whoever is providing leadership needs to be as fresh and thoughtful and reflective as possible to make the very best fight." Her only complaint is that her demanding schedule leaves little time for her daughter. She spends a great deal of time on the road, lecturing and appearing on television and radio talk shows and usually working at least twelve hours a day. She reserves the weekends for herself and her daughter.

André Watts

Pianist
Born June 20, 1946, Nuremberg, Germany

"It's possible I have inner wounds, but as a result of these experiences, you have feeling within you, certain emotions that come out when you play."

The only child of an African American father and a Hungarian mother, André Watts is one of America's most gifted pianists. He burst on the scene in 1963 when CBS-TV aired a concert at which he performed with the New York Philharmonic Orchestra under conductor Leonard Bernstein. Watts was only sixteen at the time. Since then he has played with major orchestras throughout the world.

Noted for his fiery temperament and emotional playing, Watts is especially admired for his impeccable technique. His large hands, with their strong, long fingers can span twelve keys, enabling him to play octaves with the utmost ease, thundering out the notes as nimbly as he handles rippling runs. He is particularly celebrated as a performer of works by Franz Liszt and Frédéric Chopin.

In childhood, practiced three or four hours a day

André Watts is the son of a career soldier, Sergeant Herman Watts, who was stationed in

Germany after World War II. André's mother, Maria Gusmits, was living in Germany at the time, and after the couple met and married they stayed on until Sergeant Watts completed his tour of duty in 1954.

Watts was eight years old when his parents returned to the United States, and he was already showing talent as a musician. His mother, who came from a musical family, started him on the piano at the age of five. Since he did not take to it willingly, she bought him a miniature violin, which he learned to play by the time he was six. At seven he again took up the piano, and this time discovered he enjoyed it. "Soon I knew I preferred the piano," he has said. "I had the hands for it and I was more at home at the keyboard."

Watts's parents settled in Philadelphia, where Watts took piano lessons at the Philadelphia Musical Academy, studying under the noted teacher Genia Robinor. He made such remarkable progress that when he was nine he performed as a soloist, playing a Haydn concerto, at one of the Philadelphia Orchestra's Children's Concerts. The following year he again performed with the Philadelphia Orchestra, playing a Mendelssohn concerto at the Robin Hood Dell summer concert. This was followed by several more appearances in Philadelphia during the next few years.

A lot of hard work lay behind these concert performances. From an early age, Watts practiced for three or four hours each day, as well as going to school like any other child. He attended private elementary schools and a Roman Catholic high school, before enrolling at Lincoln Preparatory School. When he graduated in June 1963, around the time of his seventeenth birthday, he was already a celebrity, having recently hit the headlines.

Career as concert pianist earned many prestigious honors

Two concerts in January 1963 had brought Watts sudden fame. The first was a televised Young People's Concert performed with the New York Philharmonic Orchestra on January 12 and broadcast three days later. At this concert Watts played Liszt's Concerto no. 1 in E-flat so skillfully that he was hailed as a genius. A music critic who heard him play the same piece at a recital a week later enthused, "Only a prodigy could have amassed the technique and musical insight at the age of sixteen as were demonstrated at this recital."

Watts confirmed this reputation at his next major concert—a concert he performed through a lucky accident. Reknowned Canadian pianist Glenn Gould had been scheduled

André Watts

to play at a subscription concert at New York's Philharmonic Hall on January 31, but he fell ill two days before the performance. Who could replace such a major pianist at short notice? The New York Philharmonic's conductor, Leonard Bernstein, immediately thought of Watts, who had played the Liszt concerto so brilliantly a few weeks earlier. As a result, Watts became the first black soloist to play at a regular concert of the New York Philharmonic since the turn of the century. His performance was again masterly, winning a standing ovation from both audience and orchestra.

Watts was invited back for further concerts that season, and he also played at the Hollywood Bowl in September. He then enrolled at the Conservatory of Music of the Peabody Institute in Baltimore, Maryland, where he studied part time for the next two years. During these years Watts performed relatively few concerts—he devoted most of his time to study and practice—but whenever he performed he always drew packed audiences. Of all the young American concert musicians, he was one of the top box-office attractions.

In 1966 Watts made his debut in Europe with a concert in London, England. He then went on to the Netherlands, where he was a tremendous success. After further successful performances in the United States and Canada, Watts returned to Europe in 1967 and for the first time gave a concert in the land of his birth. In June 1967, around the time of his twenty-first birthday, he gave two concerts with the Berlin Philharmonic Orchestra under guest conductor Zubin Mehta. As usual, it was Watts's technique that impressed his audience as much as the fiery passion of his playing. "The chains of trills were never heard so quick-marching and clear," reported the newspaper *Die Welt*. "The octaves fell like cataracts but with machine precision."

Throughout these years Watts practiced for about six hours each day and continued to study periodically at the Peabody Conservatory, where he was taught by Leon Fleisher. Although Watts's technique was superb, he was aware that he needed to improve the musicality of his playing. With Fleisher's help, he gradually did so, and in 1973 Watts himself began to teach the piano as a member of the faculty of the Berkshire Music Center at Tanglewood.

Meanwhile, Watts's concert performances continued. In 1973 he made a U.S. State Department tour to the Soviet Union as a soloist with the San Francisco Symphony Orchestra. In 1976, at the Avery Fisher Hall in the Lincoln Center in Washington, he gave the first solo recital ever to be broadcast live on national televesion. For ten years he appeared in the "Great Performers" series at the Lincoln Center.

Watts has received many honors over the years, including an honorary doctorate of music from Yale University and the Gold Medal of Merit (1982) from the National Society of Arts and Letters. One of his most precious honors is one he received from Africa—the Order of Zaire—which was presented to Watts in 1970 by the president of Zaire, Sese Seko Mobutu, after Watts performed for him and other dignitaries at a state dinner.

Keenen Ivory Wayans

Comedian, filmmaker, writer, actor
Born 1958, New York, New York

"In order to see images black people are yearning to see, blacks must be in control. We need more black creative writers, more black directors, producers, etc..... I don't think it's fair to rely on studios to represent [us]. They are all owned by corporations, not individuals like [top box-office draw] Eddie Murphy."

Some call it outrageous, some call it racist, others call it sexist. But no matter what you call it, *In Living Color* is one of the most popular shows currently on television. In the forefront of the show is writer, host, and producer Keenen Ivory Wayans. He began his career as a standup comic before writing and producing several successful films. His unique style caught the attention of the fledgling Fox Television Network, which offered him his own show. The result, *In Living Color,* has set the Hollywood establishment on edge with its no-holds-barred humor.

Started as a standup comic

Wayans was born in 1958 in New York City to Howell and Elvira Wayans. His father was a salesman and his mother was a social worker. After attending Tuskegee Institute, Wayans worked as a standup comic at clubs in New York and Los Angeles. In 1989 he worked with Robert Townsend on the acclaimed feature *Hollywood Shuffle.* It documented the experiences of many black actors when they try to break into the entertainment industry and are typecast as muggers, pimps, and street punks.

The next year Wayans was the writer and producer of *Eddie Murphy Raw*, which became the highest-grossing concert film ever. He finally showcased his own comic talents in 1989 in the self-written and self-directed film, *I'm Gonna Git You Sucka!* Wayans told *Interview* that he was "not satirizing black people, but bad moviemaking. The inspiration came from [the 1980 farce] *Airplane!*" United Artists, which produced the film, believed the movie would offend black audiences and limited its release in larger cities. Wayans thought the film would initially attract a black audience, but eventually cross over to appeal to whites. Although he argued with United Artists officials to give it wider distribution, his arguments fell on deaf ears. "I could have set myself on fire, and it wouldn't have changed their minds," Wayans said in an *American Film* interview. "I think [the studio was] unfair and that we were treated with a lot of callousness. There are times when you ask yourself, 'What does a black man have to do?' But you have to channel those feelings into something productive."

In 1989 an executive at the newly formed Fox Television Network saw an advance screening of *I'm Gonna Git You Sucka!* and was impressed with Wayans's writing and delivery. He offered Wayans his own television show, but he wasn't interested, feeling television did not offer him enough opportunity to showcase his talents. Fox executives continued to offer him the show, and finally he decided to take it.

Wayans presented Fox with his sketch show, *In Living Color*. It premiered in 1990, and it was immediately clear that this was different from other sketch-comedy shows like "Saturday Night Live" and "SCTV." The show featured an interracial cast, but the format was geared toward black Americans. It poked fun at many influential blacks such as Jesse Jackson, Oprah Winfrey, and Arsenio Hall and didn't pull many punches with its humor. In one sketch, "The Equity Express Card: Helping the Right Sort of People," a successful black man is treated like a criminal when he tries to use a charge card. Wayans introduces each week's installment.

Making an impact

Right from the beginning, *In Living Color* made an impact on the viewing audience. *TV Guide* described the show as having "a wicked political edge." Harris Katleman, a Fox executive, was also quoted in the same article: "Two years ago, no one would have aired *In Living Color*. It's too different, too ethnic, and brings up too many issues that standards and practices [the network term for the censors] has never had to deal with before." In 1990 the show received an Emmy Award for outstanding comedy/variety series.

Not everyone has been impressed with the series. *In Living Color* has faced charges of homophobia, racism, and sexism. Wayans has denied many of these charges, but has acknowledged that some elements of the show could be sexist. In *Newsweek* he said, "I'll admit my sensibilities probably are slanted toward a more male point of view.... If the show picked only on one group, I could un-

Keenen Ivory Wayans

derstand people being uptight. But we get *everybody*." However, Wayans does have a line he won't cross—he won't do AIDS or crack jokes.

Wayans is a member of Hollywood's so-called "Black Pack"—a group of comics and writers including Eddie Murphy, Arsenio Hall, Robert Townsend, and Spike Lee. The group reportedly meets on occasion to network and hone their material. Some have heralded this group as evidence of a new black influence in the entertainment industry. Wayans dismisses this type of talk. "This town [Los Angeles] has not embraced the black creator," he told *People*. "How can I explain this? You can't look at four or five guys as a wave, you know? That's not even a ripple in the water. Compared to the days when there were zero, that's a significant step. But it's only a step. It's not like we're off and running. It's not like Hollywood is going 'Come on down!'" Wayans emphasizes that there should be more black creative writers, directors, and producers in order to change the thinking in Hollywood.

Until this change occurs, Wayans is content to continue producing *In Living Color*. It is the culmination of a lifelong dream he has had to be the center of attention. "When I was six and saw Richard Pryor on TV, I said, 'That's what I want to do.' Damon [his brother] and I used to do things like go out in character as the homeboys. It would flip people out."

As for his personal philosophy on life, Wayans equates his situation with a Jake LaMotta fight scene in the 1980 film *Raging Bull*. "[It's when] LaMotta is fighting Sugar Ray Robinson, and he's just getting beaten to a pulp," he told *People*. "At the end of the round, he walks over and his face is bloody and he says, 'I never went down, Ray. I never went down.' He knew he couldn't win, but he wasn't going to let this guy beat him. His objective was to stay on his feet. As far as his attitude was concerned, he was victorious. That's the kind of attitude I have."

Ida B. Wells Barnett

See **Barnett, Ida B. Wells**

Phillis Wheatley

Poet
Born 1753 or 1754, West Africa
Died December 5, 1784, Boston,
    Massachusetts

"In every human Breast, God has implanted a Principle, which we call Love of Freedom; it is impatient of Oppression, and pants for Deliverance."

Taken from her home in Africa and sold as a slave at the age of eight, Phillis Wheatley was America's first black woman poet and the second woman in America to publish poetry (the first being the English-born Anne Bradstreet).

Wheatley's poetry attracted considerable attention, and her fame spread from New England to Europe—though not on account of the quality of her work. The main interest was that the poetry was written by a black woman. A later age paid more attention to the poems themselves, but criticized Wheatley for writing in the conventional English manner and accepting the values of her white owners instead of expressing her own feelings. More recently, scholars have taken a closer look at Wheatley's work and have argued that it is far more original than it seems and that it does express her feelings, criticizing slavery and oppression in many subtle ways.

Slave of the Wheatleys

It is thought that Wheatley was by birth a member of the Fulani tribe from the extreme west of Africa in what is now Gambia and Senegal. Kidnapped and brought to New England in 1761, she was put on sale at the slave market in Boston, where she was bought by John Wheatley as a present for his wife, Susanna. The Wheatleys called the little girl Phillis because that was the name of the ship that brought her from Africa.

As a household servant, Phillis Wheatley received far better treatment than slaves on plantations in the South. Her room was well heated, she was well fed and well clothed, and was taught to read and write. When she proved to be a bright student, she was given a thorough education, which included Latin and some of the classics. By the time Wheatley was a teenager, she was far better educated than most other women in Boston. She was also a devout Christian, having been carefully instructed in the Bible.

The Wheatleys delighted in showing off Phillis Wheatley to their friends, whom she was free to visit whenever she liked. She also paid occasional visits to her black friend Obour Tanner, who lived in Newport, Rhode Island. In many ways, Phillis was treated like one of the family, yet the fact remains that she was a slave. Although the Wheatleys were caring, kindly people, Phillis Wheatley was totally dependent on their whims.

The young poet

Wheatley started writing poetry when she was about twelve, and her first poem was published in the *Newport Mercury* when she was fourteen. She wrote mainly in heroic couplets, which strongly reflected the style of Alexander Pope, one of her favorite poets.

Many of Wheatley's poems were elegies or verses addressed to famous figures. Her best-known early work was an elegy she composed on the death of George Whitefield, the evangelical preacher. Published as a pamphlet in 1770 and distributed on both sides of the Atlantic, it attracted the attention of the Countess of Huntingdon, who arranged for a col-

Phillis Wheatley

lection of Wheatley's poems to be published in England. This book, which was published in 1773, was given the title *Poems on Various Subjects, Religious and Moral. By Phillis Wheatley, Negro Servant to Mr. John Wheatley of Boston, in New England.*

In the summer of 1773, shortly before the book was published, the Wheatleys sent Phillis Wheatley on a trip to England. There she had a marvellous time. She was treated as a celebrity, entertained by the aristrocracy, and given a copy of Milton's *Paradise Lost* by a future Lord Mayor of London. When Wheatley's book came out shortly afterwards, the English reviewers had high praise for it, but upbraided John Wheatley for keeping the poet as a slave. As a result, he gave Wheatley her freedom in the fall of 1773.

Phillis Wheatley stayed on with the Wheatleys and continued to write poetry, though she had difficulty getting her work published from then on. This was partly because her patron, Mrs. Wheatley, died in 1774, but the bigger problem was the outbreak of the Revolutionary War. In those troubled times, people had more on their minds than poetry.

The following year the Wheatley household moved to Providence, Rhode Island, to get away from the turmoil in Boston. Like many other New Englanders, Wheatley was aglow with patriotic fervor in the struggle for independence, and she wrote to George Washington in 1775, enclosing the poem "To His Excellency General Washington." This poem is one of the earliest ever written in praise of Washington, and it hails him as a "great chief, with virtue on thy side." Some scholars have seen this as a personal poem in which, beneath the surface, Phillis Wheatley was writing about freedom from slavery. Washington wrote her a polite thank-you letter, saying, "If you should ever come to Cambridge, or near headquarters, I shall be happy to see a person so favored by the muses."

A change of fortune

Phillis Wheatley's life with the Wheatley family came to an end in 1778, when John Wheatley died and the household was broken up. One month later, she married John Peters, a free black Bostonian. Peters has been variously described as a lawyer, a grocer, a baker, and a doctor, and he may have tried all those professions. It is said that under the title "doctor" he sometimes served as a lawyer, pleading the cases of blacks who had been called before a tribunal. However, he most often had no job at all and had great difficulty supporting his wife and the three children she bore him.

For a short while after their marriage, Wheatley stayed with a niece of the Wheatley family in Wilmington, Massachusetts, though this was largely to avoid the fighting in Boston. By the end of 1779, she was back in Boston, trying to find a publisher for her collection of thirty-three poems. She never did get the collection published, though she did succeed in having two long poems printed as pamphlets in 1784. One was an elegy to Samuel Cooper, and the other was *Liberty and Peace,* an ode celebrating the end of the Revolutionary War.

By that time, Wheatley was on her own. Her marriage had not been a happy one. Two of her babies had died, and her husband had left her without providing any means of support. The whites who had made such a fuss over the "sable muse" when she was with the Wheatleys now did little to help. Only ten years after being lionized in London, Phillis Wheatley was friendless and alone. She spent her last days working as a scullery maid in a rooming house and died at the young age of thirty-one.

L. Douglas Wilder

Governor of Virginia
Born January 17, 1931, Richmond, Virginia

"I am concerned about the direction this country is headed. I have the vision, experience and fortitude that is necessary to help reverse this dangerous trend and put this great nation of ours on the right track again."

From a poor and segregated area of Richmond, Virginia, L. Douglas Wilder rose up through the political ranks to become state senator. The grandson of slaves, Wilder works in an office that is just a few blocks away from where the old White House of the Confederacy once stood. Yet race was not the chief issue in his election campaign. Wilder won for his support of a woman's right to an abortion. His media campaign cast the issue in terms of government intervention and personal privacy, and it illustrated Wilder's abortion rights views by using such symbols as the American flag and Thomas Jefferson's Monticello. "As a boy," he told *News Leader,* "I read the writings of ... Abraham Lincoln about freedom and equality, and I knew they were referring to me. My victory fulfils all of the dreams that could be dreamed by any person."

Served in an integrated army

Wilder was born on January 17, 1931, in Richmond, Virginia, to Robert, a salesman and supervisor of agents for a black-owned insurance company, and Beulah Wilder, a homemaker. Wilder used to help the family by shining shoes, delivering papers, and waiting tables. He attended the all-black Armstrong High School, where he acted in plays, was a sergeant in the cadet corps, and earned good grades.

After high school Wilder attended Virginia Union University, a private all-black school in Richmond. He studied chemistry and waited on tables to pay for tuition. He overheard the racist jokes made by white patrons while he waited tables. He eventually became so out-

L. Douglas Wilder

raged that he told the *Washington Post* he half-seriously considered "sprinkling poison in the salads" of these diners.

In 1952 Wilder graduated from university and was drafted into the army to serve in the Korean war. Since the army was desegregated by presidential order, it was Wilder's first experience in an integrated environment. In 1953 he and another soldier dodged enemy fire to hurl smoke grenades into a North Korean bunker at Pork Chop Hill, capturing nineteen enemy soldiers in the battle. Wilder was promoted to sergeant and won the Bronze Star for heroism.

Returning to the United States, Wilder applied for a job as chemist-technician for the state of Virginia. He was told the job was not available, but he could become a cook at a state school for troubled boys. It was a humiliating experience. When the U.S. Supreme Court issued its 1954 *Brown v. Board of Edu-*

cation decision outlawing segregation of public schools, Wilder said his faith in the system was restored. The ruling also prompted him to attend law school.

With no Virginia law schools open to blacks, Wilder attended Howard University in Washington, D.C. His roommate, Henry Marsh, who later became Richmond's mayor, told the *Washington Post:* "Doug was one of the more outstanding members of the class. He was articulate and intelligent. He had a lot of skills." In 1959 Wilder returned to Richmond to open a law practice. He soon became known for his fancy convertibles, trendy clothes, and for winning difficult criminal defense trials.

First black ever elected to Virginia State Senate

In 1969 Wilder announced his intention to seek election to a vacant state senate seat. Although no black had ever been elected to that body, Wilder, a Democrat, won a three-way race with less than 50 percent of the vote. Over the next sixteen years he was never opposed in his reelection bid for the seat.

Wilder made his first state senate speech in February 1970, calling for an end of the state song, "Carry Me Back to Old Virginia." The song glorified slavery and was offensive to blacks, he said. His bill never passed, and the song remains Virginia's official, if rarely sung, anthem. The debate immediately established Wilder as one of the chief spokesmen for black Virginians.

Over the years Wilder earned a reputation as an astute politician who used his personality, sense of humor, and clout with black voters to become entrenched in the senate's inner circles of power. In 1982 Democratic Governor Charles Robb wanted to nominate Owen Pickett, then a member of the state House of Delegates, to run for the U.S. Senate. Wilder felt Pickett was too conservative, so he announced his intention to run against Pickett as an independent. Wilder's threat ended Pickett's intentions of running.

By 1985 Wilder was a committee chairman and ranked among the five most influential senators. Later that year he announced his bid to become the lieutenant governor of Virginia. Many Democrats felt the public would not want a black in this position and that Wilder's defeat would bring down the rest of the Democrats on the statewide ticket. Wilder believed he could win and rented a station wagon to visit each of the state's ninety-five counties. His personal approach worked—in a state where only 19 percent of the voting population is black, Wilder beat his Republican opponent, 52 percent to 48 percent. He was the first black candidate ever elected to statewide office.

Since the lieutenant governor's job had limited duties, Wilder concentrated on politics. He drew praise from conservatives after urging blacks to assume more responsibility for eliminating social problems in the black community. In 1989 Wilder was in such a strong position to run for governor that only Democratic state senator Daniel W. Bird, Jr., of Wytheville offered a challenge for the party's nomination. He withdrew early, allowing Wilder to be unanimously nominated.

Conducted abortion rights gubernatorial race

In the general election Wilder faced Republican J. Marshall Coleman. Abortion became the overriding issue of the campaign. Coleman's staff included activists from antiabortion organizations, and Wilder's media consultants came from a national abortion-rights group. Wilder campaigned hard in white neighborhoods, especially in the rural regions of southern Virginia. He spent a record $7 million; most polls placed Wilder comfortably in the lead. When the votes were finally counted, he beat Coleman by only 6,741 votes.

As governor Wilder gained a reputation for being secretive in the way he conducted matters in Richmond, vengeful toward his adversaries, and inconstant in his political agenda. But some have also praised him for trimming the state's budget and cutting the bureaucracy during a recession in early 1990. "Instead of rasing taxes," *Time* correspondent Laurence I. Barrett wrote, "(Wilder) deftly shaved expenses without cutting major arteries. He also created a $200 million contingency fund as a buffer against a 1992 deficit."

On September 13, 1991, Wilder announced his intention to seek the 1992 Democratic presidential nomination. He soon came under fire for vague policy promises and for Virginia's weakening financial situation. In January 1992 Wilder withdrew his candidacy, saying it was too difficult to act as governor and conduct a presidential campaign at the same time. Some analysts felt he withdrew because of a lack of voter confidence and because he had less than a $1 million campaign treasury. His term as governor ends in 1994, and Wilder announced his intention to run for fellow Democrat Charles Robb's seat in the U.S. Senate in the 1994 elections.

Roy Wilkins

Civil rights activist
Born August 30, 1901, St. Louis, Missouri
Died September 8, 1981, New York, New York

"We have believed in our Constitution. We have believed that the Declaration of Independence meant what it said. All my life I have believed these things, and I will die believing them."

Head of the National Association for the Advancement of Colored People (NAACP) for more than twenty years, Roy Wilkins was an instrumental figure in the ending of segregated schools. He used every constitutional means possible to enable black Americans to enjoy the same rights as white citizens. Because of Wilkins's involvement and the involvement of many men and women of his generation, the NAACP is widely regarded as one of the most prestigious and influential black civil rights organizations in the United States.

Arrested for marching in Washington

Wilkins was born on August 30, 1901, in St. Louis, Missouri, to William and Mayfield Wilkins. His mother died when he was young and his father became an alcoholic, so he was sent to St. Paul, Minnesota, to live with his uncle Sam and aunt Elizabeth Williams. Wilkins said his uncle "was the warmest, kindest man I have ever met. Over the years he taught me that the world was not the universally hostile place my own father had taken it to be; that a man could get along if he had faith in the goodness of other people, kept his eye peeled for their weakness—and believed in himself." Wilkins had similar respect for his aunt and remembered that she taught him the value of an education.

In St. Paul the color of Wilkins's skin was not an issue; people cared about character. He excelled in high school and served as president of the Literary Society and editor of the high school paper, *The Cogwheel*. Then he attended the University of Minnesota, supporting himself with a variety of odd jobs. He also worked as night editor of the college paper, the *University Daily,* and edited a black

Roy Wilkins

weekly. He became interested in the Urban League and the NAACP, organizations dedicated to improving black civil rights. After receiving his B.A. in 1923, he joined the staff of the *Kansas City Call,* a leading black weekly.

Wilkins left the paper in 1931 to become the NAACP's assistant secretary in New York City, and he became more active in the cause for black rights. In 1934 he was arrested for participating in a march in Washington, D.C., protesting the failure of the attorney general to include lynching on the agenda of a national crime convention. Later that year he succeeded W.E.B. Dubois as editor of *Crisis,* the NAACP's national magazine.

Headed the NAACP and pursued vigorous course

In 1945 Wilkins served as an adviser in the War Department and was a consultant to the American delegation at the United Nations conference in San Francisco. He became acting executive secretary for the NAACP in 1949 for a year's term, and he also chaired the National Emergency Civil Rights Mobilization, a pressure group that sent numerous lobbyists to Washington, D.C., to campaign for civil rights and fair employment legislation.

He and the NAACP experienced an incredible sense of accomplishment on May 17, 1954, when the U.S. Supreme Court overturned, in *Brown v. Board of Education,* the fifty-eight year old *Plessy v. Ferguson* ruling that permitted separate but equal facilities for whites and blacks. The Court ruling ended segregation in public schools and heralded the end of legalized segregation nationwide.

Wilkins became the NAACP's executive director in 1955. He believed the NAACP had "become the oldest, wiliest, and best-organized civil rights group in the country." When Rosa Parks was arrested in Montgomery, Alabama, for refusing to give up her seat on a bus, the NAACP took up her case and won. They also successfully defended Autherine Lucy, who was refused admittance to the University of Alabama.

Many white intellectuals were cautioning blacks to go slow and give whites some breathing space, but Wilkins wanted to keep the pressure on. He believed that only strength and persistence were effective against racism. Wilkins depended on the courts, and especially the Supreme Court, to serve the Constitution. He also testified before innumerable congressional hearings, conferred with all the Presidents, and wrote extensively for many publications.

Praised by a new generation of black Americans

Wilkins steered the NAACP down a more militant course during the 1970s. At the annual meeting of the black National Newspaper Publishers Association in 1971, for example, he criticized President Richard Nixon's policy on housing discrimination as a "timid tightrope walking act of the greatest kind." He challenged President Nixon to exert more "positive federal power" to help blacks move to the suburbs in search of jobs. "The issue of the 1970s now appears to be whether the black population will be able to move into the suburbs in pursuit of jobs that are moving to the suburbs," he declared. Although Wilkins and

the NAACP were taking tougher stances, he and his organization were attacked by more radical groups, such as the Black Muslims.

For several years Wilkins chaired the Leadership Conference on Civil Rights, a group composed of more than 100 national civic, labor, fraternal, and religious organizations. He was a trustee of the Eleanor Roosevelt Foundation, the Kennedy Memorial Library Foundation, and the Estes Kefauver Memorial Foundation. He also served on the board of directors of the Riverdale Children's Association, the John LaFarge Institute, and the Stockbridge School, as well as Peace with Freedom—an international organization working toward the goals described in its name.

Among the accomplishments that occurred while he was at the helm of the NAACP was that the term "Negro" became a "dirty" word. "There's no word in the English language," he once said, "that couldn't be considered a white man's word." He later added that on the positive side, "Two of the best words are 'freedom' and 'liberty'. 'Negro' is not the bad word. 'Hatred' is the bad word and 'hatred' and 'enslavement'."

Wilkins received many honorary degrees and numerous awards, including the Spingarn Medal from the NAACP in 1964; the Freedom Award, 1967; the Theodore Roosevelt Distinguished Service Medal, 1968; the Presidential Medal of Freedom, 1969; the Zale Award, 1973; and the Joseph Prize for Human Rights, 1975. In 1972, Jesse Jackson, director of Operation Push, joined other militants who increasingly praised Wilkins. Jackson told the NAACP convention that blacks need both the vitality of groups like the Black Panthers and the wisdom of Wilkins.

Toward the end of Wilkins's life, younger black Americans reappraised their view of Wilkins and acknowledged the many positive things the NAACP accomplished for blacks during his leadership. Wilkins retired from the NAACP in 1977 and spent his remaining years in declining health.

In 1978 an article in the *Atlanta Daily World* claimed that Wilkins had worked in an undercover operation with the FBI in an attempt to discredit Martin Luther King, Jr. Joseph Lowery, president of the Southern Christian Leadership Conference, called this claim a vicious effort on the part of the FBI to weaken the civil rights movement.

Wilkins died quietly in New York City on September 8, 1981. President Ronald Reagan ordered American flags flown at half-mast on all government buildings and installations. *Newsweek* magazine said about Wilkins, "He was among the last of a generation of civil rights leaders who pulled and tugged and cajoled the nation through decades of change so profound that many Americans cannot imagine, still less remember, what segregation was like."

Daniel Hale Williams

Surgeon
Born January 18, 1856, Hollidaysburg,
  Pennsylvania
Died August 4, 1931

he late 1800s were an exciting time in medicine. Louis Pasteur was experi-menting with bacteria, and Joseph Lister was creating new antiseptics. Daniel Hale Williams was keenly interested in these new techniques and used them to revolutionize the medical practice. In 1893 he became the first physician to successfully perform open-heart surgery by operating on a patient who was stabbed in the heart.

Williams was also responsible for creating new opportunities for black doctors and nurses by opening Provident Hospital in Chicago, the first interracial hospital in the United States. He also served as the chief surgeon for the Freedmen's Hospital in Washington, D.C., and greatly improved its operating conditions. He later helped form the National Medical Association, a medical association for black doctors.

Barbering a family tradition

Williams was the son of Daniel and Sarah Williams. His grandfather was a preacher and owned a barbershop. His father carried on the barber business and was a civil rights activist who crusaded for better education among blacks. He was also active in the Equal Rights League, which sought to gain equal rights for blacks after the Civil War. On Williams's maternal side, his grandmother had been a slave who lived on the same plantation in Maryland as orator and abolitionist Frederick Douglass. Williams's mother claimed black, white, and Indian ancestry.

Soon after the family moved to Annapolis, Maryland, in 1867, Williams's father died of tuberculosis. His death caused the family to break up, and Williams was sent to Baltimore to live with a family friend and apprentice as a

Daniel Hale Williams

shoemaker. The ten-year-old Williams hated shoemaking and ran away from home. He received a railroad pass from an agent who had been a friend of his father. Williams took the train to Rockford, Illinois, to join his mother and sisters. He quickly learned the barber trade, and then found work in Edgerton and later Janesville. After graduating from high school, he briefly studied law, before apprenticing in the office of Dr. Henry Palmer, a widely respected physician who had directed the largest military hospital in the country during the Civil War.

Williams was twenty-two when he went to work with Palmer. At this time, very few physicians received formal training at a medical school. Most served as apprentices and then formed their own practice. Williams served with Palmer for two years and then decided in 1880 to attend Chicago Medical School. He graduated three years later and opened his own practice in Chicago.

The field of medicine was making rapid advances at this time. Louis Pasteur in France was laying the foundations of bacteriology by investigating the relationship between certain microorganisms and specific diseases. Joseph Lister in England was applying Pasteur's theories by using antiseptics to kill germs when treating wounds. Williams was keenly interested in these techniques and scrubbed his clinic with soap and water. He also sprayed carbolic acid, a strong germ killer, and sterilized all his instruments in hot water and steam to reduce the chances of infection.

Williams's reputation as a capable surgeon spread, and he accepted a position with the surgical staff of the South Side Dispensary in Chicago. He also became a clinical instructor and demonstrator in anatomy at the Chicago Medical College. One of his students was Charles Mayo, who went on to found the renowned Mayo Clinic. During the late 1800s Williams became the City Railway Company's first black surgeon, and he was appointed to the Illinois State Board of Health.

Founds Provident Hospital

Although black doctors could not gain admission to hospitals or receive hospital appointments, Williams starting working on establishing an interracial hospital. In January 1891, he established the Provident Hospital and Training School Association, where young black doctors could practice and nurses could train. When the hospital opened, 7 of 175 applicants were accepted for the eighteen-month nurses' training program. But by 1893 the hospital was threatened with closure due to tough economic times. Black leader

Frederick Douglass attended the World's Columbian Exposition in Chicago that year and urged blacks to contribute to the hospital. The money raised kept the hospital in operation.

Williams gained a national reputation later that year for saving a man's life. James Cornish was stabbed in a fight and rushed to Provident Hospital with a one-inch wound in his chest near his heart. Williams decided to put his surgical reputation on the line by operating. Without the benefit of X rays, blood transfusions, or antibiotics, Williams opened the patient's chest cavity and saw the knife had penetrated the heart about a tenth of an inch. The pericardium (the sac that surrounds the heart) was also cut. Williams decided the heart muscle didn't need sewing, but he sutured the pericardium. It was the first time a surgeon had successfully opened and explored the chest cavity. Cornish remained in the hospital for fifty-one days, but it was clear sailing after that. He lived for another fifty years, outliving his surgeon by twelve years.

Shortly after the operation, Williams was appointed chief surgeon at Freedman's Hospital in Washington, D.C. It had been established after the Civil War to serve the medical needs of the black community, but it had fallen on hard times. While preparing to move, Williams was wounded in the leg while on a quail hunting trip in southern Illinois. The wound became infected, and his friend, Dr. Christian Fenger, treated him for six months. Williams arrived in Washington in 1894 looking tired and frail.

The hospital facilities were not in much better shape. The wards were five wooden buildings that were built as emergency barracks. Funding was low, the patient death rate was high, and there were no trained nurses on staff. Williams reorganized the hospital into seven departments, established pathology and bacteriology divisions, and introduced modern surgical methods. To overcome the hospital's image as a facility only for the poor, Williams started holding open clinics in surgery. He lectured and allowed the public to observe operations in an amphitheater. By 1896 Freedman's Hospital was admitting five hundred surgical cases a year and had one of the lowest mortality rates. Dr. Williams A. Warfield, a student and Williams's eventual successor, had high praise for Williams. "Before Dr. Williams came to the hospital in 1894, there was no real surgical department. It can be said that with the arrival of Dr. Williams, surgical development began in all forms, especially abdominal. He was laying the foundation for more and better surgical work. By the time he left the hospital, a great impetus had been given to all branches of surgery."

Leaves Freedman's Hospital

Williams resigned from Freedman's in 1898, married Alice Johnson, and returned to Chicago to work at Provident Hospital. In 1899 he conducted annual surgical clinics at Meharry Medical College in Nashville, which eventually led to that city's first interracial hospital. Around this time he met Booker T. Washington, the president of Tuskegee Institute and an influential black leader of the time. Williams was in Atlanta to organize the National Medical Association, an alternative organization for blacks, who at the time were restricted from participating in the American Medical Association. Williams became the NMA's first vice-president.

In 1912, Williams became associate attending surgeon at St. Luke's Hospital, Chicago's largest, wealthiest, and most important hospital. He served until his retirement from medicine, and then lived for several years with his wife in northern Michigan. In 1926 he suffered a stroke that left him partially paralyzed. He died on August 4, 1931.

John A. Williams

Writer
Born December 5, 1925, Jackson,
  Mississippi

"The plain, unspoken fact is that the Negro is superfluous in American society as it is now constructed. Society must undergo a restructuring to make a place for him, or it will be called upon to get rid of him."

A superb storyteller and one of the best African American novelists of his generation, John A. Williams gained international recognition with the publication of his novel *The Man Who Cried I Am* (1967). Fifteen years later he again produced a masterpiece with *!Click Song* (1982), which won the American Book Award.

Williams is the author of more than 20 books, including various works of nonfiction, yet he is not as widely known as some writers of lesser talent. Williams puts this down to racial discrimination—a major theme through-

out his works—but the writer Ishmael Reed has another explanation: "John A. Williams can write circles around those permanent token writers who are so beloved by the critical and academic bureaucracy.... But Williams will never become a permanent token, for not only does he write well, he tells the truth in a society which prefers that its permanent slaves lie to it."

Won—and lost—the Prix de Rome

Raised in Syracuse, New York, John Alfred Williams is the son of John and Ola Williams. His father was a laborer, and higher education seemed out of the question when Williams was growing up. But because of his service in World War II he was able to obtain funding to complete high school after the war and then to study journalism at Syracuse University. He graduated with a bachelor's degree in 1950.

Williams did his war service in the navy, serving in the Pacific, where he experienced all the racism that was then rife in the military. As he pursued his career in journalism and publishing, he came across many other forms of racism, which he later exposed in his novels. Williams began his career in public relations, then worked for radio and television in Hollywood, and then went into publishing in New York City, where he was publicity director for vanity publisher Comet Press (1955–56) and assistant to the publisher at Abelard-Schuman Ltd. (1957–58). During this period he wrote two novels. One has never been published, but the other was published as *The Angry Ones* in 1960.

The Angry Ones (which was reprinted in 1975 under the title *One for New York*) drew on many of Williams's own experiences. It is the story of a young African American who has difficulty finding a job in New York City and ends up working for a vanity publisher. Racism is an underlying theme throughout the book, as it is in Williams's second novel, *Night Song* (1961). Based on the life of the great jazz player Charlie Parker, *Night Song* attracted considerable attention. It was considered such a good novel that Williams was named winner of the American Academy of Arts and Letters' Prix de Rome, which included a sum of money and a year in Rome. But in fact Williams never received the prize.

At the time, Williams was the divorced father of two boys, and he was about to marry a white woman, Lorrain Isaac. He mentioned this detail at his interview with the director of the American Academy—and shortly afterwards he was informed that he would not, after all, get the Prix de Rome. It was given

John A. Williams

instead to poet Alan Dugan. Dugan courageously exposed the whole affair during his acceptance speech at the awards ceremony, thereby sparking such a scandal that the Academy had to discontinue the prize.

This brought Williams some satisfaction, and he even got to Rome because he spent the early 1960s traveling through Europe and Africa as a correspondent for *Ebony, Newsweek,* and other magazines. After his marriage to Lorrain Isaac in 1965, he settled back in the United States as a university teacher. Over the years he has taught at several universities, including Rutgers, where he was appointed professor of English in 1979. He has also been an interviewer for the "Newsfront" program on National Education Television.

Wrote best-selling novel *The Man Who Cried I Am*

Whether Williams was traveling as a journalist or teaching at a university, he continued to write novels, bringing out a book every few years. He published *Sissie* in 1963, followed in 1967 by his powerful best-seller, *The Man Who Cried I Am.* This is a chilling story of an African American writer, Max Reddick, who discovers a government plot to round up all the black people in the United States and put them in concentration camps. Reddick is dying of cancer as the story unfolds, and the cancer destroying his body is paralleled by the cancer of racism corrupting American society. Williams believes very strongly in the message he is communicating through this novel. He has said, "The plain, unspoken fact is that the Negro is superfluous in American society as it is now constructed. Society must undergo a restructuring to make a place for him, or it will be called upon to get rid of him."

Williams's next two novels, *Sons of Darkness, Sons of Light* (1969) and *Captain Blackman* (1972), also are dark and despairing. The former is a story of militancy and murder, the latter is about a black soldier in Vietnam and the difficulties faced by black soldiers throughout history. But next came two novels that were more upbeat: *Mothersill and the Foxes* (1975) and *The Junior Bachelor Society* (1976), which was made into the television movie *Sophisticated Gents* in 1981.

Undoubtedly the most powerful novel of Williams's later years is *!Click Song* (1982), a story about two writers who have long been friends. One is Jewish and the other is African American. Whereas the Jewish writer wins awards and has a successful literary career, the African American struggles to make a living. Yet his life is far happier and more fulfilling than that of his successful friend, who commits suicide at the beginning of the book. *!Click Song* is so totally absorbing and so well constructed that Williams's next two novels, *The Berhama Account* (1985) and *Jacob's Ladder* (1987), seem anticlimactic. Yet they are extremely readable like all his books, including his works of nonfiction.

Williams's nonfiction books include *Africa, Her History, Lands, and People* (1962) and *If I Stop I'll Die: The Comedy and Tragedy of Richard Pryor* (1991). One of his most controversial books is *The King God Didn't Save: Reflections on the Life and Death of Martin Luther King, Jr.* (1970), which criticizes the civil rights leader's philosophy. Williams has also collected the writings of others, which he has published in several editions of *The Angry Black,* and he has contributed stories and articles to numerous anthologies. An extremely versatile writer, he is above all a storyteller—the type of writer whose stories live on in memory for years after one has closed the book.

Montel Williams

Television talk show host
Born about 1956, Baltimore, Maryland

"You'd think this is something you'd see in another type of show, but in the way we format our field pieces, there's time for conversation, time for discussion, time for questions. I think our viewing audience wants to see a little difference."

With his shaved head and imposing six-foot, two-inch and 210-pound stance, Montel Williams has become a recognizable personality on television. Although he is best known as host of the *Montel Williams Show,* a talk show that looks at serious issues without being sensational, he is also well known as a former motivational speaker and intelligence agent. Williams also helped form the Reach the American Dream foundation, which assists underprivileged children.

Living near the dump

Williams is the son of Herman and Marjorie Williams and grew up in a large black ghetto of Baltimore called Cherry Hill. "We lived three blocks from the dump," Williams told the *Washington Post*. "My parents were poor, but they worked very hard to give us the appearance of a lower-middle class lifestyle." His father worked three jobs and eventually became the city's commissioner of transportation, while his mother often held two jobs.

During his teenage days, Williams spent his summers working at a McDonald's restaurant during the day and playing with a band at night. After graduating from Andover High School in Linthicum, Maryland, in 1974, he decided to become a full-time musician. His band, Front Row, made quick money by playing in clubs around the city, so Williams put further education on the back burner. He applied to some colleges, but didn't pursue it. Then two band members were arrested, and the band dissolved.

Williams considered two options. He could either go to a vocational technical school to learn a trade or join the military, as many other young blacks were doing. He decided to enlist in the navy, and within six months, he received two meritorious promotions. When boot camp ended, Williams became the first black to be accepted into the U.S. Naval Academy Preparatory School. Forty marines entered the program in 1976, and Williams was one of only four to graduate. He stayed with the U.S. Naval Academy and earned a bachelor's degree in engineering with minors in international security affairs and Mandarin Chinese in 1980.

Williams became a special intelligence officer and traveled across the globe on top-secret missions. He later learned Russian at the Defense Language Institute in Monterey, California. The Russian skills coupled with his mastery of Chinese made Williams an invaluable officer. During his military career, he was decorated nine times, including two Meritorious Service Medals.

After a time, Williams started recruiting minorities for officer training in the navy. While stationed at Norfolk, Virginia, he was asked by a friend to speak at a black leadership conference in Kansas. The presentation there drew a dozen requests for Williams to speak at other schools. He was so impressed with the response that he began a campaign to lecture kids on the importance of education and the perils of drug abuse.

Reach the American dream

The more talks he gave, the more requests came in. In 1988 Williams was featured on the *Today Show* and *NBC Nightly News,* prompting another round of requests. He decided to form the Denver-based, non-profit Reach the

Montel Williams

American Dream foundation, which provides everything from personal counseling to college scholarships for underprivileged teens.

Williams was a lieutenant commander in the navy at the time, and he knew he couldn't keep up his current pace. He had to make a decision between the military and a speaking career. With only nine years left until retirement and without a steady income, Williams resigned from active duty. He said in a *Parade* interview that it was the toughest decision of his life. "Since kids are listening to me," he said. "I know this is what I'm supposed to be doing. Maybe I won't win the war, but I'll liberate a lot of prisoners."

Williams embarked on a motivational speaking tour, working twenty-six days each month. With such a hectic schedule, it did not take him long to reach more than seven hundred schools and two million students. But it was not only students who were interested in hearing him; many adults started attending as well. They were interested in Williams's speech about the three R's—responsibility, restraint, and respect. After hearing him speak, Margaret Friedrich wrote in the *Baltimore Sun,* "each parent should follow his 'three R's'— taking the responsibility to show children how to use restraint and delay gratification, to assume responsibility for the future of the community and to show self-respect and respect for others."

When Williams lectured at a school in Jacksonville, Florida, the school district wanted to televise his talk on a local station, WTLV, owned by the Gannett Company. After giving his talk, Williams added an informal discussion at the end. The show was so successful that it garnered a Best of Gannett Award.

Other television specials followed, including ones in the large markets of Washington, D.C., and Detroit, Michigan. In 1990 he hosted a program in Denver called *The 4th R—Kids Rap About Racism,* which won a local Emmy Award. Pepsico helped sponsor some of Williams's speeches, and when they needed someone to narrate an introduction to a special version of the 1991 film *Glory,* they looked no further than Williams. The film, a chronicle of a troop of black soldiers during the Civil War, was used as an educational tool in schools.

Williams soon caught the attention of Hollywood entertainment executives. When *Glory* director Freddie Fields saw Williams's one-minute introduction, he was impressed. After watching Williams on a talk show, Fields realized that Williams should have his own show. In the summer of 1991, they launched the *Montel Williams Show* on nine stations across the country. It was produced and taped in Los Angeles by Out of My Way Productions, which is half-owned by Williams. Although it debuted in only a few cities, they were some of the biggest, including New York, Los Angeles, and Dallas. The show got off to a shaky start, but it was not long before the ratings turned around, and the number of stations carrying the show increased.

Serious, not sensational

The show attracted a following because of its informal town-meeting approach. The one-hour program usually dealt with one topic of a serious nature. Williams approached a variety of subjects—rape, child molestation, drug abuse, and suicide—but was not sensationalistic. "If we are talking about rape, for example, and have a panel of rape survivors, we don't belabor what actually happened during the rape," he told the *Washington Post*. "Other shows will spend three or four segments going over every gory detail. Our aim is to find out how the survivors are handling the experience."

Since his Los Angeles location created a three-hour time difference between his and similar shows, Williams decided to move the show to New York City. As he went head-to-head with his competition, he realized the show would have to develop something unique if it wanted to stand out. Williams tries to focus on topics that are not normally covered by daytime talk shows.

Despite his on-screen success, Williams has not forgotten the crusade that brought him to the public eye. In 1992 he hosted *Mountain! Get Out of My Way!*—a prime-time television show that looked at AIDS, drugs, crime, and suicide from a kid's perspective. *The Detroit Free Press* gave it three stars: "Most of *Mountain!* takes place outside the talk-show format. There's a fine line between exploring this painful stage in life and exploiting it; Williams walks the line well."

The best example of Williams's style is when he and his crew spent almost twenty-four hours traveling through Manhattan interviewing homeless people and their advocates at soup kitchens, shelters, and subway stations. Williams summed up his decision to carry the show to the *Baltimore Sun:* "That's part of the reason we are so different. You'd think this is something you'd see in another type of show, but in the way we format our field pieces, there's time for conversation, time for discussion, time for questions. I think our viewing audience wants to see a little difference."

Sherley Anne Williams

Writer
Born August 25, 1944, Bakersfield, California

"I wanted specifically to write about lower-income black women.... We were missing these stories of black women's struggles and their real triumphs."

The critic, poet, and novelist Sherley Anne Williams has focused much of her writing on lower-income black women, chronicling their sufferings and triumphs. Such women were strong and supportive influences during her early years, and she felt they should be represented more fully in American literature.

Williams's works also reflect her own experiences. "I am the women I speak of in my stories, my poems," she says. Her works include a book of literary criticism, *Give Birth to Brightness: A Thematic Study in Neo-Black Literature* (1972); two volumes of poetry, *The Peacock Poems* (1975) and *Some One Sweet Angel Chile* (1982); and the novel *Dessa Rose* (1986).

In addition to writing, Williams has supported herself with a career in teaching. Since 1973 she has taught at the University of Cali-

Sherley Anne Williams

fornia, San Diego, where she is currently professor of Afro-American literature.

Managed college education despite austere beginnings

Williams was brought up mainly by women—by her mother and then by an older sister and her sister's women friends. Williams's father, Jessee Williams, died of tuberculosis when she was seven, and nine years later her mother, Lelia (Siler) Williams, also died. The sixteen-year-old Williams was then cared for by Ruise, the eldest of her three sisters, who became her strong support and role model. Ruise was also the model for some of the indomitable women in Williams's books.

Williams's early life did little to prepare her for a career in literature. Her mother actually discouraged her from reading, because it did not help provide for the family's needs. The Williamses lived in a low-income housing project in Fresno, California, and they made what money they could as seasonal workers, traveling from farm to farm. From her earliest childhood, Williams spent long hours in the fields picking cotton and fruit.

When Williams was at high school she read the autobiographies of Richard Wright and other black authors, and this made her realize that she too could be a writer. However, she did not begin to write seriously until after she had completed college. Williams attended Fresno State College, where she earned a B.A. in history in 1966. She then did a year of graduate study at Howard University, and in 1972 graduated M.A. from Brown University, where she had been teaching a black studies program.

Peacock Poems nominated for National Book Award

Williams's first major work was the book of literary criticism *Give Birth to Brightness* (1972). It was well received by the reviewers, one of whom wrote: "Miss Williams has written a readable and informative survey of black literature. In using both her knowledge of Western literature and her understanding of black life, she provides insight into the sadly neglected area of reversed values that plays such a significant role in much black literature."

Williams dedicated the book to her son, John Malcolm, who was the main subject of her first volume of poetry, *The Peacock Poems* (1975). The opening poem, "Say Hello to John," was about the boy's birth, and later poems recorded his development as he grew older. Other poems explored Williams's personal feelings as a single mother or recalled her early family life. Throughout the book Williams was "singing the blues" in verse, which she did so poignantly that she was nominated for the National Book Award in 1976.

In Williams's next book, *Some One Sweet Angel Chile* (1982), she took the blues theme a step further by devoting a whole section to poems about the life legendary blues singer Bessie Smith. Another section details the experiences of a black woman soon after the Civil War. Other sections express the feelings of modern black women, including Williams herself, who recalls various events from her childhood. Like the blues poems of her first volume, the poems in *Some One Sweet Angel Chile* sing of hard times and the hard life of women.

Dessa Rose novel hits best-seller lists

The sufferings of women form the main theme of Williams's powerful novel, *Dessa Rose* (1986). The story follows the life of Dessa, a slavewoman whose back is scarred from all the whippings she has received. When Dessa's white master kills her lover, Dessa kills the master. She is then arrested and chained to a line of other slaves, from which she eventually escapes. Tracked down and caught, Dessa is sentenced to die—but not before her child is born. Since Dessa is pregnant, her owners want to obtain her child to bring up as a slave. Every slave they have adds to their wealth.

While waiting in prison for her baby to be born, Dessa is interviewed by a journalist who asks her why she kills white men. "Cause I can," she says. It is for this same reason that a white woman later gives Dessa and other escaped slaves refuge—because she can. Much of the story revolves around the bond that is formed between Dessa and her white friend, who is also disadvantaged, being poor and female.

The character of Dessa is based on a real person—a pregant slave who led a rising in 1829. The lust and brutality of the slaveowners is also based on fact. This is what makes the story so powerful and so very moving. In *Dessa Rose* Williams gives far more detail about the abusive treatment of women slaves than is usual in novels about slavery, or even in nonfiction works on the subject.

These qualities, together with Williams's skills as a writer, made *Dessa Rose* an instant success. Praising the book for its "unflinchingly realistic portrayal of American slavery," the *New York Times* placed it for two weeks on its recommended reading list. Other newspapers and magazines gave equally glowing reviews, with the result that the book quickly became a best seller and was sought for paperback rights and film rights.

Williams suddenly found that she was famous—much to her surprise. She had simply been continuing the process she had started many years earlier with her books of poetry: "I wanted specifically to write about lower-income black women.... We were missing these stories of black women's struggles and their real triumphs.... I wanted to write about them because they had in a very real sense educated me and given me what it was going to take to get me through the world."

August Wilson

Playwright
Born 1945, Pittsburgh, Pennsylvania

*"What I try to do is an inward examination....
I think the black Americans have the most
dramatic story of all mankind to tell."*

A ugust Wilson has twice been honored with the Pulitzer Prize for Drama, in 1987 for his play *Fences* and in 1990 for his play *The Piano Lesson.*

The prize recognizes the most outstanding plays that best show the power and educational value of the stage. All Wilson's plays have a strong educational impact in the unforgettable way they portray the black experience. They do this in personal terms, exploring the inner feelings of the characters concerned. "I think that black theater of the sixties was angry, didactic, and pushing outward," Wilson has said. "What I try to do is an inward examination.... I think the black Americans have the most dramatic story of all mankind to tell."

Dropped out of high school

August Wilson grew up in a family of six children in one of the poorest districts of Pittsburgh, Pennsylvania. He hardly knew his father, a German baker who did not live with the family. Wilson's mother, Daisy, did her best to support the children by working as a cleaner, but there was never enough money to go round. The family scraped by, crowded into a two-room cold-water apartment.

During Wilson's teenage years his mother married David Bedford, a fellow African American. The family then moved into a better neighborhood in a largely white part of town, where they were clearly not welcome. Bricks were thrown through the window, and at school Wilson found notes on his desk saying "Nigger, go home." When he wrote a term paper on Napoleon, he was accused of cheating because "it seemed a bit too good to have been done by a black boy."

Wilson had learned to read when he was barely four year old and had shown promise at elementary school, but the atmosphere at his high school put him off, and he dropped out when he was fifteen. From then on his main source of education was the public library, where he read the works of Langston Hughes, Richard Wright, Ralph Ellison, and other black writers. Already Wilson had decided that he, too, would be a writer.

August Wilson

To support himself Wilson took whatever jobs he could get—usually low-paying jobs such as coffee shop cook. When he was twenty he bought a typewriter for the twenty dollars he earned helping one of his sisters with her term paper on poets Robert Frost and Carl Sandburg. Wilson's passion for reading included poetry, and he was familiar with the works of all the major American poets. He had also begun to write poetry, and over the next few years some of his verses were published in small magazines such as *Black Lines*.

Wins Critics Circle Award for *Ma Rainey's Black Bottom*

In 1968 Wilson moved to St. Paul, Minneapolis, where a friend of his was involved in the theater. Realizing what a powerful medium the theater was for getting his message across, Wilson founded the Black Horizons Theater Company and set to work writing a play. Like many other African American intellectuals of the 1960s, Wilson was a black nationalist who wanted to use his creative talents to make important political statements. He called himself "a cultural nationalist … trying to raise consciousness through theater." The Black Horizons Theater Company put on various cultural programs as well as Wilson's early plays, but it did not bring in a regular income. Wilson supplemented his income with work at the Science Museum of Minnesota, writing scripts for short theatrical pieces that accompanied the museum's exhibitions.

In 1982 Wilson's first major play, *Jitney,* was accepted for workshop production at the National Playwrights Conference held in the O'Neill Theater Center. Later that year it was staged in Pittsburgh by the Allegheny Repertory Theater. Set in a Pittsburgh taxi station, *Jitney* is a realistic drama about city life. Wilson was so encouraged by the attention it attracted that he soon completed the script of *Fullerton Street,* another play in the same realistic style, but it was far less effective and did not take off in the same way. Meanwhile, he was putting the finishing touches to a work he had begun in the 1970s—a play about famous blues singer Ma Rainey. He called the play *Ma Rainey's Black Bottom* (black bottom was a popular dance of the 1920s, when Ma Rainey was in her heyday).

Ma Rainey's Black Bottom takes place during an imaginary recording session in 1927. Some of the scenes are set in the studio, where an arrogant Rainey heaps abuse on the other musicians, and some are set in the rehearsal room, where the musicians discuss Rainey's behavior. The rehearsal room episodes are the crux of the play, for the musicians' discussion of Rainey's verbal abuse leads to a discussion about other forms of abuse, most notably the various experiences of racism that all of them have suffered. The play was first staged in 1984 by the Yale Repertory Theater in New Haven, Connecticut. There it garnered such glowing reviews that before the end of the year it had opened on Broadway. Wilson was hailed as a "promising new playwright" and "a major find for American theater." Meanwhile, the play itself went on to win several awards, including the New York Drama Critics Circle Award.

Racks up more prizes with *Fences* and *The Piano Lesson*

Wilson's next drama, *Fences* (1985), also had its first performance with the Yale Repertory Theater. It then played in Chicago, Seattle, and San Francisco before opening on Broadway in 1987. From the first, *Fences* received rave reviews. It was especially praised for its perceptiveness, strength, and passion. "Wilson's greatest gift is his ability to make sense of anger," wrote the drama critic for *Time* magazine.

The anger is expressed most forcibly through the character of Troy Maxson (played by James Earl Jones), a garbage collector and former baseball player. Troy was a baseball star in the days when African Americans had to play in the Negro Leagues rather than in the majors, and his resentment over this injustice causes him to forbid his teenage son to accept an athletic scholarship.

Fences won the 1987 Pulitzer Prize for Drama as well as a host of other prizes, including the New York Drama Critics Circle Award and four Tony Awards. Some reviewers compared *Fences* to the Arthur Miller classic, *Death of a Salesman,* and all agreed that Wilson himself was a major talent. He confirmed this reputation with his next drama, *Joe Turner's Come and Gone,* which opened on Broadway in 1988 and was yet another winner of the New York Drama Critics Circle Award. The play is about an ex-convict's efforts to find his wife. It is also an allegory for all uprooted black Americans.

The Piano Lesson, which opened on Broadway in 1990, was the second of Wilson's plays to win a Pulitzer Prize. It is about a brother and sister who quarrel over a piano that has been in the family for generations. Boy Willie wants to sell the piano to buy the land on which their ancestors were slaves, but his sister Berenice wants to keep the piano because of the family history carved on it. *The Piano Lesson* was first produced in 1987 at the Yale Repertory Theater, which has represented the birthplace of so many of Wilson's dramas. In 1990 the Yale Repertory Theater continued the tradition of introducing Wilson's plays by staging the first production of *Two Trains Running,* which opened on Broadway in 1992. Set in Pittsburgh in 1968, *Two Trains Running* takes place at a lunch counter where the regulars discuss the issues of the times—the civil rights movement and the Vietnam War.

Like Wilson's earlier plays, *Two Trains Running* is part of his project to portray the central issues facing African Americans in all ten decades of the twentieth century. Wilson looks particularly at the choices people face and the many ways in which they cope. In total, he draws a magnificently broad picture of African American life—what a *New York Times* critic has called "a teeming canvas of black America ... and a spiritual allegory."

Oprah Winfrey

Broadcasting executive, talk show host, actress
Born January 2, 1954, Kosciusko, Mississippi

"My mission is to use this position, power and money to create opportunities for other people."

Every week day, millions of American flip on their television sets to *The Oprah Winfrey Show.* Winfrey's down-to-earth interviewing style has created a huge following, and she has been a big winner at the Daytime Emmys. While most associate her with being a talk show host, Winfrey is also in charge of Harpo Productions Inc., a movie production company. She is generally acknowledged as one of the most affluent and powerful black women in America.

Lives with her grandparents

Winfrey was born on a farm near Kosciusko, Mississippi, on January 29, 1954. Her father, Vernon Winfrey, was only twenty and was in the armed forces. Her mother, Vernita Lee, was eighteen and eager to leave the state. Winfrey was named Orpah from the Book of Ruth in the Bible, but she eventually became known as Oprah because it was easier to pronounce.

Winfrey lived with her maternal grandparents on the farm until she was six years old. Her mother moved to Milwaukee to find work as a housecleaner, and her father didn't know she was alive until he received a birth notice in the mail, with "send clothes" scribbled on the back. She was reading by the time she was two and a half and was soon reciting in church on holidays. Some say she wrote to her kindergarten teacher requesting that she be moved to the first grade, and the next day it happened.

At age six Winfrey moved in with her mom, who was rarely at home because of her work. Vernita had a difficult time looking after Winfrey, and Winfrey made up several stories to get her mother's attention. One time her mother refused to buy her a new pair of glasses, because she couldn't afford them, so Winfrey staged a fake burglary at her home, alleging that she had been knocked unconscious and her glasses had been broken in the scuffle. Another time she ran away from home, found Aretha Franklin's limousine, and convinced the singer that she was an abandoned child. It's reported that Franklin gave her one hundred dollars.

Sexually abused as a youngster

Her mother's lack of supervision enabled several men to sexually abuse Winfrey. When she was nine she was abused by a teenaged cousin and then by other male relatives and friends. The abuse caused her to run away from home on many occasions. Her mother gave her an ultimatum when she was fourteen—live with her father and stepmother or be sent to a juvenile detention center. She went to live with her father in Nashville, Tennessee. Her father and his wife, Zelda, were a tremendous help to her, and she flourished under their care. Her father was a barber, an elected city councillor, a grocery store owner, and a church deacon. He was a high achiever who expected responsible behavior from his daughter. Her days of wearing heavily applied makeup and revealing dresses and of breaking curfew were over. In an interview with the *Washington Post Magazine,* she credited her father and his wife for saving her. "If I hadn't been sent to my father, I would have gone in another direction. I could have made a good criminal. I would have used these same instincts differently."

Winfrey joined the drama club in school and became a prizewinning orator, winning a

Oprah Winfrey

$1,000 college scholarship for her two-and-a-half minute speech titled, "The Negro, the Constitution, and the United States." She was the first black person to win Nashville's Miss Fire Prevention title. In 1971 she became a part-time radio newscaster on Nashville's WVOL and was named Miss Black Tennessee. In 1973, while still attending Tennessee State University on a scholarship, she was hired by WTVF-TV, the CBS affiliate in Nashville, as a reporter and anchor. From there, she moved to WJZ-TV, an ABC affiliate, from 1976 to 1983. She started out as a news anchor, but did poorly and was soon fired. She was given a chance to cohost a Baltimore morning talk show called *People Are Talking,* where she was an instant hit. The ratings soared, but Winfrey was having personal problems, which caused her to overeat. The station wanted her to change both her name and her look. She was told her eyes were too far apart, her nose was too wide, and her chin was too

long. To thin out her hair, she underwent a French permanent at an expensive salon, which was so badly botched that she was temporarily bald.

Despite these "shortcomings," Winfrey's popularity continued to increase (and so did her size). In 1984—weighing in at 160 pounds—she joined WLS-TV's *AM Chicago.* Her experience with broadcasting executives in Baltimore had convinced her that no one should manipulate her appearance or personality again.

Chicago AM

When Winfrey joined *Chicago AM,* it seemed the odds were stacked against her. She was pitted against the legendary *Phil Donahue Show,* and the 5 feet 6 inch, 180-pound Winfrey seemed an unlikely candidate to topple his successful ratings. Undaunted, Winfrey studied improvisation with Chicago's Second City comedy troupe, and her down-home style of interviewing captured the audience's attention. Where Donahue would dance around the morality of a pornographic actress, Winfrey would simply blurt out, "Don't you get sore?" Her show was so successful that it was quickly syndicated to television stations in more than 120 American cities. Within a year of Winfrey's arrival, Donahue relocated to New York and switched to an afternoon time slot.

In 1985 Winfrey made her acting debut in the film *The Color Purple.* Producer Quincy Jones saw her show in his hotel room and immediately cast her in the part of Sophia. Winfrey did so well in the role that she received nominations for a Golden Globe and an Academy Award for best supporting actress.

The next year, *The Oprah Winfrey Show* made its national debut. Within five months it was the third highest rated show in syndication, and the number one rated talk show. It has touched on a variety of topics including divorce, child rearing, sexual abuse, racism, breast cancer and suicide—just to name a few. Winfrey has received three Daytime Emmy awards for excellence in the talk/service broadcasting field. When her original contract ended in 1988, she told executives she was considering discontinuing her show, unless she could own and produce the show. She called her new company, Harpo Productions (Harpo is Oprah spelled backwards), and it made at least $50 million during the 1988-89 season. As her popularity increased, so did her profits. By 1991, she was earning $80 million and was third on *Forbes* magazine's 1990-91 list of the richest entertainers in the business.

New productions

In addition to her television show, Winfrey has been involved in other productions. In 1989 she coproduced and starred in the Harpo endeavor, "The Women of Brewster Place," a miniseries based on an award-winning novel about a group of ghetto-based women. The show was well received, and Winfrey decided to follow it up with a weekly television show. The pace was too much for Winfrey, and the show was cancelled in its first season.

Winfrey has overcome this failure and thrown herself into new endeavors. She owns the screen rights to *Beloved,* Toni Morrison's Pulitzer Prize-winning tale of slavery, and Winfrey intends to play the lead. She also owns the screen rights to *Kaffir Boy,* an anti-apartheid autobiography by South African writer Mark Mathabane. As well, Winfrey has part-ownership of three network affiliated stations and an interest in The Eccentric, a Chicago restaurant.

Despite her busy schedule—she frequently works fourteen hours a day—she still finds time and money for many charitable causes. She regularly meets with a group of teenage girls from Chicago's Cabrini-Green housing project and takes them to movies, dinner, or shopping sprees. As the creator and sponsor of the "club," she sets the rule: stay in school and don't get pregnant. She has also established scholarships at Tennessee State University and Atlanta's Morehouse College. Winfrey keeps in touch with the scholarship recipients to monitor their grades and progress in school. She gives dozens of speeches each year, dousing them with her practiced wit, anecdotal flair, and recognizable style.

Stevie Wonder

Singer, songwriter, instrumentalist
Born May 13, 1950, Saginaw, Michigan

"There's so much music in the air. You hear this music in your mind first; that's the way it is for me, anyway. Then I go after getting it exactly the way I imagined it."

One of the most original and compelling pop musicians, Stevie Wonder has had hit after hit since the 1960s when, as a child prodigy, he first burst on the scene as "Little Stevie Wonder." His records have won him more than fifteen Grammy Awards, including Album of the Year in 1973, 1974, and 1976.

Wonder has made ingenious use of electronic synthesizers and keyboard technology to produce a series of remarkable albums that are performed entirely by himself—not only as singer and instrumentalist, but as composer and arranger as well. In his concert performances, too, he bounces from piano to drums to synthesizer, playing an amazing number of instruments as he provides the background music for his songs.

The style of Wonder's songs is unique. As *Time* magazine pointed out, he "has distilled a wide array of black and white musical styles into a hugely popular personal idiom." Although Wonder is now performing less than in the 1970s, he still draws huge crowds and his records continue to sell year after year. Many of his albums have sold well over a million copies.

Little Stevie Wonder

Stevie Wonder was the middle child in a family of five, with two older brothers and a younger brother and sister. He was born Stevland Judkins, but after his mother divorced and remarried, he took his stepfather's surname and was called Stevland Morris. His blindness may have resulted from the fact that he was a premature baby. "I have a dislocated nerve in one eye and a cataract on the other," he has said. "It may have happened from being in the incubator too long and receiving too much oxygen."

Despite being blind, Stevie had a happy childhood, living first in Saginaw and then in Detroit, where his mother moved on her re-

marriage. He showed a love of music at a very young age. When he was two, he enjoyed banging pots and pans with spoons, accompanying the music played on the radio. By the time he was four, he was playing the drums and learning the harmonica and piano. Stevie wore out his toy drums so often that the local Lion's Club gave him a set of real drums.

Stevie sang in the choir at the Whitestone Baptist Church in Detroit and became a soloist at the age of nine. But he was expelled from the choir after a member of the congregation heard him playing rock and roll music with some friends. It was around this time that a friend's older brother took Stevie to visit the Motown recording studio in Detroit. This black record company became a regular haunt of Stevie, and he would drop in after school to try out the various instruments and play songs he had composed. The people at Motown called him "the little boy wonder."

When Stevie was thirteen, the president of Motown, Berry Gordy, signed a contract with him and promoted him as "Little Stevie Wonder." That same year, Stevie had his first big hit with the Motown song "Fingertips Part 2," which he sang while accompanying himself on the harmonica. During the summer of 1963, this record sold over a million copies and made Stevie an instant star. From then on, he traveled with the Motown entertainers, taking private tutoring for three or four hours each day. When not on tour, he studied at the Michigan School for the Blind in Lansing.

As Stevie grew older, he dropped the "Little" from his name. Meanwhile, Motown managed his money for him and decided what songs he would sing. Although most of the songs were typical of Motown black soul music, Stevie's voice gave them an extra dimension. He had an unbelievable number of hits during the 1960s, including "Uptight," "Blowin' in the Wind," "I Was Made to Love Her," "Yester-me, Yester-you, Yesterday," "For Once in My Life," and "My Cherie Amour."

Creative composer

When Wonder was twenty-one, he decided to break free from Motown control. "I had gone about as far as I could go," he explained in an interview with *Stereo Review.* "I wasn't growing; I just kept repeating 'the Stevie Wonder Sound,' and it didn't express how I felt about what was happening in the world. I decided to go for something else.… I wanted to see what would happen if I changed."

What happened was that Wonder continued to score hits, though with a different sound. Using modern recording techniques and synthesizers, he came up with the one-man album *Music on My Mind* (1972), in which he accompanied himself on the drums, piano, harmonica, organ, and clavichord. He negotiated a new contract with Motown that allowed him complete control of his music, which took on a deeper meaning as well as a new sound. Many of his songs now touched on issues of personal concern.

Throughout the 1970s, each album Wonder produced sold more than a million copies, and each had at least one song that was a major hit, from "Superstition" to the more cheerful "You Are the Sunshine of My Life." Even though he produced far fewer albums in the 1980s, his records continued to be enor-

mously popular, and by the end of the decade his total record sales stood at almost 70 million.

In 1971 Wonder married Syreeta Wright, from whom he has since been divorced. He has three children, and his love for them has often served as an inspiration for his music. A bad car accident in 1973 affected Wonder deeply, causing him to pause and consider the direction his life was taking. "It became very clear to me," he said later, "that it wasn't enough just to be a rock and roll singer or anything of that nature. I had to make *use* of whatever talent I have."

One of the uses to which Wonder has put his talents has been benefit concerts for AIDS research. He has also campaigned against drunken driving. A very moderate drinker himself, he popularized the song "Don't Drive Drunk" and sponsored a poster that read "I Would Drive Myself Before I Would Ride

Stevie Wonder

with a Drunken Driver." The poster was displayed in all schools throughout the country.

Wonder was at the forefront of the movement to get Martin Luther King's birthday made a national holiday. As he told *Jet* magazine, he looks forward to the day when there will be no more racism and people will live in harmony: "Neither this country nor the world will be right until people begin to accept people as being people and not let their insecurities determine the future of this society, this country, this world."

Carter G. Woodson

Historian, educator
Born December 19, 1875, New Canton,
  Buckingham County, Virginia
Died April 4, 1950, Washington, D.C.

"The achievements of the Negro properly set forth will crown him as a factor in early human progress and a maker of modern civilization."

Before Dr. Carter Godwin Woodson began his work as a recorder of black history, the achievements of African Americans were almost totally ignored by the country's historians. Black Americans figured in the history books chiefly as slaves—a people with no cultural history and no promise for the future.

Woodson turned this situation around by researching and documenting the subject with great diligence and by promoting the study of the African American culture in every way possible. He formed the Association for the Study of Negro Life and History, founded and edited the *Journal of Negro History* and the *Negro History Bulletin,* established a publishing company to print books about African Americans, and himself wrote more than a dozen books and numerous articles. Through his work he laid the foundation for the widespread adoption of black studies programs that have since been established in American schools and universities.

Finally able to attend high school— at age thirty

The son of former slaves, Carter Woodson had little chance of education during his childhood, yet he became the second African American to earn a Ph.D. in history. This achievement took him years of study and a great deal of perseverance.

Woodson's parents, James and Anna (Riddle) Woodson, were so poor that they could not afford to allow their many children to attend school regularly. All available hands were needed to work on the Woodson farm, a hardscrabble farm that barely supported the family. Woodson helped out with farmwork from the age of about seven, and as a teengager he brought in money by working in the West Virginia coal mines.

In 1895, when Woodson was twenty, he at last had the chance to attend school regularly. He enrolled at West Virginia's Douglass High School, and after receiving his diploma in 1896 he spent two years at Berea College, Kentucky, which at the time accepted both black and white students. Woodson then taught in Winona for a year before being appointed principal of Douglass High School, where he remained from 1900 to 1903. During this period he completed the work for his B.Litt. degree, which he received from Berea College in 1903.

For the next ten years Woodson taught and traveled while continuing to study for higher degrees. He taught for four years in the Philippines (where he learned Spanish), studied for a year in Europe (where he learned French), and in 1909 accepted a position at a high school in Washington, D.C., where he taught English, history, Spanish, and French. Meanwhile he graduated from the University of Chicago with a B.A. in 1907, an M.A. in 1908, and in 1912 earned his Ph.D. from Harvard University.

Established African American history as a reputable discipline

Having earned his doctorate, Woodson continued to teach at the high school in Washington, but already his main interest was the study of black history. In 1915 he and four friends formed the Association for the Study of Negro Life and History (now known as the Association for the Study of Afro-American Life and History). This was the first association ever formed to promote research on African Americans.

In 1916 Woodson founded the *Journal of Negro History,* a quarterly which printed scholarly articles on the black experience. The articles were based on oral history and personal letters and diaries as well as on more formal records such as census data. They thus presented black history from a black point of view—a totally new approach, since history books were commonly written from the view-

Carter G. Woodson

point of the masters rather than the slaves. Because of this approach and the new light it shed on the past, the journal became an important reference for white as well as black historians. Woodson remained editor of the journal until his death.

In 1919 Woodson accepted a university appointment as professor of history and dean of liberal arts at Howard University, and from 1920 to 1922 he held a similar position at West Virginia State College. He then gave up teaching in order to concentrate on promoting black history through his association and through the publishing company he had recently formed. In 1921 Woodson had founded Associated Publishers in order "to make possible the publication and circulation of valuable books on the Negro not acceptable to most publishers."

Besides editing and publishing the works of others, Woodson published more than a dozen books of his own, including *History of* the Negro Church (1921), *The Negro in Our History* (1922), *Negro Makers of History* (1928), *The Miseducation of the Negro* (1933), and *African Heroes and Heroines* (1939). His most famous book is *The Negro in Our History,* which has been widely used as a textbook in schools and universities.

In 1926 the Association for the Study of Negro Life and History succeeded in getting the government to establish Negro History Week, which gradually developed into today's Black History Month—a time in February each year when schools and libraries mount special projects and exhibitions, and the entire nation celebrates the achievements of black Americans. By this time Woodson was totally engrossed in the work of the Association. "The Association was his life," wrote Jim Finch, deputy postmaster general, when in 1984 a postage stamp was issued in honor of Woodson. "To him, no task was too small or unimportant if it helped the Association. Whether he was scrubbing the office floors or taking books to the post offices for mailing to other historians, Carter G. Woodson immersed himself in the Association's activities."

In 1937 Woodson founded another journal, the *Negro History Bulletin,* which gave a simplified view of history that was more readable, and thus more suitable for students, than the scholarly *Journal of Negro History.* In his last years he also edited the six-volume *Encyclopedia Africana.*

Woodson never married. "I don't have time to marry. I'm married to my work," he said whenever anyone broached the subject. His work has had a lasting impact in the attention it has focused on black culture and his-

tory. Because of Woodson's trailblazing efforts, there are now black studies programs in schools and universities throughout the country. And there is one month each year when the entire nation celebrates its African American citizens. Author and civil rights leader W. E. B. Du Bois saluted Woodson when he said, "I know of no one man who in a lifetime has, unaided, built up such a national celebration."

Richard Wright

Novelist
Born September 4, 1908, near Natchez, Mississippi
Died November 28, 1960, Paris, France

"I swore to myself that if I ever wrote another book, no one would weep over it; it would be so hard and deep that they would have to face it without the consolation of tears."

One of the most important American authors of the twentieth century, Richard Wright was the first African American novelist to write of black life in the northern cities. He was also the first to express the anger of black Americans over the way whites excluded blacks from so many areas of life. His best-selling books forced whites to realize just what it was like to be black, shocking them out of their complacency.

Works such as *Native Son* (1940) and *Black Boy* (1945) not only opened the eyes of white readers, they set a new standard for black writers. James Baldwin, Ralph Ellison, and other emerging authors of the time were deeply influenced by Wright's approach and by his eloquent exposure of bigotry and racism.

Wright's works include novels, short stories, plays, poems, histories, and a large number of articles. While most focus on the racial situation in the United States, some look at racism and persecution on a wider scale.

A Southern childhood

Richard Nathaniel Wright had a miserable childhood in which he was always hungry, often beaten, and frequently moved from place to place. The son of a sharecropper, he was born on a plantation in Roxie, about twenty miles east of Natchez, Mississippi. When he was three, his father, Nathan Wright, took the family to Memphis, Tennessee, where he then deserted them. Richard's mother, Ella Wright, was left to support Richard and his brother on whatever she could earn. After struggling for four years, she took them to live with her sister in Arkansas. This proved to be a disaster for, soon after their arrival, the sister's husband was murdered by whites who wanted his land. Terrified, the family fled to rented rooms in another town.

Wright's teenage years were no better. His mother suffered a stroke when he was eleven, and from then on he lived with various relatives, who were very strict and tried to make him submissive and religious. As a result, he became rebellious and unreligious. The frequent moving from town to town meant that he had very little schooling, and his formal education did not really begin until he entered a fifth-grade class in Jackson, Mississippi. Five years later he dropped out of school

and went back to Memphis, where he supported himself by washing dishes, sweeping streets, waiting on tables, and doing other odd jobs.

Professional writer

Wright spent two years in Memphis, two very important years because he developed a passion for reading. He read *Harper's* and *Atlantic Monthly.* He borrowed books from the whites-only library by forging a note that read, "Dear Madam: Will you please let this nigger have some books by H. L. Mencken?" Wright was particularly impressed by Mencken's books, especially his writings on prejudice.

Wright continued to read avidly after he moved to Chicago in 1927. There he found a job in the post office and began to write in earnest. His first story had been published three years earlier, in a Jackson newspaper, and he was determined to become a writer. In 1932, he joined a left-wing literary group, and the contacts he made there led to his joining the Communist party. Wright saw communism as a means of battling racial oppression, and for several years he was an active member of the party, writing revolutionary poems and articles. On moving to New York in 1937, he became Harlem editor of the Communist newspaper, *The Daily Worker.* But as the years passed, he became disenchanted by the rigid views of many of the members, and in 1944 he resigned from the party.

During much of the 1930s, Wright was working on his first novel and trying in vain to get it published. It was not published until after his death as *Lawd Today* (1963). Meanwhile, he was also writing short stories, and in 1938 he won a $500 prize for a collection of stories based on the life of a black communist he had known in Chicago, treating the violence inflicted by whites on blacks and on black retaliation. Published later that year as a book entitled *Uncle Tom's Children* (in reference to Harriet Beecher Stowe's 1852 novel, *Uncle Tom's Cabin*), the stories gave the stern message that members of the younger generation would not be passive like Uncle Tom; they would fight back.

Uncle Tom's Children sold so well that Wright was able to support a wife, and in 1939 he married a white woman, Dhimah Meadman. The marriage was not a success, and the couple divorced a year later. In 1941, Wright embarked on a far more successful marriage with another white woman, Ellen Poplar. The first of his two daughters was born the following year.

Best-selling author

Early in 1939, Wright was awarded a Guggenheim Fellowship, which helped support him while he worked on the novel *Native Son* (1940). With its shocking account of the life of the murderer Bigger Thomas, *Native Son* is likely to remain Wright's best-known work. It was an instant success, selling two hundred thousand copies in the first three weeks. Like the stories in *Uncle Tom's Children,* the book shows how violence begets violence, and it, too, focuses on a black victim who is the hero of a racial war. But the shocking thing about *Native Son* is that the victim-hero is not a "good" person; the victim-hero is the brutal Bigger.

Native Son was produced as a play in 1941 and later made into a film. While adapting the book for the theater, Wright was also researching and writing *Twelve Million Black Voices: A Folk History of the Negro in the U.S.* (1941). During the next few years he was very busy working on a variety of projects. The most important of these was his autobiography, which was published in two parts. The first part, about his early life, was *Black Boy,* which came out in 1945. The second part did not appear until some years after his death, when it was published as *American Hunger* (1977).

Like Wright's earlier works, *Black Boy* was concerned with racism and bigotry. While telling his own story, the story of one hungry and unhappy black boy, Wright revealed the larger picture, showing how the legacy of slavery still haunted the South, with its restrictive laws and inhuman attitudes. He portrayed the

Richard Wright

Southern whites as totally inhuman, but he also criticized Southern blacks, implying that they had cooperated in their own oppression by being so meek and subservient. This drew criticism from some black reviewers, though most were greatly impressed by the book. Wright had put into words what many African Americans had felt for many years.

Black Boy was another best-seller and, like *Native Son,* it was a Book-of-the-Month Club choice. *Black Boy* brought Wright international fame, and in 1946 he was invited to France, where he became friends with a number of French intellectuals, including Jean-Paul Sartre and Simone de Beauvoir. Finding a less racist atmosphere in France, Wright moved his family to Paris in 1947, and France remained his home base for the rest of his life.

The first book Wright wrote in France, *The Outsider* (1953), was an existentialist novel that was not primarily concerned with racial matters. Neither was *Savage Holiday* (1954), but Wright returned to the racist South of his youth in *The Long Dream* (1958). His most important nonfiction works during the last years of his life were *Black Power* (1954), about a visit he made to Africa in 1953, and *White Man Listen!,* a collection of essays.

Wright's books have been translated into many languages, bringing the African American experience to people throughout the world. He was one of the most significant American writers of the twentieth century, a strong influence on American culture, and especially on African American literature, which was changed forever after the publication of *Na*

Coleman Young

Mayor of Detroit
Born May 24, 1918, Tuscaloosa, Alabama

"Today the big debate is whether the country's heading into another damned depression—the truth of the matter is, Detroit never came out of depression. Since I've been mayor, our unemployment level has been twice the national average. That's why we need to take radical steps to preserve this city—but this city is worth preserving."

Coleman Young can best be summarized as a fighter. Early in his life he fought against poverty, discrimination, and poor labor conditions. He continued to fight against these issues in the Michigan state senate, where he became popular with the black clergy and unions. He took his fight a step further in 1973 by becoming the mayor of Detroit. Although much has been said of the city's sagging economy, high crime rate, and dwindling population, Young has fought to balance the budget despite federal and state cutbacks, attracted new business to the city, and revitalized several downtrodden neighborhoods.

HUAC investigates him for his union organizing

Young was born on May 24, 1918, in Tuscaloosa, Alabama, to Coleman and Ida Young. He spent his early years in Huntsville, but his father took the family to the Black Bottom section of Detroit in the late 1920s to establish a dry cleaning business. Although

Young had excellent grades in public school, he was denied financial aid to the University of Michigan because of his race. He decided to help support his four brothers and sisters by enrolling in an apprentice electrician program at Ford Motor Company in the late 1930s. Although he finished at the top of the program, he was passed over by a white applicant for the only available electrician's job.

In the early 1940s Young worked on the Ford assembly line and became an underground union organizer and civil rights activist. After a few months he became the target of racial comments by "company goons," who eventually led him into a fistfight that caused him to be fired.

Young found new work with the post office and continued his union activities. By the time he was drafted into World War II, he had established a name for himself by demanding equal employment and fair treatment in the automobile industry. During the war Young became a second lieutenant with the Tuskegee Airmen, an elite black flying unit, and flew missions as a bombardier-navigator. Near the end of the war he was arrested and jailed with several other black officers for demanding service at a segregated officers' club. The army eventually integrated the club, in part due to the publicity generated from the event.

When the war ended Young returned to Detroit where he spent the next decade drifting from job to job. His main interest during the 1950s was union organizing, and campaigning for the Progressive party. He also founded the National Negro Labor Council, an organization dedicated to civil rights in the workplace. Young's activities brought him to the attention of the House Un-American Activities Committee, which investigated him for possible Communist ties. Rather than hand his membership list over to the U.S. attorney general, Young disbanded the organization. The negative publicity over his actions made it difficult for him to keep a job.

By the end of the 1950s Young was making a decent living as an insurance salesman. He became active in the Democratic party, and in 1960 he was elected a delegate to the Michigan Constitutional Convention. Young's popularity slowly rose, and by 1964 he won a seat in the state senate. He fought for open housing legislation and for busing to integrate public schools. His views garnered him widespread support from Detroit's black clergy and the unions.

In 1973 Young declared himself a candidate for mayor. He faced stiff competition from John F. Nichols, a white police commissioner. Nichols promised to bring law and order, while Young stated the police force was being unduly harsh on the black community. Young promised he would promote better race relations. A mere 17,000 votes decided the election, with Young coming out on top. He took 92 percent of the black vote, while Nichols took more than 91 percent of the white vote.

"We are going to turn this city around," Young said in his inaugural address. He called for a coalition of business and labor to help business remain in the city and to attract new ones. He also began reforming the police department by adding more black officers and promoting those already within the ranks. Police officers, as well as the rest of Detroit's civil servants, were required to live within the city. William Beckham, Young's former deputy mayor, told the *Detroit Free Press* that the early years of Young's administration were marked by a sense of struggle against a common enemy. "When Coleman took office, he was fighting (to reform) the Police Department, fighting federal cutbacks and the recession—real big enemies. This is still a strong administration because of its foundations. But it has lots of pitfalls based on its longevity."

Landslide victories marked his mayoral reelection bids

Since 1973 Young won every election by a landslide. He is the only mayor in the city's history to serve five consecutive terms, for which some journalists have dubbed him "mayor for life." When close ally Jimmy Carter became U.S. president, he asked Young to become a cabinet member in Washington, D.C. Young turned down the offer, feeling there was more he could accomplish in Detroit.

Young was a harsh critic of federal cutbacks instituted by the Ronald Reagan and George Bush administrations, but his own administration has occasionally faced complaint. The Young government has been investigated on more than six different charges, including improprieties in awarding city contracts and illegal use of city funds by the police department. Young has never been implicated during these investigations, and some feel his reputation has actually been bolstered by never being charged with any wrongdoing.

During his years in office, Young has had many accomplishments. The riverfront was expanded to bring in new conventions and

Coleman Young

tourists; and tax abatements have attracted new business—including two major automobile plants—to the city. Young intends to diversify the area's economy to overcome the booms and busts of the automotive industry. Even his strongest critics admit that Young is a tireless worker who has the best interests of the city at heart.

Despite Young's achievements, Detroit faces many problems, with a dwindling population base being the chief concern. Members of the middle class are living in the suburbs, causing the city to lose tax revenue. Some critics charge Young's management style is autocratic and he is only concentrating on cosmetic changes to the city, rather than making structural changes. Young defended his actions in *Newsweek*. "I'm not going to stay in office by being a Teflon goddam mayor, taking positions to enhance my popularity."

Young told the *Detroit Free Press* he considered retirement in 1985 but held off. On

June 24, 1993, he announced that he would not seek reelection to a fifth term, saying that he lacked the energy to continue leading the city. He feels there is still a great deal more to be accomplished and that what he has "set out to do has been done and is taking place."

Whitney M. Young

Civil rights activist, author
Born July 31, 1921, Lincoln Ridge, Kentucky
Died March 11, 1971, Lagos, Nigeria

"We're all militants in different ways. I can't afford the luxury of a completely dogmatic position that says, 'I won't make any compromises,' because I'm dealing with the real world."

While many young blacks were seeking militant ways to further the black civil rights movement, Whitney M. Young decided a more cautious approach was needed. As the director of the National Urban League, Young worked with influential business and political leaders to improve the economic fortune of blacks. Young served on seven presidential committees and numerous other boards and committees. His approach opened many doors for the organization as its budget increased from $300,000 to $35 million, and thirty-five new chapters were formed in the span of a decade.

Despite his success, he was often criticized as an "Uncle Tom" who gave into the wishes of the white establishment. Young, however, was far from an Uncle Tom. He spoke out forcefully, right up to his untimely death, against the slow pace at which businesses and government agencies were fulfilling their promises to blacks. To Young, the most important point in the movement was to maintain communication with the country's financial and political centers.

Mediates with army officers

Young was born on July 31, 1921, in Lincoln Ridge, Kentucky, to Whitney and Laura Young. His father was the headmaster of a preparatory school and his mother was a teacher. Young received his bachelor of science degree at Kentucky State University in 1941 and later did graduate work at the Massachusetts Institute of Technology. From 1941 to 1945 he served with the armed forces, rising to the rank of first sergeant and seeing action overseas. He was a member of an all-black engineering company that was officered by whites. The young blacks did not want to be accorded second-class status and refused to obey their officer's orders. "The officers could see their lieutenant's bars, captain's bars, going down the drain. So they set down with me to try to straighten things out. That was the beginning of my work in that field—being an intermediary between whites and blacks," Young told the *New York Times Magazine*. Several of Young's fellow soldiers accused him of being overly accommodating with the white authorities—a charge that would dog his entire career. Since no one else would negotiate with the officers, Young stuck it out to benefit both sides.

In 1947 Young received a master of arts degree in social work from the University of

Minnesota. From 1954 to 1961 he served as dean of the Atlanta University School of Social Work. During the academic year 1960–61 he was a visiting scholar at Harvard University under a Rockefeller Foundation grant. He left his position as dean in 1961 to become the executive director of the National Urban League. He sought to increase black civil rights through more established, traditional channels. During his ten-year tenure with the Urban League, Young opened thirty-five new chapters and pushed the organization to become more involved with helping those in urban slums. Using his connections with the white business establishment, Young managed to increase the annual budget from $300,000 in 1961 to almost $35 million in 1971. At the height of the civil rights era, Young, along with Martin Luther King, Jr., Roy Wilkins, and James Farmer, were the movement's "Big Four" leaders.

Young was personally acquainted with many captains of industry, including Henry Ford II, chairman of the Ford Motor Company. He was also an advisor with direct access to President Lyndon Johnson. Young was so popular with the Johnson and Kennedy administrations that he was called upon to sit on seven presidential commissions. He was also president of the National Association of Social Workers and the National Conference on Social Welfare. He served on a variety of boards and advisory committees including: the Rockefeller Foundation, Urban Coalition, and the Urban Institute. Using these connections, Young was able to secure agreements from businesses to open up the industrial job market to blacks.

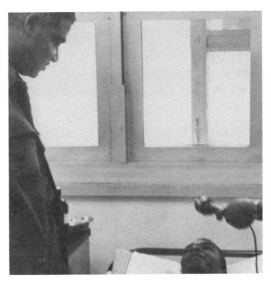

Whitney M. Young

Labeled an Uncle Tom

Despite his success, Young's political and business friendships often stirred controversy in the black civil rights movement. Many young blacks called him an "Uncle Tom" for accommodating the white establishment. They felt the Urban League was being held hostage by Young and his supporters and that they were too middle class in their outlook. Young was often the target of personal attacks that accused him of abandoning the principles of the black civil rights movement. Tom Buckley in a 1970 *New York Times Magazine* article described Young's reputation in the black community: "The white media do in fact usually describe Young as a moderate, responsible black leader, and it listens to what he says with respect. Young is certainly responsible and moderate... but he leads few blacks."

Young did not take this criticism lying down. He responded to Buckley's article by saying, "Nobody who's working for black people is a moderate....We're *all* militants in different ways. I can't afford the luxury of a completely dogmatic position that says, 'I won't make any compromises,' because I'm dealing with the real world....Somebody's got to deal in a very practical way with the issues that are before them, and there's nobody else who's got the entree with the decision makers."

Young frequently spoke out against the slow pace with which businesses and government agencies were fulfilling their promises to blacks. He felt the most important part of the civil rights movement was to maintain the lines of communication with America's centers of financial and political power, no matter how tense race relations might become in the nation's streets and schools. In 1969 he was one of twenty Americans selected by President Johnson to receive the Medal of Freedom, the nation's highest civilian award.

Besides his work with the Urban League, Young was also an accomplished writer. He completed his first book, *To Be Equal,* in 1964 and published *Beyond Racism* five years later. He also wrote *Status of the Negro Community* (1959), *Integration: The Role of Labor Education* (1959), and *Intergroup Relations as a Challenge to Social Work Practice* (1960). His column, "To Be Equal," was syndicated in thirty-five daily and weekly newspapers.

Hoped to work with Nixon administration

Shortly before his death, Young had hoped to join the Nixon administration as an intermediary between the White House and black America. He wanted guaranteed direct access to the president and his cabinet and to be able to consult with other black leaders in drawing up an agenda to assist the black community. Young was unsuccessful in this attempt, so he began to openly criticize the adminstration. He said it was inconsistent in its dealings with blacks and should end the Vietnam War because it siphoned away money needed for social reforms. Young also lobbied the government to implement a "domestic Marshall Plan" that would help blacks recover from the economic inequalities perpetrated by white America for more than three hundred years. "I haven't lost the hope that right will win out," he said.

In 1971 Young and a group of other Americans, white and black, attended an African American conference in Lagos, Nigeria, designed to bridge the gap between Africans and Americans, particularly black Americans. Young drowned at the conference on March 11 while swimming at a party which included former U.S. Attorney General Ramsey Clark. President Richard Nixon expressed his sorrow upon hearing of Young's death: "I have lost a friend, black America has lost a gifted and commanding champion of its just cause."

In a tribute to Young, *Time* reported that Young once described his place in the civil rights movement as not being "the loudest voice, or the most popular. But I would like to think that, at a crucial moment, I was an effective voice of the voiceless, an effective hope of the hopeless."

Index

Volume number appears in **bold**.

Art

Hunter, Clementine **2**
Lawrence, Jacob **3**
Parks, Gordon **3**
Tanner, Henry Ossawa **4**

Business

Bing, Dave **1**
Eldridge, Elleanor **2**
Gaston, Arthur **2**
Gordy, Berry, Jr. **2**
Johnson, John H. **2**
Owens, Jesse **3**
Proctor, Barbara Gardner **3**
Randall, Dudley **3**
Sims, Naomi **4**
Walker, Madame C.J. **4**
Walker, Maggie L. **4**
Winfrey, Oprah **4**

Dance

Ailey, Alvin **1**
Dunham, Katherine **1**
Hines, Gregory **2**
Jones, Bill T. **2**

Education

Asante, Molefi Kete **1**
Baker, Augusta **1**
Baraka, Amiri **1**
Barnett, Marguerite Ross **1**
Bethune, Mary McLeod **1**

Chisholm, Shirley **1**
Clark, Joe **1**
Cobb, Jewel Plummer **1**
Cole, Johnnetta Betsch **1**
Collins, Marva **1**
Cooper, Anna J. **1**
Craft, Ellen **1**
Davis, Angela **1**
Derricotte, Juliette **1**
Diggs, Irene **1**
Du Bois, William Edward
   Burghardt (W.E.B.) **1**
Futrell, Mary Hatwood **2**
Gates, Henry Louis, Jr. **2**
Hill, Anita **2**
Lewis, Elma **3**
Madgett, Naomi Long **3**
McClellan, George Marion **3**
Robeson, Elsanda Goode **3**
Rollins, Charlemae Hill **3**
Scott, Gloria **4**
Steele, Shelby **4**
Sudarkasa, Niara **4**
Terrell, Mary Church **4**
Washington, Booker T. **4**
Woodson, Carter G. **4**

Exploration and adventure

Coleman, Bessie **1**
Henson, Matthew **2**

Fashion

Campbell, Naomi **1**
Houston, Whitney **2**
Johnson, Beverly **2**
Keckley, Elizabeth **3**
Kelly, Patrick **3**

Malone, Annie Turnbo **3**
Sims, Naomi **4**

Film

Belafonte, Harry **1**
Berry, Halle **1**
Campbell, Naomi **1**
Davis, Ossie **1**
Davis, Sammy, Jr. **1**
Givens, Robin **2**
Glover, Danny **2**
Goldberg, Whoopi **2**
Gregory, Dick **2**
Hall, Arsenio **2**
Hines, Gregory **2**
Horne, Lena **2**
Houston, Whitney **2**
Ice-T **2**
Jackson, Janet **2**
Johnson, Beverly **2**
Jones, James Earl **2**
Lee, Spike **3**
McDaniel, Hattie **3**
McQueen, Thelma
   "Butterfly" **3**
Murphy, Eddie **3**
Parks, Gordon **3**
Poitier, Sidney **3**
Pryor, Richard **3**
Robeson, Paul **3**
Ross, Diana **3**
Singleton, John **4**
Snipes, Wesley **4**
Townsend, Robert **4**
Van Peebles, Mario **4**
Washington, Denzel **4**
Wayans, Keenen Ivory **4**
Winfrey, Oprah **4**

Bethune, Mary McLeod   **1**
Bond, Julian   **1**
Brown, H. Rap   **1**
Carmichael, Stokely   **1**
Cleaver, Eldridge   **1**
Clements, George   **1**
Cole, Johnnetta Betsch   **1**
Cosby, Bill   **1**
Craft, Ellen   **1**
Davis, Angela   **1**
Diggs, Irene   **1**
Douglass, Frederick   **1**
DuBois, William Edward
    Burghardt (W.E.B.)   **1**
Dunham, Katherine   **1**
Edelman, Marian Wright   **2**
Evers, Medgar   **2**
Farmer, James   **2**
Garvey, Marcus   **2**
George, Zelma Watson   **2**
Gregory, Dick   **2**
Hale, Clara   **2**
Hamer, Fannie Lou   **2**
Height, Dorothy   **2**
Hernandez, Aileen   **2**
Hill, Anita   **2**
Hooks, Benjamin L.   **2**
Innis, Roy   **2**
Jackson, Jesse   **2**
Jacob, John   **2**
Johnson, James Weldon   **2**
Jordan, Vernon E., Jr.   **2**
Kennedy, Flo   **3**
King, Coretta Scott   **3**
King, Martin Luther, Jr.   **3**
King, Yolanda   **3**
Lowery, Joseph E.   **3**
Malcolm X   **3**
Mason, Biddy   **3**

McKissick, Floyd B.   **3**
Meredith, James   **3**
Moore, Audley   **3**
Muhammad, Elijah   **3**
Murray, Pauli   **3**
Newton, Huey   **3**
Parks, Rosa   **3**
Randolph, Philip A.   **3**
Robeson, Eslanda Goode   **3**
Robeson, Paul   **3**
Rustin, Bayard   **3**
Scott, Dred   **4**
Seale, Bobby   **4**
Shabazz, Attalah   **4**
Sharpton, Al   **4**
Simmons, Althea T.L.   **4**
Steele, Shelby   **4**
Taylor, Susie Baker King   **4**
Terrell, Mary Church   **4**
Toussaint-Louverture   **4**
Trotter, William Monroe   **4**
Truth, Sojourner   **4**
Tubman, Harriet   **4**
Turner, Nat   **4**
Vesey, Denmark   **4**
Waddles, Charleszetta   **4**
Walker, Madame C.J.   **4**
Wattleton, Faye   **4**
Wilkins, Roy   **4**
Young, Whitney M.   **4**

Sports

Aaron, Hank   **1**
Abdul-Jabbar, Kareem   **1**
Ali, Muhammad   **1**
Ashe, Arthur   **1**
Bing, Dave   **1**
Bonilla, Bobby   **1**
Bowe, Riddick   **1**

Campanella, Roy   **1**
Chamberlain, Wilt   **1**
Gibson, Althea   **2**
The Harlem Globetrotters   **2**
Johnson, Earvin "Magic"   **2**
Jordan, Michael   **2**
Joyner-Kersee, Jackie   **2**
Lewis, Carl   **3**
Louis, Joe   **3**
Mays, Willie   **3**
O'Neal, Shaquille   **3**
Owens, Jesse   **3**
Paige, Satchel   **3**
Robinson, Jackie   **3**
Rudolph, Wilma   **3**
Russell, Bill   **3**

Television

Bradley, Ed   **1**
Cornelius, Don   **1**
Cosby, Bill   **1**
Goldberg, Whoopi   **2**
Gregory, Dick   **2**
Gumbel, Bryant   **2**
Hall, Arsenio   **2**
Rowan, Carl T.   **3**
Simpson, Carole   **4**
Taylor, Susan   **4**
Townsend, Robert   **4**
Wayans, Keenen Ivory   **4**
Williams, Montel   **4**
Winfrey, Oprah   **4**

Theater

Gordone, Charles   **2**
King, Yolanda   **3**
Robeson, Paul   **3**
Shabazz, Attalah   **4**
Torrence, Jackie   **4**